The films of Luc Besson

CW01262182

MANCHESTER
1824

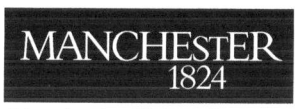

Manchester University Press

The films of
Luc Besson

Master of spectacle

edited by Susan Hayward and Phil Powrie

Manchester University Press
Manchester and New York
distributed exclusively in the USA by Palgrave

Copyright © Manchester University Press 2006

While copyright in the volume as a whole is vested in Manchester University Press, copyright in individual chapters belongs to their respective authors, and no chapter may be reproduced wholly or in part without the express permission in writing of both author and publisher.

Published by Manchester University Press
Oxford Road, Manchester M13 9NR, UK
and Room 400, 175 Fifth Avenue, New York, NY 10010, USA
www.manchesteruniversitypress.co.uk

Distributed exclusively in the USA by
Palgrave, 175 Fifth Avenue, New York,
NY 10010, USA

Distributed exclusively in Canada by
UBC Press, University of British Columbia, 2029 West Mall,
Vancouver, BC, Canada V6T 1Z2

British Library Cataloguing-in-Publication Data
A catalogue record for this book is available from the British Library

Library of Congress Cataloging-in-Publication Data applied for

ISBN 978 0 7190 7029 7 *paperback*

First published 2006

First reprinted in paperback 2009

Produced by Lightning Source

Contents

List of tables and figures	*page* vii
List of contributors	viii
Preface	x
Introduction *Susan Hayward and Phil Powrie*	1
1 Three French neo-baroque directors: Beineix, Besson, Carax from *Diva* to *Le Grand Bleu* *Raphaël Bassan*	11
2 *Du côté d'Europa*, via Asia: the 'post-Hollywood' Besson *Rosanna Maule*	23
3 Musical narration in the films of Luc Besson *Gérard Dastugue*	43
4 Hearing Besson: the music of Eric Serra in the films of Luc Besson *Mark Brownrigg*	57
5 Of suits and men in the films of Luc Besson *Phil Powrie*	75
6 From rags to riches: *Le Dernier combat* and *Le Cinquième élément* *Susan Hayward*	91
7 The sinking of the self: Freudian hydraulic patterns in *Le Grand bleu* *Laurent Jullier*	109
8 Imprisoned freedoms: space and identity in *Subway* and *Nikita* *Mark Orme*	121
9 *Nikita*: consumer culture's killer instinct and the imperial imperative *Hilary Ann Radner*	135
10 *Léon* and the cloacal labyrinth *Phil Powrie*	147

11 *Jeanne d'Arc*: high epic style and politicising camp
   Susan Hayward 161
12 An unpublished interview with Luc Besson
   Gérard Dastugue 175

Filmography 179
Select bibliography 189
Index of proper names and film titles 193

Tables and figures

Tables

3.1	Music and screentime in Besson's films	*page* 47
3.2	Musical themes in *Léon*	50
10.1	Shot-by-shot breakdown of the final explosion in *Léon*	155

Figures

3.1	Léon's theme	52
3.2	The death theme in *Léon*	52
3.3	The romantic theme in *Léon*	52
5.1	Besson's system of male attire	87

Contributors

Raphaël Bassan is a film journalist who has written on experimental cinema (amongst other forms of cinema) in specialist journals such as *Écran* and *La Revue du Cinéma*, in national dailies such as *Libération*, and in dictionaries and encyclopedias, for example *L'Encyclopaedia Universalis* (since 1996), *Une encyclopédie du court métrage français* (2004). He is the co-founder of the Collectif Jeune Cinéma in 1971, and has made three short films: *Le Départ d'Eurydice* (1969), *Prétextes* (1971) and *Lucy en miroir* (2004).

Mark Brownrigg is a lecturer in Film and Media Studies at the University of Stirling. He has published articles on Howard Shore's music in the *Lord of the Rings* trilogy and, with Peter Meech, on the changing nature of music in UK television channel identifiers. He is currently researching the relationship between notions of authorship in film-scoring and the role of convention in mainstream film music.

Gérard Dastugue has completed a PhD at the University of Toulouse II (France) on the viewer's reception of film music in the Hollywood Golden Age. He is a contributor to TraxZone.com, a web magazine devoted to film music, and executive producer for Lympia Records.

Susan Hayward is the Established Chair of Cinema Studies at Exeter University where she is the Director of the Department of Film Studies. She is the founder and co-editor with Phil Powrie of *Studies in French Cinema*. She is the author of *French National Cinema* (Routledge, 2nd edition, 2006), *Cinema Studies: The Key Concepts* (Routledge, 3rd edition, 2006), *Luc Besson* (Manchester University Press, 1998), *Simone Signoret* (Continuum Press, 2005), *Les Diaboliques* (IB Tauris, 2006).

Laurent Jullier is Professor of Film Studies at the University of Paris III-Sorbonne Nouvelle. His most recent publications include *Star Wars, anatomie d'une saga* (Armand Colin, 2005), and *Hollywood et la difficulté d'aimer* (Stock 2004, Prix du meilleur essai 2004 du Syndicat Français de la Critique de Cinéma). He collaborated on *The French Cinema Book* (BFI, 2004) and *For Ever Godard* (Blackdog, 2004).

thinkers had turned to the baroque sensibility with its emphasis on monstrous form and lighting effects during the 1980s (see Buci-Glucksmann, 1984 and 1986; Calabrese, 1992; Deleuze, 1988; Scarpetta, 1988), so that Besson's films were part of a larger cultural and intellectual development. Although Bassan's piece covers all three of the look directors (so Jean-Jacques Beineix and Leos Carax as well), it is an important article which signalled a change in perception of this type of filmmaking. However, it places Besson within a specific 1980s context, which many of the subsequent chapters will question.

The new way of filming exemplified by Besson is paralleled by a new way of producing and financing films, an area of Film Studies which is not generally explored in much detail, but which is vital for an understanding of how Besson has transformed French filmmaking. Rosanna Maule focuses on Besson's second production and distribution company alongside Leeloo (which he retains for his own films), Europa, intended to fulfill the European dream of creating an alternative to Hollywood. Besson, like French cinema more generally, has always had a love–hate relationship with Hollywood, from the distribution litigation with Fox for *Le Grand bleu* to the unsatisfactory or unproductive relations with Warner, Sony and Fox. With Europa, Besson expanded his distribution branch, created the sophisticated post-production studio Digital Factory, and began producing a more diverse set of films. Some of his production efforts are geared to the international mainstream circuit, as is the case for *Baiser du dragon* (*Kiss of the Dragon*, Chris Nahon, 2001) and *Wasabi* (Gérard Krawczyk, 2001). In France, Europa produces more culturally oriented films, directed by arthouse directors (such as the Italian Mimmo Calopresti). Maule's chapter shows how Besson uses strategies of production development and marketing promotion that have for many years been recommended by economic experts as the best way of overcoming the crisis of European cinema. Seen by most film critics as the most Americanised filmmaker of his generation, Besson learned the rules of the contemporary film market with his own films, and applies them to the promotion of projects aimed at the international market. The production and distribution strategies of Besson's companies reflect the coherence of a director who has always struggled to maintain his autonomy from the American as well as the French studios and corporations. Maule shows how the post-Hollywood Besson has overcome the inextricable set of conflicting interests that link European cinema, especially the French cinema, to Hollywood. His production and distribution initiatives view new forms of partnership in the international arena and in France as the only effective counterweights to the North American monopoly.

Our next two chapters consider another area of Film Studies which tends to be addressed less frequently than the visual – music, which has assumed increasing importance since the late 1980s. Long the poor relation in Film Studies, because of the primacy of the visual for theorists of spectatorship, music emerged as a concern from the work devoted to the soundtrack. The 1980 *Yale French Studies* special issue on sound edited by Rick Altman was a key early work (about half of it dedicated to music), as was the work of the French theorist Michel Chion (whose foundational 1980s work has been translated by Claudia Gorbman; see Chion, 1994 and 1999). Scholarship in this area has expanded rapidly as specialists in musicology and Film Studies have explored it, and the vitality of the area is exemplified by the publication of recent anthologies (Donnelly, 2001; Dickinson, 2003), as it is by volumes which attempt to give overviews of complex arguments (for example, Davison, 2004, Duncan, 2003). Although the key work has tended to be on pre-existing classical music and on music composed specifically for the screen (for example, Gorbman 1987; Flinn 1992; Kalinak 1992; and Brown 1994), there has also been a move to explore popular music and film (Kassabian 2000; Wojcik and Knight 2001; Inglis 2003; Powrie and Stilwell 2005).

Besson's films are good examples of the way in which music is a key component of the film. His films, often considered as flashy videoclips, have musical scores which guide audience reception: actions on screen are paralleled by a musical response on the soundtrack. Even though reviews underline Eric Serra's wall-to-wall music in Besson's films, they avoid analysing it, when it seems obvious that it cannot be considered as a mere aesthetic accompaniment. As in melodrama, it establishes a new depth of focus as well as an emphasis on the characters' inner feelings. Gérard Dastugue shows how the music's syntagmatic line unfolds in parallel with the narration, from *Le Dernier combat* through to *Jeanne d'Arc*, but with a particular emphasis on *Léon*, which, as is the case with all of Besson's later films, has music for approximately 90 per cent of the screentime. Mark Brownrigg adopts a more directly musicological analysis, examining the development of Eric Serra's compositional style throughout his association with Besson. He traces a clear progression from the early pop scores, which rely heavily on repeating riffs and set-piece song sequences, to the later full-blown orchestral work on *Le Cinquième élément* and *Jeanne d'Arc*. Brownrigg shows how Serra becomes more ambitious, replacing his Euro-rock riff style with an increasing grasp of orchestral/quasi-orchestral writing. Notwithstanding this development process, Serra has also retained links to his pop roots, most notably through the incorporation of pop songs either as numbers in their own right in the films, or playing over the closing credit crawl, and can still be heard to use the riff-style backing, only using more grandiose riff constructions (as for example in Le Cinquième élément).

During the 1990s, work developed on costume in films. There was an influential collection on costume and the female body (Gaines and Herzog 1990), and later in the decade, Pam Cook explored British Gainsborough films, where she showed how a flamboyant 'Europeanness' betokened a scandalous urge to search for hybrid identities (Cook, 1996). Stella Bruzzi's landmark work considered broader issues of gender and costume, and opened up discussion on masculine costume (Bruzzi, 1997). In that volume, Bruzzi wrote some perceptive pages on gangster costume in Léon. Phil Powrie expands this work on masculine costume by focusing on what could be called Besson's 'sartorial system' of masculine costume, in this case suits of various kinds (including the frequently occurring 'diving suit'), and shows how the stability normally associated with the suit is destabilised in Besson's films. His chapter suggests that Ruby Rhod in Le Cinquième élément is a key figure in this sartorial system.

The following chapters move away from the broader overview of Besson's output to a closer focus on individual films. These are dealt with in broadly chronological order, although some films are dealt with in the same chapter. This is the case, for example, with Susan Hayward's chapter on Le Dernier combat and Le Cinquième élément, which she considers from the generic perspective of the science-fiction film, showing how there are considerable similarities between them, in that they both suggest an ambivalent relationship to technology. However, Le Dernier combat is, she shows, fundamentally dystopian in its ecological critique of various forms of consumption, whereas Le Cinquième élément is more utopian, but also less critical in its play with technology, whether at the level of production (the use of digital images), or at the level of representation (the fascinating issue of Leeloo's 'techno-body').

Laurent Jullier returns to the issue raised by Bassan, that of the new type of anomic 'sad young man', with particular reference to Le Grand bleu. Unlike Bassan, however, he shows how there is some continuity between the protagonists of the New Wave and Besson's films. Jullier focuses on the sea as metaphor, and uses classical psychoanalytic models and evolutionary psychology tools (those of denial and self-deception in particular) to show how Jacques denies reality in his attraction to the sea, which functions as a metaphor for extinction. His form of denial, Jullier suggests, is a combination of projection – where the subject denies aspects of the self which are unacceptable, and projects them onto others – and magical thinking, whereby Jacques considers that he is no longer human, and can live deep under the sea.

As is the case with music and costume in Film Studies, space is also a recent focus, relying principally on the work of André Gardies (Gardies, 1993). Mark Orme analyses *Subway* and *Nikita* from this perspective, showing how the interaction of space and identity is fundamental to the psychological intensity of both films. He shows how Besson exploits the films' settings to reveal the (emotional) state of characters, and how space is used as a vehicle for communicating a sense of 'imprisoned freedom' on which each film pivots. Focusing on the relationship between physical environment and personal psychology, his chapter demonstrates how claustrophobia in *Subway*'s subterranean setting is hijacked and rerouted as an alternative space. It may be an enclosed space, but it assumes for Fred and his fellow eccentrics the magical qualities of a haven liberated from the constraints of convention. In *Nikita*, by contrast, the film's enclosed spaces mirror Nikita's own psychological enslavement.

Several chapters in this volume explore the relationship between the 'French' Besson and the 'American' Besson. Hilary Ann Radner looks in detail at *Nikita* to show how the film creates paradoxes and tensions. It exemplifies an emerging feminine culture that is global in its scope, grounded in consumer competence and the cult of violence. To that extent it undermines its role as an auteur film that exports 'Frenchness'; moreover, despite the fact that Besson's obsession with the disintegrating family may be one of the marks of his auteur vision, in this film, the solitary individual that this vision produces – a single girl without national or familial ties – paradoxically supports the structures that may appear to 'cause' this same disintegration. The key tension of the film, however, is that it tries both to suggest new feminine ideals of autonomy based in consumer culture, while at the same time trying to contain that autonomy. Additionally, like Jullier, Radner suggests that there may be far more links between the New Wave and Besson than the *Cahiers* critics allowed for, in that the consumer-culture femininity that the film exemplifies so well has its roots in the films of the New Wave.

Like some of the areas previously mentioned – music, costume, space – the representation of masculinity in films is another area which came to the fore in Film Studies from the mid-1980s onwards, and is thus, like the other areas mentioned, broadly contemporary with Besson's work. Phil Powrie has already written on masculinity in *Subway* (Powrie, 1997); here, he turns to *Léon*, partly to offset the debates on the troubling heterosexual relationship between Léon and Mathilda at the time of the film's release. Returning to an issue adumbrated in studies of the baroque, mentioned above in relation to Bassan's work, and related to Orme's discussion of spatial configurations in Besson's films, Powrie focuses on the traditionally feminine metaphor of the labyrinth to show how they are as intestinal as they are uterine in Besson's films. He links the labyrinth to Calvin Thomas's work on 'scatontological anxiety' (Thomas, 1996), and through a close analysis of the scene of Léon's death, he shows how the film can be read quite differently, as a rectal and homoerotic fantasy, where the salient relationship is as much that between Stansfield and Léon, as between Léon and Mathilda.

In this volume on Besson, Susan Hayward deals with *Jeanne d'Arc*, a film she was unable to treat in her 1998 monograph. Joan of Arc is one of France's great myths, and has generated a considerable number of film adaptations, with no less than eight in the silent period as well as the better-known sound films.[2] Surprisingly perhaps, Besson's version was mostly well received in the critical press in France, signalling to some extent the acquisition of critical respectability. Hayward provocatively, given this context, explores the spectacular, performance and excess in the film, and their relationship to camp. Camp is historically associated with display by French courtiers. Like Nikita before her, Jeanne is a transgressive female. However, she cross dresses much more than Nikita, and because she also gives orders and wins battles, unlike the courtiers of the period who used camp as part of their abdication of any political responsibility, her performance of androgyny politicises camp. Hayward's argument helps us to see how Besson's film is more radical than its critical acceptance might have led us to believe, and suggests another reason why Jeanne was burnt as a witch.

We complete the volume with an unpublished interview with Besson, undertaken by Dastugue, that dates from late 1999 when *Jeanne d'Arc* was released. In that interview, when asked to explain his statement that he would only make ten films as a director, Besson recalls that there are Ten Commandments, and muses: 'I've always wondered why "Thou shalt not kill" is sixth position rather than first. Rather than saying "You must believe in me",[3] we should have started with that'. His throw-away line is characteristically revealing, with its simultaneous foregrounding and backgrounding of violence in a framework – the Ten Commandments – which could not be more spectacular. Besson as a campy Moses with his ten tablets of stone; the image is as spectacular and knowingly self-deprecating as the films themselves.

References

Bassan, R. (1989), 'Trois néobaroques français', *Revue du cinéma*, 449, pp. 44–50.
Brown, R. S. (1994), *Overtones and Undertones: Reading Film Music* (Berkeley

and London: University of California Press).
Bruzzi, S. (1997), *Undressing Cinema: Clothing and Identity in the Movies* (London and New York: Routledge).
Buci-Glucksmann, C. (1984), *La Raison baroque* (Paris: Galilée).
Buci-Glucksmann, C. (1986), *La Folie du voir: de l'esthétique baroque* (Paris: Galilée).
Calabrese, O. (1992), *The Neo-Baroque: A Sign of the Times* (Princeton: New Jersey, Princeton University Press). Originally published in Italy as *L'età neobarocca* (Roma: Laterza, 1987).
Chion, M. (1994), *Audio-Vision: Sound on Screen*, ed. and trans. by C. Gorbman (New York: Columbia University Press).
Chion, M. (1999), *The Voice in Cinema*, ed. and trans. by C. Gorbman (New York: Columbia University Press).
Cook, P. (1996), *Fashioning the Nation: Costume and Identity in British Cinema* (London: BFI).
Degli-Esposti, C. (1998), 'Postmodernism(s)', in C. Degli-Esposti (ed.), *Postmodernism in the Cinema* (New York and Oxford: Berghahn), pp. 3–18.
Deleuze, G. (1988), *Le Pli: Leibniz et le Baroque* (Paris: Éditions de Minuit). Translated as *The Fold: Leibniz and the Baroque*, trans. T. Conley (London: Athlone, 1993).
Dickinson, K. (ed.) (2003), *Movie Music: The Film Reader* (London and New York: Routledge).
Donnelly, K. J. (ed.) (2001), *Film Music: Critical Approaches* (Edinburgh: Edinburgh University Press).
Flinn, C. (1992), *Strains of Utopia: Gender, Nostalgia and Hollywood Film Music* (Princeton: Princeton University Press).
Gaines, J. and C. Herzog (eds) (1990), *Fabrications: Costume and the Female Body* (London and New York: Routledge).
Gardies, A. (1993), *L'Espace au cinéma* (Paris: Méridiens Klincksieck).
Gorbman, C. (1987), *Unheard Melodies: Narrative Film Music* (Bloomington: Indiana University Press).
Gunning, T. (1990), 'The cinema of attractions: early film, its spectator and the avant-garde', in Thomas Elsaesser and Adam Barker (eds), *Early Cinema: Space, Frame, Narrative* (London: BFI, 1990), pp. 56–62.
Hayward, S. (1998), *Luc Besson* (Manchester: Manchester University Press).
Inglis, I. (ed.) (2003), *Popular Music and Film* (London: Wallflower).
Kalinak, K. M. (1992), *Settling the Score: Music and the Classical Hollywood Film* (Madison: University of Wisconsin Press).
Kassabian, A. (2000), *Hearing Film: Tracking Identifications in Contemporary Hollywood Film Music* (London and New York: Routledge).
Powrie, P. (1997), '*Subway*: identity and inarticulacy', *French Cinema in the 1980s: Nostalgia and the Crisis of Masculinity* (Oxford: Clarendon Press), pp. 121–9.
Powrie, P. (2001), *Jean-Jacques Beineix* (Manchester: Manchester University Press).
Powrie, P. and R. Stilwell (eds) (2005), *Changing Tunes: The Use of Pre-exist-*

ing Music in Film (Aldershot: Ashgate).
Scarpetta, G. (1988), *L'Artifice* (Paris: Grasset).
Thomas, C. (1996), *Male Matters: Masculinity, Anxiety, and the Male Body on the Line* (Urbana and Chicago: University of Illinois Press).
Vincendeau, G. (1996), *The Companion to French Cinema* (London: Cassell and BFI).
Wojcik, P. R. and A. Knight (eds) (2001), *Soundtrack Available: Essays on Film and Popular Music* (Durham, NC, Duke University Press).

Notes

1 The term is Tom Gunning's; see Gunning 1990: 58.
2 In chronological order, and excluding several TV films, these are directed by Alfred Clark (USA, 1895), Georges Hatot (France, 1898), Georges Méliès (France, 1900), Albert Capellani (France, 1908), Mario Caserini (Italy, 1909), Nino Oxilia (Italy, 1913), George Willoughby (Australia, 1916), Cecil B. DeMille (USA, 1917), Carl Dreyer (France, 1928), Marc de Gastyne (France, 1928), Gustav Ucicky (Germany, 1935), Victor Fleming (USA, 1948), Roberto Rossellini (Italy/France, 1954), Jean Delannoy (France, 1954), Otto Preminger (USA, 1957), Robert Bresson (France, 1962), Gleb Panfilov (USSR, 1970), Ulrike Ottinger (Germany, 1989), Jacques Rivette (France, 1994).
3 The First Commandment is in reality 'Thou shalt have no other gods before me'.

Three French neo-baroque directors: Beineix, Besson, Carax, from *Diva* to *Le Grand Bleu*

Raphaël Bassan[1]

In terms of film production, the 1980s[2] has become characterised by a so-called *cinéma du look* and, more specifically, associated with the work of three young filmmakers: Jean-Jacques Beineix, Luc Besson and Leos Carax. Their work has caused much ink to flow, and broke with the chronic naturalism of French cinema. The aims of these three auteurs are not necessarily identical, and the term *neo-baroque* used here to describe their work is perhaps convenient shorthand; but then to analyse their work we must start somewhere. What follows is therefore necessarily fragmentary, contradictory, just like the work of these new wonderboys of the cinema.

Jean-Jacques Beineix was the first of the three to emerge. Unlike Besson and Carax whose work is neo-baroque from their second film, Beineix began to work in this vein from his first film, *Diva* (1981), which can be seen as the founding film of the genre. He has predecessors in the French cinema: Téchiné (*Barocco*, 1976), Rivette (*Duelle*, 1976), Garrel (*Le Berceau de cristal*, 1976). These pioneers only occasionally worked the neo-baroque vein. Beineix is also the only one of the three to adapt novels to the screen. He adds non-functional motifs, arabesques, digressions in excess of the film's initial meaning. The meaning is displaced from narrative to a visual language which carries other messages.

Rift with the critics

It is no coincidence that we should feel the need to integrate the work of Beineix, Besson and Carax in the national and international intellectual environment of the 1980s. The decade has seen the collapse of a number of doctrines and ways of life, whether they be political or aesthetic. Postmodernism rejects artistic progress; it places so-called minor modes of expression (cartoons, graffiti, advertisements) on the same footing as major modes (painting, classical music, art films). This does not mean the end of civilisation as we know it, as so many purists and nostalgics maintain, but informs real discussion about art. There are a thousand and one ways of being *postmodern*.

It is said that the work of the three directors with whom we are concerned here is too hip to be sincere. But they are not so much hip as dependent on the ephemeral nature of their time. For some critics, *Diva*, *Subway* or *Mauvais sang* (Carax, 1986) – the three most neo-baroque films – have no more cultural value than would an advertisement for pantyhose or a popular TV show. But this is to disregard the way in which such material is structured, as well as to disregard the urge to make films, neither of which are the case for the promoters of pantyhose or TV show producers. Let us say no more about this aspect. These so-called intellectuals forget that artists of all ages have made use of the signs available around them. It is hardly possible to ignore the presence of videos, music clips and the new strip cartoons. Are we supposed to carry on using basic sociology and out-of-date humanism at the expense of the cinema, the visual art par excellence? Critics, unable or unwilling to revitalise their discourses, and believing that a 'film with a message' is superior to a highly visual work, have lost some of their influence faced with the multiplicity of printed and recorded images. It is not unusual these days for a film poster to give more clues about the meaning of a film than many articles. The way in which meaning is created has changed, and it is time for those who want to guide spectators in their choices to take account of this.

The heterogeneity of registers in a film is not a sign of weakness. It is important to recognise this if we want to construct a coherent critical system which can map onto the work under scrutiny. If we do not recognise it, that way incoherence lies for the unsuspecting journalist, however competent he or she may be. For example, Michel Perez, one of the most professional of reviewers, used the same arguments at relatively close intervals to praise *Boy meets girl* (Carax, 1984) and to demolish *Mauvais sang*, two films constructed on the same basis:

> The protagonists of *Boy meets girl* show all the contempt that the younger generation has for conventional ideas of beauty, for Hollywood-style glamour which we thought was chiselled in marble and imperishable. But Leos Carax, knowing exactly how to make use of fashion, is careful not to throw his characters into punk, and the miracle happens: these characters become beautiful. (Perez 1984: 23)

A couple of years later, Perez writes as follows: 'Visually the signs of *Mauvais sang* are casual chic, destructuring (as ready-to-wear designers might still say) and carefully calculated grunge . . . Mess and narrative incoherence are turned into an aesthetic system' (Perez, 1986).

This example, one amongst many, is not an isolated instance. When you read the 300 or so pages written on the eight films in our corpus, you feel a real unease in them. Their admirers – not always sincere; you can sense it in the flowery epithets which dispense with any serious reflection – like their detractors get bogged down in anecdotes. These are the expressions that come time and again: 'young filmmakers', 'iconoclasts'; 'have incorporated the lessons of their predecessors', or (a variant) 'have corrupted with impunity the art of their elders'; 'long videoclips'; 'the story does not matter as long as there is poetry' or 'incapable of mastering a story'. The disapproval, the inability to admit a different type of cinema, are sometimes accompanied by bad-temperedness and intolerance which do not reflect well on the critic:

> If you really must go and see Leos Carax's film, do like me, choose the right kind of film theatre. A hundred or 30 uncomfortable seats in the *quartier des Halles*, the smell of joints, a few shaved heads, and, especially, at the back, a tall guy who looks like a wardrobe and who whinnies every time something happens on screen. Don't worry, nothing much happens in Leos Carax's film and you can do what mostly everyone does, just doze off in peace. (Poulle 1985: 40–1)

This nasty review, stuck in the rut of analysing a film by its 'themes', auteurist and sociological, sounds off furiously when faced with something new which it does not understand.

Advertising and creativity

And yet things are slowly changing. When I went to see *Diva* again on 4 January 1986 in the Paris Vidéothèque, I saw a few cinephiles who had refused to go and see the film when it came out. Not long before, when the film was shown on TV, Serge Daney, no lover of Beineix, but a supporter of Carax, situated the debate where it needed to be situated:

> The public supported *Diva* while critics reproached Jean-Jacques Beineix for having made a film of 'applied advertising'. The debate never got anywhere because the wrong questions were asked. Advertising is more than an aesthetic, it is a way of being and seeing, of evaluating and judging, in short a vision of the world. *Diva* was successful because Beineix was the first to address the legacy of advertising philosophically by proposing a separation between pre-existing commodities (objects and clichés) and what cannot be commodified (the soul, creation). (Daney, 1988: 47)

Before proceeding, let us use *Diva* as a yardstick for analysis as it contains the same themes and the same aesthetic treatment of those themes as in the eight films of our corpus. Jules, the young postman, is a sophisticated music lover. He records, without her knowing, the performance given by Cynthia, a black singer. This is the 'artistic' track, the one which really interests Beineix. A thriller plot is grafted onto this central track – a rite of passage for any first-time director at the beginning of the 1980s – which 'darkens' the atmosphere and moves the action along. Nadia, a call-girl, slips an audiocassette denouncing the evildoings of Saporta, the police commissioner, into the young man's satchel. The postman becomes the point of convergence for the antagonist forces in the film. Some Taiwanese businessmen are chasing the recording of Cynthia – a rarity given that she has never made a recording. Saporta's henchmen are also on Jules's trail to get hold of the compromising audiocassette. The young man lives in a loft which he has transformed into a technological paradise.

Beineix plays wonderfully on the tonal and colour contrasts, emphasising light and shadow, loading each frame with decorative effects. Every location, every object is fetishised (and not the products as in advertising) in a new urban mythology, becoming non-functional emblems. We return with *Diva* to the themes of courtly love. During the film, Jules meets up with Cynthia. Do they sleep together? It is vaguely hinted at. What interests the boy is Cynthia's voice, in other words Art with a capital A, one of the few things which still interest young people. It is clear, returning to Daney's point, that art is not commodified for Beineix. Cynthia refuses to commercialise her voice, and Jules steals her dress to seal his lonely pleasure as a music lover.

What does advertising seek to do? It seeks to seduce potential customers, to oblige them to purchase consumer products. How? By a brief, allusive and metaphorical montage, using disparate elements of reality, so as to bring together the promise of personal well-being and the impersonal industrial sphere. What benefits might potential customers obtain? They will get younger (thanks to creams and cosmetics); they will feel better (thanks to beer which quenches thirst, lingerie which magnifies the body's natural contours); they will be able to make love without risks (thanks to condoms). The messages are anonymous; you receive them whether you are rich or poor, young or old, even though only a fraction of the population will use what is being sold, but they address the reality of the individual (a diabetic would fall into a coma if he or she ate too much ice-cream). This is basic advertising, what you see in the intermission between two films at the cinema. Then there is the clip, a more sophisticated version of the ad, which promotes the product artistically.

However creative the clip might be, in the end the aim is purely commercial.

Beineix, Besson and Carax have grown up in a world where ads and clips are everywhere. They were amazed by this non-verbal way of expressing things, and have used it, although only moderately, given that their films all have, whatever people might think, a classical narrative framework. They have not attempted to 'sell' anything in the usual sense of the word. Jules's loft is too excessively decorated to be copyable; Isabelle Adjani's 'Iroquois' hairstyle in *Subway* is no more than a distinguishing mark, a meaningless affectation. Lofts, hairstyles, jewellery, and so on, are already all around us, so why not use them? They are, as Daney says, pre-existing commodities. Moreover, the seductive and flexible language of advertising, in tune with the times, can transmit messages. The most important of these is the revaluation of art, last refuge against the barbarity of the urban metropolis. Jules the postman magnifies his miserable existence, as we have seen, through his passion for opera. He transforms his loft into a work of art by decorating it with all sorts of incongruous objects. Betty is fascinated by Zorg's novel in *37°2, le matin* (Beineix, 1986), and sacrifices her mental equilibrium so that it can be published. After a nuclear holocaust, the old doctor (Jean Bouise) teaches the man he has saved how to speak again by daubing paint onto the walls of his laboratory like a caveman. Jacques Mayol, the diver, abandons everything for his art in *Le Grand bleu*, the art of deep-sea diving. As for Alex, dandy haunted by despair and main protagonist of the two films by Carax (*Boy meets girl* and *Mauvais sang*), he turns his life into a work of art.

Difficulties of communication

There is another important point: these films show young people who cannot communicate, and who find it impossible to love. Jules is enthralled by the diva's voice, and even if he touches her shoulder on one occasion, we presume that the only thing that moves him is her voice. Traumatised by the death of his sister who was raped and murdered, Gérard the docker, another of Beineix's anti-heroes, finds it impossible to establish a relationship with a woman in *La Lune dans le caniveau* (Beineix, 1983). *37°2, le matin*, Beineix's most physical film, shows the decline of a girl in love, destroyed by the talent of her writer boyfriend. His writer's gift makes of him a superior being in her eyes, despite his vapidity. Between these two types of relationship, as slight as they are unhappy, the almost autistic Alex compensates for his existential malaise in *Boy meets girl* and *Mauvais sang* by a tragic drift.

And what about Besson? Woman is a sketchy, almost hidden figure in *Le Dernier combat*. Adjani is brilliant with the coldly distant seductiveness of a fashion model (*Subway*). Fred (Christophe Lambert) declares his love to her:

> FRED: Why do I love you?
> HÉLÉNA: Because I'm a fantastic girl.
> FRED: Why don't you love me?
> HÉLÉNA: Because I can't be bothered.
> FRED: You're lazy.
> HÉLÉNA: Terribly lazy!

Besson de-dramatises the situation by using laconically hip dialogue. The end of the film, which refers to the end of *À bout de souffle* (*Breathless*, Godard, 1960), shows that the situation is more tragic than it seems.

Diva, the first film of our corpus, insisted in a major way (the opera) and in a minor way (the 'look', the décor) on the importance of art (and of artifice) for the youth of today. *Le Grand bleu*, the last film in our list, sketches in close detail the existential portrait of the new generations. Mayol prefers the ocean's depths to Johana's body (Rosanna Arquette, the prettiest breasts in Hollywood). The film was demolished by the critics. But the journalists were wrong. Besson was 'neo-baroque', in the same flashy way as Beineix, but only in *Subway*, even if in other ways (the mix of heterogeneous elements, hyperreal locations) all of his films fall into that category. People wrote that *Le Grand bleu* was nothing more than one long pop video. It is difficult to see how. The film is a realist drama (the beginning in black and white recalls the pared-down feel of *Le Dernier combat*) where the mythical dimension only appears in Jacques Mayol's excessive passion for the ocean depths.

Once the hue and cry had died down, the psychoanalyst Daniel Sibony gave some clues for reading the film differently (as well as potentially those of Beineix and Carax):

> She (Johana) falls in love; he (Mayol) is also 'in love', in inverted commas, because he does not know what it is to be 'in love', he has never had a mother, nor a father whose desire would have transmitted to him the desire for a woman (because these things, the possibility of these things, are transmitted) . . . The only thing the girl who falls in love has is a heart which beats to the rhythm of another world. It is a symbol of a very contemporary unhappiness: there are all the signs of life, the heart beats, but not enough for an affair of the heart . . . The woman wants to bring warmth to the man whose is psychically frozen. But this man has a very modern illness: he finds it as difficult to warm up his cold heart, as to accept his psychic inertia. The woman wants to give him her tenderness, but nothing

Rosanna Maule is Assistant Professor of Film Studies at the Mel Hoppenheim School of Cinema, Concordia University (Montreal, Canada). Her articles on French and Spanish contemporary cinema, as well as early cinema, have appeared in a number of film journals and books. She is also the editor of three journal issues on topics related to early and silent cinema. She is now completing a book on authorial film practices in French and Spanish cinemas since the 1980s. She is a member of the GRAFICS, a research group on early cinema based in Montreal, and of the editorial board of *CinemaS*.

Mark Orme is Principal Lecturer in Languages at the University of Central Lancashire, UK, where he teaches and pursues research in French cinema and twentieth-century French culture. He recently co-organised an international and interdisciplinary conference on Albert Camus in Paris, and is currently preparing the publication of the proceedings. He has also published several articles on Camus, and is completing a book on Camus and Justice, forthcoming by Fairleigh Dickinson University Press.

Phil Powrie is Professor of French Cultural Studies at the University of Newcastle upon Tyne. He has published widely in French cinema studies, including *French Cinema in the 1980s: Nostalgia and the Crisis of Masculinity* (Oxford University Press, 1997), *Contemporary French Cinema: Continuity and Difference* (editor, Oxford University Press, 1999), *Jean-Jacques Beineix* (Manchester University Press, 2001), *French Cinema: An Introduction* (co-authored with Keith Reader, Arnold, 2002), and *The Cinema of France* (editor, Wallflower Press, 2006). He is the co-editor of several anthologies: *The Trouble with Men: Masculinities in European and Hollywood Cinema* (Wallflower Press, 2004), *Changing Tunes: The Use of Pre-existing Music in Film* (Ashgate, 2005), *Composing for the Screen in the USSR and Germany* (Indiana University Press, forthcoming 2006). He is the general co-editor of the journal *Studies in French Cinema*, and co-author of a monograph on film adaptations of the Carmen story.

Hilary Radner is Professor of Film and Media Studies in the Department of Communication Studies at the University of Otago, New Zealand. She is the author of *Shopping Around: Feminine Culture and the Pursuit of Pleasure* (Routledge, 1995), and co-editor of *Film Theory Goes to the Movies* (Routledge, 1993), *Constructing the New Consumer Society* (St Martin's, 1997) and *Swinging Single: Representing Sexuality in the 1960s* (University of Minnesota, 1999). She is completing a book-length manuscript on the post-feminist girly film. Her research interests include feminist film theory, film melodrama in American and French cinema, and the representation of celebrity in French culture.

Preface

This volume arose from a panel at the Popular European Cinema conference entitled 'The Spectacular', held in the University of Warwick in March 2000, where Stella Bruzzi, Susan Hayward, and Phil Powrie each gave a paper on the films of Luc Besson. We are very grateful to Ginette Vincendeau and Richard Dyer for allowing us to do this. Susan Hayward and Phil Powrie subsequently commissioned papers from a wide range of international scholars to continue the work done by Susan Hayward in her 1998 book on Besson. The editors are grateful to the contributors to this volume for their commitment to popular French cinema.

Note that when Besson's films are mentioned in this volume, only the original French title is given, on the assumption that readers will be familiar with those films. We give the translated titles here for the films made by Besson as a director, and which are considered in detail in this volume; all other details for the films are given in the filmography at the end of the volume. English titles for all other non-English films are given in the text.

1983	*Le Dernier combat*	(*The Last Battle*)
1985	*Subway*	
1988	*Le Grand bleu*	(*The Big Blue*)
1990	*Nikita*	(*La Femme Nikita* [USA])
1994	*Léon*	(*Leon* [GB]; *The Professional* [USA])
1997	*Le Cinquième élément*	(*The Fifth Element*)
1999	*Jeanne d'Arc*	(*The Messenger: The Story of Joan of Arc*)

The reader will also find a select bibliography at the end of the volume.

Introduction

Susan Hayward and Phil Powrie

Excess and stylisation are the two major hallmarks of Besson's films. We are most vividly aware of this in characterisation, décor and genre. The characters are larger than life, often powerful physically, whether male or female, at the same time as they seem to lack psychological or historical depth, much like the comic-strip characters to whom they owe a great deal, and with whom critics are often, rather sniffily, prone to compare them. Much as the characters seem to be spectacular images cut loose from any clear historical context – spectacle for spectacle's sake – so too the décor in Besson's films is in excess of the referent, to the point of overriding the narrative. The Paris Métro in *Subway*, or space-age New York in *Le Cinquième élément* become more significant than the original to which they refer; they also become excessive in relation to the décor to which they often obliquely refer: Trauner's Paris in his 1930s films with Marcel Carné for *Subway*; or *Metropolis* (Fritz Lang, 1927) and *Blade Runner* Ridley Scott, 1982) for *Le Cinquième élément*. Excessive in relation to the real as well as imagined cities, Besson's décor is, in a way, too dense, spectacularly real, indeed postmodernly hyperreal.

Excess is one of violence and points to a lack, to an emptiness of meaning. Thus, as we have said, the characters – though larger than life – are in fact empty and ahistorical; similarly, the décors reduce the topography to which they refer to the supremely ugly or the dizzyingly grandiose. The *outer* abundance of the subject points to the lack *within*: characters and décor mirror each other in their excess and their violence until, finally, characters literally become the embodiment of violence, monstrous (in the old sense of freakish) and dazzling cataclysms. We are warned, in Besson's films time and again, of the effects of technology and the drive to control death through making life (bringing Nikita and Leeloo back to life, for example).

Besson's use of excess and stylisation is not just a metaphor for violence and death. It is also extremely playful. He mixes violence with humour (and did so long before Tarantino). He blends the intertexts of early cinema with the comic strip for the best of entertainment effects. The slapstick and gags of early cinema sit well with the bare narrative offered by the comic strip, something that brings Besson closer to Jean-Luc Godard in terms of practice, even though the comparison is not one readily admitted by critics. The combination works to propel the spectator helter-skelter from one violently spectacular event to another – the cinema of attractions at its best.[1]

Despite Besson's stature as a popular filmmaker during the late 1980s and 1990s, there was during this period little major academic work on his films. The single exception was Susan Hayward's monograph which opened MUP's French Directors series in 1998. Since that volume appeared, Besson's work has been explored by academics in more detail, as our bibliography shows. The purpose of this volume is to supplement that pioneering work by covering a broad range of issues in Besson's films, which have not yet been substantially covered by academic analysis; and, moreover, wherever possible, to use analytical tools developed in Film Studies during the same period as Besson's work.

We begin with a key article on the *cinéma du look* for the *Revue du cinéma* in 1989 by experimental filmmaker and film critic Raphaël Bassan, translated here for the first time. During the 1980s, the *cinéma du look* was roundly despised by establishment critics connected with the major film journal in France, the *Cahiers du cinéma*, who considered his films (and those of fellow *cinéma du look* director Beineix) to be simplistic exercises in style, bereft of any substantial 'message' (see Powrie 2001: 10–21 for an exploration of this issue). Ginette Vincendeau's description of this style of filmmaking reflects to some extent this view: 'Youth-oriented films with high production values . . . The "look" of the *cinéma du look* refers to the films' high investment in non-naturalistic, self-conscious aesthetics, notably intense colours and lighting effects. Their spectacular (studio-based) and technically brilliant *mise-en-scène* is usually put to the service of romantic plots' (Vincendeau 1996: 50). Bassan's reassessment was little short of revolutionary in its impact. Here was an experimental filmmaker, a director concerned with film as formal experimentation, claiming that Besson, Beineix and Carax exemplified new and vital concerns in both film form and in the way their films intersected with social concerns. Bassan argues in his article that the *cinéma du look* can be theorised as 'neo-baroque' in its emphasis on *mise-en-scène*; this is now the orthodox view of Besson in many recent film histories. As Bassan himself points out in his article, many European happens given that what allows love to speak itself is missing ... Some critics have criticised the absence of sensation, of emotion, but have not asked themselves why these things are absent; to do this they would have been obliged to put themselves on the line, instead of refusing to understand. (Sibony 1988: 2)

Besson has pinpointed a contemporary truth (which should not be taken to imply that I find the film excellent). There have been countless surveys of single men and women in magazines in recent times. We are a long way from the utopian films of the 1960s with their commitment to free love.

Questions of style

I have neither the space nor the competence to undertake a thorough analysis of the reasons for this malaise relative to the films under consideration. Briefly though, there is, as Sibony remarked, the death of the 'fathers': Betty and Zorg (*37°2, le matin*), and the zombies of *Le Dernier combat*, do not seem to have a family. Héléna/Adjani's husband (*Subway*) is despicable. Gérard has lost his sister and cannot stand his brother (*La Lune dans le caniveau*). A father asks his son to kill him if he should become senile (*Boy meets girl*). Alex's father (*Mauvais sang*) and Jacques's father (*Le Grand bleu*) die at the start of each film. The 'heroes' of these films are generally from a modest social background (postman, painter-decorator, jobless). Their desire to make good is channelled through art, whether it be admiration from afar, as is the case with Jules who, without his passion for opera, would be condemned to play cards during his lunchbreaks, or by practising an art (*Le Grand bleu*). The hero has to be available, which means that he cannot enter into a deep emotional relationship with anyone. Nuclear danger (*Le Dernier combat*) or AIDS (*Mauvais sang*), two very contemporary ills, oblige the protagonists to retreat into their cocoon. Finally, Beineix, Besson and Carax are the 'new moralists' of the 1980s. Zorg refuses to sleep with a friend because he loves Betty (*37°2, le matin*). Enzo, who has begun to flirt with Johana, leaves off when he understands that she is getting closer to Jacques (*Le Grand bleu*). It is Carax who expresses this new philosophy the most overtly in *Mauvais sang*: those who make love without love will catch 'STBO' (no need to translate).

It has been said that the style of these wonderboys is that of advertising (we shall return to this below), but the aim of their films has nothing at all to do with the advertising ethos: art and 'passion' cannot be bought and sold. This could explain the ambivalence of critics, who reject them, but are also drawn to them. There is a disjunction between form and content. When you watch a film by Antonioni, you know that it will end badly. In the case of Lelouch, on the other hand, things usually turn out all right. But with Beineix, Besson and Carax, you get a combination of playfulness and the death or failure of the 'heroes'. All the seductive elements (neon lights, extravagant hairstyles, hi-tech hi-fi, and so on) are negatively connoted. They are no longer signs of well-being, but signs of death. Paraphrasing the advert for 'Canada Dry' ('It has the taste, the colour, the appearance of alcohol, but it isn't alcohol'), we could say of *Subway* or *Mauvais sang*: they look like adverts for the young, for Paris by night, for unusual tourist attractions; but they are no more than the desperate visions of individuals who are suffocating, counter-ads for 'misfortune'.

Where style is concerned, Guy Scarpetta has written a remarkable book on the 'neo-baroque'. He writes as follows:

> It is perfectly possible for fashion which is ephemeral and art which is timeless to share the same forms, the same materials, the same states of mind. The two are demarcated not so much by the 'nature' of the signs they use as their pace (much as one might talk of the pace of an engine, which allows different speeds). This is probably not enough, however. Beyond differences of pace and of temporality, we should also define a difference in use. Art is distinguishable from fashion in its ability to arouse simultaneously a feeling of pleasure and of truth, even if this truth is the result of fiction, of artifice. (Scarpetta 1988: 126).[3]

We find this mixture of pleasure and truth in the work of Beineix, Besson and Carax, although in different degrees. It is interesting to note that these filmmakers have been attacked hypocritically for the pleasure aroused by their films (the criticism being that they are based on a disjointed formalism). This prevents critics from going any deeper, where a dystopian view of 1980s society is hidden. Advertising is rooted in the allusive language of contemporary art. Avant-garde artists at the turn of the twentieth century worked towards a new worldview through the juxtaposition of very different realities. As early as 1912, Braque and Picasso were captivated by the potential for new associations in the practice of collage (bits of material, newspaper clippings, cardboard, cut-out pictures). These practices were developed by surrealism and pop art. Advertisers found that this kind of language, which dispenses with all rational explanation, worked very well to sell their products.

Neo-baroque in spite of everything?

With *Diva*, something changed in the way that art was seen in French commercial cinema. Unlike Epstein (Impressionism) or Godard (New

Wave), Beineix was not looking to establish a 'school', or to make grand historical statements. He knew that the 1980s would not produce any new artistic language. Work produced in the 1980s borrows from all historical periods and recycles material in what has been called postmodernism. Scarpetta has defined this new state of mind by using Malraux's notion of the 'imaginary museum':

> (This kind of art) is meta-historic, autonomous, its forms can work together independently from 'art history' conceived as linear, positivist, and narrowly chronological . . . It gives us access to a perceptual universe, not just an intellectual universe, in which, as in Malraux's books, 'The Nashi Waterfall' from the Nezu Museum in Tokyo can be put side by side with the 'Lac d'Annecy' by Cézanne [1896] . . . or a voodoo statuette from Dahomey with Picasso's 'Little girl skipping' [1950]. Each painter, each artist, will of course find his own particular solution to this new perceptual situation. It is undoubtedly the case, however, that it is no longer possible to see things in the same way any more, as if this visual shock had not happened. (Scarpetta 1988: 97)

Let us consider now my hypothesis of the 'neo-baroque', which is a useful way of thinking about the work of these three filmmakers, and more appropriate than has hitherto been allowed. The dictionary definition of the word 'baroque' (which comes from the Portuguese word *barroco*, meaning an irregular pearl) is as follows:

> In art the baroque wants to astonish, touch the senses, dazzle. It does so by using effects which rely on movement and contrast of light, forms which are stretched and strained to the point where perspective is disrupted and mutates into *trompe-l'œil*. Architecture, sculpture and painting tend to blend together into a unitary spectacle whose dazzling energy conveys euphoria. (*Le Petit Larousse*, 1989)

This new version of 'neo-baroque' spectacle ('neo' because the baroque is historically dated) is common to the three filmmakers in question, although the mix differs. The most perfect example is *Diva*, which manages to maintain an equilibrium between narrative and form.[4] Decorative excess dominates *La Lune dans le caniveau*. But then as this film is about pain, loss, neurosis, its 'dys-narrative', as one might say, does not seem out of place. *37°2, le matin* is closely mapped onto its plot. The visionary side occurs at the beginning when Betty and Zorg paint the beach-houses. Beineix works with pre-existing material (novels by Delacorta, Goodis, Djian), while Besson's inspiration comes from popular genres, whether literary (science fiction, adventure stories) or graphic (cartoons). Carax depends much more on a solid cinema culture. *Le Dernier combat* seems classically balanced due to its restraint. Its baroque features are not pronounced, emerging mainly through black and white colour contrasts, and the framing which tends to magnify even the barest décor. *Subway* is Besson's most baroque film. Ephemeral on the surface, the film manages nevertheless to suggest an alternative vision. The strangeness of *Le Grand bleu* comes from the ocean depths which are rarely seen on screen. Besson's baroque is probably the least thought through of the three directors. Carax is undoubtedly the most 'theoretical'. He borrows from his predecessors (Godard, Garrel, Cocteau, Dreyer) and recycles the material within a very personal vision. His films are the closest to the 'irregular pearls' of the baroque. The linking factor is his desire to tell his own story through the characters and the situations he has come across in other people's films. This makes him somewhat different from Beineix and Besson. It could be argued that Jules in *Diva* is a distant alter ego of the director, and that Mayol in *Le Grand bleu* has more than a few points in common with Besson; but these characters are too fictionalised to be truly autobiographical. Alex, the name of the main protagonist of *Boy meets girl* and *Mauvais sang*, played on both occasions by Denis Lavant, is much more obviously Leos Carax's 'double', something underlined by the fact that the director's real name is Alex Dupont. We therefore have here a set of baroque mirror images: each time a film is referred to, it also refers to the experience of Carax-as-spectator who was going through specific life crises when he saw that film.

What will the future hold for these directors during the 1990s? A naturalist style of filmmaking is gradually developing. Zidi, in *Deux* (1989),[5] has managed to reconcile an advertising style with its utopian message: Paris is a beautiful city, and love, even frustrated, can blossom. A stylish flat in a stylish location helps things along no end. No more dirty lofts decorated with posters; no more young people living on the edge of society; no more stories about the difficulty of being in love when you live in a society which has lost its ideals. In nine months (January 1990), everything will be rose-tinted. Perhaps Beineix, Besson and Carax will yield to this facile optimism. Let us hope not.

References

Buci-Glucksmann, C. (1986), *La Folie de voir: de l'esthétique baroque* (Paris: Galilée).
Daney, S. (1988), 'Beineix Opus 1', *Libération* (21 November 1988), n.p. Reprinted in S. Daney, (1991) *'Devant la recrudescence des vols de sacs à main': cinéma, télévision, information 1988–1991* (Lyon, Aléas), pp. 47–8.
Fernandez, D. (1984), *Le Banquet des anges: l'Europe baroque de Rome à*

Prague (Paris: Plon).
Perez, M. (1984), 'Leos Carax: les habits neufs du cinema français', *Le Matin* (23 November 1984), p. 23.
Perez, M. (1986), 'Un accès de fièvre de croissance', *Le Matin* (28 November 1986), n.p.
Poulle, F. (1985), 'Mauvais sang', *Le Jeune cinéma*, 164, 40–1.
Sarduy, S. (1975), *Barroco* (Paris: Seuil). Originally published in Buenos Aires: Editorial Sudamericana, 1974; second French edition published 1980.
Scarpetta, G. (1988), *L'Artifice* (Paris: Grasset).
Sibony, D. (1988), 'Le Grand bleu de nos malaises', *Libération* (10 August 1988), p. 2.

Notes

1 Translated by Phil Powrie.
2 Editors' note: this article appeared in one of the major film journals in May 1989, under the title 'Trois néobaroques français: Beineix, Besson, Carax, de *Diva* au *Grand Bleu* ', *La Revue du cinéma*, 449, pp. 44–50. *La Revue du cinéma* ceased publication in October 1992 with no. 486.
3 There are a number of other recent books devoted to the resurgence of the baroque; see Fernandez (1984), Buci-Glucksmann (1986), Sarduy (1975).
4 *Diva* is the best film of this group along with *Mauvais sang*. If I have relegated this value judgment to a note, it is because the purpose of this article is to analyse the way these films function, independently of any artistic merit they may have.
5 Editors' note: a romantic comedy in which a composer and concert organiser falls in love with an estate agent.

2

Du côté d'Europa, via Asia: the 'post-Hollywood' Besson

Rosanna Maule

> Luc Besson has been praised and disparaged as one of the new breed of high-tech, high-gloss, Americanoid, anti-auteur filmmakers who do not wish to provide an alternative to Hollywood's blockbuster confections, but merely to embellish them with some Gallic sauce. Mr. Besson has even been described as the French Steven Spielberg. (Sarris, 1991)

Many film critics, in France and within the international film scene, share the conviction that Luc Besson is one of the most Americanised European filmmakers of his generation, a typical byproduct of Hollywood's pervasive influence over nation-state cinemas. This reputation has accompanied Besson for most of his career; and indeed, for his detractors, it constitutes a major point of critique. During the 1980s, Besson's American aura was associated with the director's penchant for action films and generic formulas, and complemented his categorisation within the *cinéma du look*, a film style allegedly aimed at younger generations accustomed to watching Hollywood blockbusters. Since the 1990s, this American image was substantiated by Besson's increasing collaboration with Hollywood, which involved the distribution of his films in the US mainstream circuit by Hollywood film companies and production/distribution contracts with Hollywood studios. To complete the picture, Besson progressively moved into multi-million dollar budgets and English-speaking productions, replete with Hollywood stars and actors.

Yet, for his part, Besson has always maintained his professional distance from Hollywood and, even though he has signed contracts with three of its studios (a two-year contract with Warner Brothers, a three-year contract with Sony and a three-year contract with 20th Century-Fox), has rarely worked on an American film set. The only film he has co-produced with an American film company is *Léon*. At the film's US release, *Variety* presented Besson as an independent player, 'a dedicated auteur' yet 'unabashedly commercial', a filmmaker who 'does not feel like a "French" director' and is happy to work in Hollywood yet is 'not sure he wants to put the sunglasses' on 'full-time' (Alexander 1994: 10). Some years later, coinciding with the release of *Jeanne d'Arc*, the entirely French-funded mega-production about France's eponymous martyr, *Variety* saluted Besson as an 'action auteur', 'largely unloved by his fellow French filmmakers' (Williams 1999: 105). His first official recognition by film critics in his own country was the 1997 César award as best director for *Le Cinquième élément*. Besson's defence against French critics' accusations that he is 'trying to emulate American "commercial" cinema' and 'selling out for the American-style movies' is based on the claim that his narrative developments would be unacceptable in Hollywood and that he had yet to make sequels of his most successful films (Williams 1999: 105).

Since October 2000, Besson's independent attitude vis-à-vis both the French and the American film contexts has concretised in the film production and distribution company Europa Corp (subsequently referred to as Europa). A studio entirely based in France, located on Besson's estate properties in Paris and Normandy, and financed through the reinvestment of box-office revenues from the films that Besson directs and produces, Europa hardly registers as a 'French comeback'. The enterprise shows a logical development within Besson's coherent trajectory of self-determination, and reinstates his assertive stance on the importance and centrality of French and European cinema to the international film market. Besson's initiatives at Europa have been enmeshed with the French–American debate over cultural exception and have punctuated some of the most salient stages in French cinema's attempt to maintain a double standard on its economic and cultural interests vis-à-vis Hollywood. Before addressing these issues, an overview of Besson's position within both the domestic and international film arenas is in order.

An American in Paris, a Parisian in New York: the trans-national Besson

An outsider to the French film system and culture, Luc Besson has, from the beginning of his career, carved out his own space and retained a margin of autonomy within the French and international film industry by combining independent and corporate systems of production and personal and standard methods of filmmaking (see Hayward 1998: 13–21). He has always chosen his own collaborators and maintained director's cut and general supervision even for the most costly and complex of his projects and at every stage of his films' pre-production and production, an endeavour that he can undertake owing to his technical competence and his indefatigable, meticulous working style.[1] In spite of the fact that he entered the mainstream circuit at a very young age and has forged tight connections with sizable studios (mainly Gaumont, France's largest film company, with whom he was associated from 1984 to 1999), he has remained a defender of independent production systems, which lie at the core of his filmmaking philosophy. His comments on his long collaboration with Gaumont are indicative of this sensibility:

> During fifteen years, my relations with Gaumont have always been both good and difficult. Gaumont is an old lady, a big, heavy firm, and I have always been small and alone. Now, the interests of a big company are not always those of a person. The people in charge at Gaumont have always been kind people, agreeable and listening, but, this notwithstanding, each film has been a battle. They are open-minded businessmen, but they are not artists. Each time, I have had the impression of making a film against them. Never have I arrived with a project to hear them say to me: 'Yes, super, brilliant!' (Besson 2001: 80).[2]

Another distinctive aspect of Besson's self-determination is his detachment from France's 'high' film culture and institutions, traditionally identified with the films circulating at film festivals and cine-clubs and discussed in film journals, as well as with academic film programmes or professional film schools. Boycotted by film journals and either scorned or ignored as a commercial phenomenon at film festivals,[3] Besson is notoriously secretive about his projects and gives very few interviews, primarily with film magazines that have proven supportive of his work, which in France includes *Première* and *Studio Magazine*.

The unresolved tension between Besson and the French art-house film context foregrounds some of the contradictions implicit in the demarcation of culturally and commercially oriented film modes, and reinstates traditional views of European and Hollywood cinemas as monolithic and antithetical film systems.[4] Hayward has suggested that Besson's attitude towards production systems and filmmaking methods situates him within the French tradition of collective film modes, particularly the 1930s poetic realist movement (Hayward 1998: 10). Undoubtedly, Besson proposes a unique blending of personal and collaborative working styles. If his political and aesthetic purposes differ considerably from those of the Popular Front cinema, they certainly offer a similarly uncompromising and autonomous stance with respect to France's state cinema and cultural establishment, inspired by national–popular ideas concerning cinema's function in modern society.

Ideologically, Besson's idea of cinema as a narrative form of expression and entertainment may appear as simply a slight variation – no matter how personalised and culturally specific – of Hollywood and mainstream cinema's enviable predicament, as 'flexible managerial culture and an open and innovative financial system' that has 'adapted to changing economic and social conditions' (Miller 1998: 371). However, a crucial difference exists between Besson's approach and Hollywood's: whereas for the latter any creative purpose remains subordinated to industrial and commercial considerations, for Besson creativity and style have primacy, as he reaffirmed in a 2002 interview with *Première*:

> The mechanism scares you in the beginning. . .But today, I detach myself, I take pleasure in the gesture, in the writing. The camera, like style, must weigh as much as a feather. A creator must have a suppleness that allows him to be more inventive. One does not have to become ossified or let oneself be grabbed by the apparatus. (Besson 2002: 94)

Without falling back into essentialist juxtapositions between industrial and artistic priorities, it is legitimate to say that Besson's markedly individualistic and anti-institutional practices are incompatible with studio-modelled modes of production. Although ignoring any recognisable gestures of intellectual justification and still at the service of the film industry, Besson's cinema is ultimately the product of a filmmaker who conceives box-office revenue as a necessary but not essential aspect of his work. In the summer of 2001, less than a year since the foundation of his new film studio, Besson made a strongly negative assessment of his relationships with Hollywood. Although his comments propose some clichés about Hollywood's assembly-plant methods, set against his self-enterprising, individually coordinated mode of production, they also capture the daily reality of a production system which Besson has personally lived through and walked away from:

> In the studio system, when you make a film, you take the risk of getting fired, so. . .everyone tries not to make films! This is the spirit of the studios. You don't make a film until you cannot do otherwise. Except for the unavoidable projects, like Spielberg or Tom Cruise, the studios practically never give the green light. I've spent three years at Warner: they have never 'greenlighted' any of my projects. At Sony, it was the same. They say: 'Super, super!' until the studio head has himself fired and a new team arrives. Everybody is paid, the weather is beautiful, the guys beat it at 4:00 pm. It's their life, but it is not mine. They have a mentality of their own. They don't want to take any risk. They want some product. And if you are not there to make their product, it doesn't work. Sure, they say they love the European artists, they only ask them to give a little tone to their films. Like, we make the cake and you put the cherry on top. (Besson 2001: 79)

Besson has a more dialectical vision of French cinema, one that acknowledges the interface of commercial and artistic constituents of a national film context largely backed by state subsidies and predicated upon cultural priorities, yet also accountable to a large mainstream audience and market. Commenting in *Première* on the present situation of the French film industry, Besson opines:

> In France, about twenty people control the cinema in its entirety. They are producers, directors, managers, people who have an economic responsibility but who must also love cinema. If they don't have this love, it's the cinema as a whole that is in deep shit. What is important is that they recognise a good equilibrium. If they are twenty people that think of nothing else but making money, it's going to be a catastrophe. If they love cinema, they are going to divide things into parts: producing certain films because economically the whole of the business needs it; then, producing other films, more demanding, because we also need those. . .I don't sufficiently know these people to know if they are all aware of this. I am aware of this and it's one hell of a responsibility. (Besson 2002: 95)

Undoubtedly, Besson's defence of a national–popular model of cinema reveals cultural roots heavily indebted to the cinematic imagination of a mainstream filmgoer. His cinematic preparation is linked to the viewing conditions offered by a film market dominated by Hollywood blockbusters and French mainstream films. His professional competence is the result of a long and humble apprenticeship on film sets, progressively moving his way up to the position of assistant director.[5] Soon after the creation of Europa, Besson reinforced his image as an independent player by means of moving into a new area of the public sphere, the Internet. Besson's official website contains a personal editorial under the rubric 'Princess L.', intended to act as Besson's alter ego or spokesperson. Princess L. makes frank observations (in Besson's style), among other things, about films that she has recently seen. Princess L.'s remarks ultimately accentuate Besson's pride in classifying himself as an ordinary filmgoer, and continue his long-established polemic against the film critics through dismissive comments about their own writings on the same films.

If Besson's cinematic preferences often stem from an aesthetically and historically naive perspective, they also suggest an unrestricted consideration of cinema and a rejection of the categorisations that have for years biased the discussion of French cinema towards its construction and commendation as the ceremonial banner of Europe's art cinema. Ginette Vincendeau reminds us that 'French cinema is *also* — and for its home audience, primarily – a popular cinema' (Vincendeau 1996. x). For Vincendeau, the most idiosyncratic character of French cinema resides in its cultural vitality, supported not only by discriminatory institutions such as film festivals, cine-clubs, and specialised film journals, but also by a wide-ranging typology of audience and media. Lucy Mazdon adds to this point by stressing the different perception of French cinema domestically and abroad. Introducing an anthology on 1990s popular French films, she explains why the distinction between art and popular cinema is problematic and concludes:

> It would seem that what we perceive to be an 'art' or a 'popular' film depends as much upon the particular context of reception as upon the identity of the film itself. This is not to suggest that such definitions are entirely redundant. Evidently some films are more aesthetically or thematically challenging than others and will demand quite different modes of reception to those invited by the mainstream product. However, such definitions are a highly complex matter, subject to change and influenced, as we have seen, by production, exhibition, and reception. (Mazdon 2001: 5)

The pre-eminent labelling of French films as art films, as films not developed for a mainstream circuit, is one of the reasons for the rare distribution of France's popular films abroad, a rule only occasionally broken by box-office phenomena such as, to pick three recent examples, the two films adapted from the Asterix comic strips and the universal hit *Le Fabuleux destin d'Amélie Poulain* (*Amelie*, Jean-Pierre Jeunet, 2001). As Mazdon notes, the box-office success *Taxi* (Gérard Pirès, 1998), produced by Besson's company Leeloo, was promoted in Britain with the slogan: 'Hollywood doesn't make them like this any more'. This particular instance of (anti-) Americanisation is the antithesis of the one that Columbia adopted in 1994 to promote *Léon* in the USA, which described the work as an 'American film by the director of *La Femme Nikita*' (the English title for *Nikita*). Whereas *Léon* is an action film set in New York and co-produced by Columbia, *Taxi* is set in Marseille, displays typical traits of French comedy, and was entirely produced and distributed by a French company. Including all the classic ingredients of the Hollywood action film, and adapting the on-wheel, speed-related plot inaugurated by *Speed* (Jan de Bont, 1994), *Taxi* foregrounds car chases and stunts, and is, as are all of Besson's films, interwoven with French cultural motifs. The British promotion of *Taxi* hits the right note in that it incidentally translates one of Besson's ambitions: making films with the same production values as Hollywood, but with a distinctive tone and setting.

The configuration of Besson's work, between auteur, art and national discourse

In her book *Luc Besson* (1998), Susan Hayward analyses Besson's films 'in context,' stressing the filmmaker's alterity with respect to the French lineage of state- and television-supported authorial cinema (Hayward, 1998). She reminds us that Besson resists the label 'auteur' and prefers to use the director's definition of himself as a *metteur-en-scène*, which in French means film director, but is also a figure that the 1950s French auteur-oriented critics juxtaposed to the auteur to delineate a stylistically talented although not conceptually unique filmmaker (Hayward 1998: 2–10). To be sure, Hayward's approach also suggests that, in so far as Besson reinstates a personal style and worldview within mainstream filmmaking practices, he could also be categorised within the tradition of the auteur directors.[6] Indeed, in spite of the scorn that auteur-oriented critics have explicitly expressed for him, Besson is the herald of authorial film practices whose cultural sanctions trespass the surreptitious boundaries of 'art' and 'popular' cinema. Ultimately, though, deciding to what film typology Besson belongs, or debating whether Besson is an auteur, is not the point. The issue at stake is verifying what pre-established assumptions and classifications of film practices and modes are subsumed under the notion of auteur, in France and in the international scene, with the awareness that, as Timothy Corrigan observes, the film author is a historically and contextually variable manifestation of an aesthetic category and a commercial strategy of promotion (see Corrigan, 1991).

Alternatively, Besson's position as a 'popular' filmmaker should be considered within a national and international context, particularly with respect to the role of European cinema in the global audiovisual market. As Stephen Crofts suggests, the 'European-model of art cinema', promoted after the Second World War to counteract Hollywood, has been modified by 'the suppression of existentialism by later 1960s political radicalism and subsequent apoliticism', as well as by 'Hollywood's development of its own art cinema' (Crofts 1993: 51). Crofts also underlines the complications of the situation; that is, the exchanges that many of these European art cinemas have established with Hollywood styles and genres, a claim that is at the centre of many critical approaches to European national cinemas, including Thomas Elsaesser's on New German Cinema and Marsha Kinder's on Spanish *Nuevo Cine*. Many scholars (Crofts 1998, Durovicová 1994, Moran 1996 and Petrie 1992) and players in the film industry (Finney 1996, Ilott 1996 and Puttnam 1997) have stressed that the idea of European cultural unity is both purely theoretical and hardly applicable to either past or present European conditions. According to Victoria de Grazia, during the post-Second World War period the logic of each European nation state was that of integrating 'Europe on a societal level around a common material culture' while maintaining its economic distinction through protectionist laws against the competition of the US cinema (de Grazia 1998: 27).

France's audiovisual policy vis-à-vis Hollywood cinema is an example of the flagrant paradox existing between Europe's claim for its cultural specificity and unity and the actuality of the nation states' economic and political orientations. In the homeland of European art-house cinema's 'mystique', two popular film types contributed to save France's film industry in the 1980s: the heritage film and the *cinéma du look*. France's protectionist policies on foreign films (in contrast to other European countries, most notably the UK) were reinforced at the same time that French film corporations were merging their distribution circuits with some US majors (including, to mention just a few of the earliest ones, Gaumont with Buena Vista in 1993, and UGC with Fox in 1995). As much as these commercial strategies were profitable for the development of French cinema abroad through international co-productions, they obviously clashed with the country's resolute stance on retaining its cultural distinction from Hollywood. For the French film industry, Besson has perennially represented a major source of box-office receipts and secured access to the US market. Indeed, Besson concretised efforts by the French Minister of Culture Jack Lang and the producer Toscan du Plantier's (the head of Gaumont in the early 1980s and then of Unifrance, the state's promotional agency for French films abroad) to reinstate France in the domestic and international circuits of film distribution. Moreover, he is the only filmmaker identified with the *cinéma du look* to overcome the crisis that this type of cinema faced in the early 1990s.[7]

Although firmly rejecting any affiliation with Europe's 'high art' or 'intellectual' film tradition, Besson has often acknowledged his position within the French and European film contexts with respect to an alleged cultural heritage. Decidedly, Besson does not align himself with the French (and European) claim for the 'cultural exception of cinema' through which France argued its position against the USA at the 1993 Uruguay Round of the General Agreement on Tariffs and Trade (GATT). To this day, the issue remains a hot topic of controversy with the USA and Hollywood representative, Jack Valenti, President of Motion Picture Association of America, as well as with different factions of the French film industry. On this issue, Besson's statements are resolute, while still coherent with his conception of cinema:

> There is no cultural exception. We have to keep the word 'culture'. That's all. The culture is the identity card of a country. Period. We don't say 'the passport exception'. We say 'passport'. With culture it's the same, we don't even have to fight over this. They can't take out an organ from us. The culture is in us, is our heart. It won't be possible to take it out from us. Or it will be necessary to kill us all. (Besson 2001: 95)

To be sure, Besson mitigates his view of cultural exception by insisting on his defence of cultural diversity. Yet, within the context of French film culture shared by film critics and art-house filmmakers and producers, a negative view of cultural exception is equivalent to an anti-nationalist declaration vis-à-vis French cinema. Some months after Besson had pronounced his opinion on the matter, Jean-Marie Messier's abrupt declaration that 'cultural exception is dead', pronounced at the time of his acquisition of Canal+, provoked a vast polemic, which echoed among French film critics and filmmakers. The discussion on cultural exception has reinforced strong partisanships within the French film system and culture. But France's claim for cinema's cultural exception is predominantly the symptom of unresolved contradictions within the French and international film industry. The widely publicised confrontation between France and the USA at the 1993 GATT showed less the struggle between the cultural values of cinema (France) versus the commercial usurper (the USA), than it did two contestants representing opposite interests in an important sector of the culture industry. Quoting Michael Chanan published in the British film journal *Vertigo*, Angus Finney concludes that the real issue behind the GATT crisis was 'the result of a move during the 1980s by the US to change the arena for international regulation of intellectual property . . . the move corresponds to the growing importance of the culture industry in the global market-place, now including not only entertainments but also information' (Finney 1996: 7). As do other observers, Finney argues that the temporary resolution of the 1993 GATT wrangling between France and the USA was an 'exception' to the inclusion of films in the trade agreement (see also Jäckel, 1996 and Puttnam, 1997). According to him, the agreement brought no substantial modifications to the pre-existing situation, in so far as it 'only sanctioned those protectionist measures that were already in place' (Finney 1996: 8). Miller argues that the international meeting that followed and replaced the GATT in 1995, the World Trade Organisation (WTO), turned the attention of the audiovisual sector toward other controversial issues, namely the TV–film nexus and satellite programming. Miller gives a Marxist-oriented interpretation of the GATT and European Union (EU) cultural politics, noting that:

> The abiding logic of the Community's audiovisual policy is commercial: it clearly favors large concerns that can be built upon further . . . the seeming discontinuity with earlier concerns, when the E.C. had a primarily economic personality, is misleading: a notion of cultural sovereignty underpins concerns vis-à-vis the US, but so too does support for monopoly capital and the larger states inside its own walls. (Miller 1998: 80)

With Europa, the 'post-Hollywood' Besson is proving that (successful) movies can be made and distributed outside of the constraints and limitations of Hollywood's global control and France's stance for cultural exception. Conceived from within a national–popular perspective, the film production and distribution company targets the international film market and thrives on the ideological inconsistencies of France's pretensions about its 'cultural' specificity. From this perspective, the studio's opening of the Asian market (sanctioned in April 2002 through the creation of Europa Corp. Japan, which linked Europa with the Japanese film distribution company Asmik-Ace) offers a way out of the inextricable set of conflicting interests that bind European cinema (and particularly France) to Hollywood, by creating new forms of partnership within the international film arena as well as in France.

Europa and the politics of France's (inter)national film marketing

Besson had this to say about the creation of Europa:

> What was your ideal in creating Europa? – Quite honestly? To have fun! It's the only thing that we thought of. The excitement of saying to ourselves: 'We are going to be able to make the films that we dream about'. After that, we had to get organised and do things seriously so as to be able to master the entire production line, from the conception of the project to its diffusion in film theatres and in video. But the first impulse was that: to have fun! (Besson 2001: 81)

Although Besson likes to present Europa as the result of a fortuitous encounter among people variously related to the film business, a calculated professionalism may be read behind the rationale in bringing together the expertise of a previous manager of Gaumont, an emerging producer, and an art-house actor turned agent. Besson's senior partner, Pierre-Ange Le Pogam, is a former Gaumont executive with eighteen years of experience in the studio's highest ranks (when he left, he was general assistant director). Among other things, Pogam is at the head of GBVI, the company that sealed the contract between Gaumont and Disney. Through him, Disney distributed Europa's first film, *Kiss of the Dragon* (*Le Baiser du dragon*, Chris Nahon, 2001), in the international film market. The other two associates do not have quite the same credentials. The young Virginie Silla (since August 2004 Besson's wife) had worked for a few years at Gaumont in the foreign office department, the distribution department, and as an assistant producer, before joining Besson's team, three years before the foundation of Europa. The third partner, Michel Feller, is a former art-house actor – the protagonist of Olivier Assayas's *L'Enfant de l'hiver* (*Winter's Child*, 1989) – who moved to Artmédia as a talent scout. Such managerial variety justifies Europa's diversification of films, genres, marketing sectors, and financial investments, alternating nationally and internationally distributed action films with small domestic comedies.

An important asset of Europa is its sophisticated post-production studio, Digital Factory, located in one of Besson's properties, a seventeenth-century castle in Normandy, where the director had also filmed some sequences of *Jeanne d'Arc*. A proud Besson said to *Studio Magazine*: 'Up to 25M$, Europa is at present able to produce a film without the help of the Americans' (Besson 2001: 79), and he claims to have turned down many offers from Hollywood studios to be involved in the production of *Kiss of the Dragon*, which was eventually bought by Fox for international distribution. Late in 2001, Europa took a dramatic twist towards a higher production volume, by signing a three-year deal with the group Vivendi-Universal, France's leading multinational corporation, run by the French financial scout and manager Jean-Marie Messier. At the time, Messier was in the middle of a spectacular financial rampage, which would eventually cause the corporation a loss of 13.6 billion Euros (US$ 11.8) and force him to resign from his post as CEO in July 2002, although he was well remunerated with a stunning $20 million dollar compensation package. Originally, Messier had created this financial empire from the privatisation of the French state-owned water company, Compagnie Générale des Eaux, and had progressively transformed the company, renamed Vivendi, into a media corporation, which had incorporated the French pay-TV Canal+ (for many years a crucial player in France's cultural film production and exhibition).[8] The consecration of Vivendi as a worldwide media corporation was the purchase of Seagram (previously controlled by the Montreal and New York-based, powerful Bronfman family and chaired by the family heir, Edgar Jr., who remained as the company's vice chair) and its subsidiaries Universal Studio and Universal Music, the US satellite television company EchoStar Communications, and Barry Diller's USA Networks, including a portion of Diller's stock share.

Besides buying exhibition rights to some of Europa's films, the deal with Vivendi aimed at financing the company's post-production studio,

Digital Factory, and building new studios for post-production, music recording, and also for the production of animation films. The negotiations with Besson were troubled by Messier's acquisition of Canal+ and, soon after, the firing of the company's director, Pierre Lescure, who was one of Besson's longstanding professional partners, but whose culturally oriented agenda was incompatible with Messier's mainstream film production interests and partnerships with the Hollywood studio Universal. This move caused enormous controversy in France and rekindled criticism of Messier, his lavish lifestyle, and his public displays of corporate power. On the Lescure affair, Besson never took an official position and did not renew the loyal affiliations that he had often demonstrated in his career, most recently with Bill Mechanic at Fox. Six months before the Lescure scandal exploded, when asked by *Studio Magazine* if Lescure's rumoured departure from Canal+ would have affected his agreement, he compromisingly answered that, although his collaboration with Canal+ was primarily the result of his long-term friendship and partnership with Lescure and Nathalie Bloch-Laîné, his contract with Vivendi had been signed and would have remained valid regardless (Besson 2001: 95). An ambiguous commentary on Vivendi's acquisition of Canal+ appeared on Besson's official website, signed by Princess L. In the note, Princess L. makes sarcastic comments about Messier's acquisition of Canal+, celebrated by a regal party at the Louvre palace, and plays with the comparison between the economic king 'J6M' (Messier) and Louis XIV, the Sun King, who at the time was featured in the French historical drama *Le Roi danse* (*The King Is Dancing*, Gérard Corbiau, 2000), the latest film production effort from Canal+.[9] Yet Princess L. is less negative on Messier per se for having 'killed' Canal+ than on Canal+ being a dead television network, lacking creativity and inspiration, and Messier not quite an art promoter, as Louis XIV was.

Despite its links with big corporations such as Disney and Vivendi-Universal, Europa started as a relatively small enterprise. In the beginning, the studio employed approximately fifty people, although the number of employees doubled within a few years. The firm rapidly increased its pool of projects, varied in both type and budget. To a certain extent, Europa is Besson's response to his problematic relationship with the Hollywood studios and the impossibility for him to create under their industrial and managerial structure and mentality. Certainly, the deal with Vivendi-Universal was a considerable test of Besson's position vis-à-vis corporate financing and the studio's production philosophy, especially when Messier was attacked by the French media for firing Lescure. Besson reacted by keeping a very low public profile, and reinforcing even more his hermetic and withdrawn attitude toward the media, giving fewer interviews and discontinuing his contributions to his official website.

To be sure, Europa pursued a growing and successful line of production, which seemed to lie far beyond the recreation of 'Bessonian' films. Besson describes his role as film producer as that of a facilitator. Europa produces and distributes films ranging across a variety of genres, and involving both international and French casts and crews. An area of specialisation in Europa's productions seems to be the big-budget action flick with martial arts elements and stars. In two years, the film company produced and distributed Chinese star Jet Li's vehicle *Kiss of the Dragon*, Hong Kong actor and director Corey Yuen's *The Transporter* (2003), co-directed with French first-time director Louis Leterrier, whose second film for Europa, *Danny the Dog* (*Unleashed*, 2005), features Li again in an unusual Scottish setting, surrounded by a prestigious, international cast including Morgan Freeman and Bob Hoskins. Other films that play with generic and transcultural hybridism (albeit often resulting in stereotyping) are *Wasabi* (Gérard Krawczyk, 2001), set in Japan and starring Besson's fetish actor Jean Reno and Japanese teenage pop idol Ryoko Hirosue, and *Yamakasi* (Ariel Zeitoun, 2001), an action movie starring a group of young people who jump from buildings and which the film promotional tag describes as: 'The samurais of the modern times'. There are also comic-strip adaptations (which, over the past few years, have become almost a subgenre in French cinema), such as *Michel Vaillant* (Bernard Bonvoisin, 2003) and thrillers, such as the sequel of Matthieu Kassovitz's successful *Les Rivières pourpres* (*The Crimson Rivers*, 2000) entitled *Les Rivières pourpres 2: Les anges de l'Apocalypse* (*Crimson Rivers 2: Angels of the Apocalypse*, Olivier Dahan, 2004).

The studio caters to audiences across Europe, North America and Asia, and also addresses different types of domestic audiences, producing France's veteran director Bertrand Blier's *Les Côtelettes* (2003), French comedies such as Patrick Alessandrin's *15 Août* (*August 15th*, 2001) and *Moi César, 10 ans 1/2, 1 m 39* (*I Cesar*, Richard Berry, 2003), as well as international art-house films such as the Italian filmmaker Mimmo Calopresti's *La felicitá non costa niente* (*Happiness Costs Nothing*, 2002) and the Québécoise filmmaker Manon Briand's *La Turbulence des fluides* (*Chaos and Desire*, 2002), and two actors' directorial debuts, *Peau d'ange* (*Once Upon an Angel*, 2002, by French star Vincent Perez) and *Cheeky* (2003), by British actor David Thewlis.

Since *Jeanne d'Arc*, Besson has put an emphasis on European themes and projects that champion new French filmmakers and actors turned filmmakers, many of whom come from his own professional team. This is the case of Aruna Villiers, a veteran script supervisor for international film productions, who worked for him on *Jeanne d'Arc*, and completed her first film, *À ton image*, in 2004. Perez finished his first film directly before acting in two Europa productions, the intimate drama *La felicitá non costa niente* and the spectacular remake of *Fanfan la Tulipe*, directed by Krawczyk (one of the most prolific filmmakers of the team Europa), with Perez in the main role and Penélope Cruz. Other French actors' projects include Bernie Bonvoisin's costume adventure film with western variations and an all-star French cast *Blanche* (2002), Richard Berry's already-mentioned *Moi, César, 10 ans ½, 1 m 39*, and Isabelle Doval's *Rire et châtiment* (*Laughter and Punishment*, 2003), featuring Doval's husband José Garcia (who also appears in *Blanche*) and the director herself in the main roles. At the same time, Besson has co-produced films outside France, some of which are by critically acclaimed but not commercially viable directors, such as the Québécoise Briand and the Italian Calopresti, and some of which are by genre directors for the mainstream circuit, for example Hong Kong action directors such as Corey Yuen, and the Pang Brothers, whose *Jian gui* (*The Eye*, 2002) was released in France by Europa.

Europa is not simply the fulfilment of Besson's individual and professional conception of cinema; it realises an aspiration that many film production companies have always pursued in Europe, generally with poor results: that of constituting an industrial and commercial alternative to and competitive with Hollywood. With Europa, Besson challenges Hollywood on his usual terms, playing the big studios' game with fewer and more diverse means, which allow him more flexibility and freedom. In this respect, the studio responds to the needs of Europe's reconfiguration, involving new strategies of development and promotion, management-oriented decision making, marketing diversification, transnational co-operation, and investments in structures, infrastructures, human resources, technologies and cultural organisations. In many European countries, these strategies are developed by state and EU programmes to aid audiovisual production and distribution, new independent and corporate film structures, and international co-productions among TV networks and film companies. In this regard, Europa is an exceptional and quite unique entity.

Europa also reflects the tension of a director who has always maintained his autonomy from the American as well as the French studios and corporations, and has never shared the old continent's guilt about combining cultural and economic interests while being part of the same economic systems at play in the international market. Besson's studio is moving into the interface of local and global film production and distribution from a position outside of corporate structures, although not completely free from their sphere of influence. In this respect, Europa's most original trait is its diversification of production scales and marketing niches, something that the Hollywood majors or any large European studio cannot easily do.

Besson's Americanised image is based on the premise that European cinema would be nationally based and Hollywood globally oriented, something which overlooks an important aspect of global film practices and industries: namely, that they debunk the flimsiness of national specificity and promote a distinctively transnational and cross-cultural agenda. In the same way that a Besson film may be promoted as an American or American-looking product, Hollywood studios may try and adapt their films to a specific market. As Miller puts it:

> Part of the talent of international cultural commodities is their adaptability to new circumstances: the successes and meanings of Hollywood films need to be charted through numerous spatial, generic, and formatting transformations as they move through US release to Europe and Asia then domestic and international video, cable, and Network television . . . The Ford Motor Company has long worked with the adage 'To be a multinational group, it is necessary to be national everywhere'. (Miller 1998: 337)

Europa seems to be working with the Ford maxim particularly as far as the Asian market is concerned. The studio's most internationally driven productions, such as *Kiss of the Dragon* and *Wasabi*, apply the laws of globalisation to the letter. The former is an action film that transposes the Chinese martial arts star Jet Li into a US context and narrative. Li, who had formerly taken the lead in two Hollywood blockbusters, *Lethal Weapon 4* (Richard Donner, 1998) and *Romeo Must Die* (Andrzej Bartkowiak, 2000), decided to work with Besson and co-produce *Kiss of the Dragon* on the basis of a conception of production very similar to Besson's. Like Besson, Li wants a project to come together quickly and special effects to be realistic.[10] *Wasabi* is an action thriller with comic undertones, clearly indebted to the classic male-buddy film (here two French cops, the hero and his goofy pal), but adding to the mix an adolescent Japanese girl, and set against the cluttered urban environment of contemporary Tokyo. The script was 'commissioned' by Besson for his longtime friend and collaborator Jean Reno, who wanted to make a film in a country where he has had immense popularity since *Nikita* and *Léon*. Reno's female co-star, Ryoko Hirosue, one of Japan's youngest upcoming stars, is an actress and singer whose cultural disparity with Reno is overplayed throughout the film. *Wasabi* deploys all the clichés of the cultural clash between France and Japan, and exploits the two stars' typical screen personas, thus playing to a variety of audience expectations from different cultural locations.

Europa's ambition is to celebrate the impossible marriage between commerce and art upon which cinema is predicated: a self-sufficient, vertical organisation including post-production facilities, the collaboration of a dependable professional entourage, and a personal network of connections in the French and international film industry, the studio is the expression of Besson's idiosyncratic view of cinema as a personal form of expression and a form of social consumption. The escalation of the Franco-American polemic over cinema's cultural exception and, more importantly, Europa's consolidation with Vivendi-Universal, may have a negative impact on Besson's vision. He may have circumvented the question of cultural exception by upgrading his public profile to a filmmaker that blends artistic and businesslike attitudes toward cinema with production and distribution practices equally attentive to the domestic and the international markets from an economically autonomous standpoint. Yet the studio's compromise with corporate interests and positions on cultural exception also raises questions over Europa's own image of the cottage factory-style bearing connections with the mainstream film circuit. Intermittent revelations about cases of professional exploitation and managerial unscrupulousness, some of which have had legal consequences, cast shadows on Besson's intentions to keep Europa as an independent pole of production and distribution.[11]

References

Alexander, M. (1994), 'A Gaul in Hollywood', *Variety*, 356 (10 October), p. 10.

Besson, L. (2001), 'Le plus grand défi de Luc Besson: entretien avec Jean-Pierre Lavoignant et Christophe d'Yvoire', *Studio Magazine*, 169, pp. 72–83.

Besson, L. (2002), 'Je n'ai plus peur: entretien avec Lionel Cartégini et Olivier de Bruyin', *Première*, 300, pp. 92–7.

Corrigan, T. (1991), *A Cinema without Walls: Movies and Culture after Vietnam* (New Brunswick, New Jersey: Rutgers University Press).

Crofts, S. (1993), 'Reconceptualizing national cinemas', *Quarterly Review of Film and Video*, 14:3, pp. 49–68.

Crofts, S. (1998), 'Authorship and Hollywood', in J. Hill and P. Church Gibson (eds), *The Oxford Guide to Film Studies* (Oxford: Oxford University Press), pp. 310–24.

de Grazia, V. (1998), 'European cinema and the idea of Europe, 1925–95', in G. Nowell-Smith and S. Ricci (eds), *Hollywood and Europe: Economics, Culture, National Identity: 1945–95* (London: BFI), pp. 19–33.

Durovicová, N. (1994), 'Some thoughts at an intersection', *Velvet Light Trap*, 34, pp. 3–9.

Finney, A. (1996), *The State of European Cinema: A New Dose of Reality* (London, Cassell).
Hayward, S. (1998), *Luc Besson* (Manchester: Manchester University Press).
Ilott, T. (1996), *Budgets and Markets: A Study of the Budgeting of European Film* (London and New York: Routledge).
Jäckel, A. (1996), 'European co-production strategies: the case of France and Britain', in A. Moran (ed.), *Film Policy: International, National, and Regional Perspectives* (London and New York: Routledge), pp. 85–100.
Lequeret, É. (2002), 'Les inconnues de l'après-Canal+' (dossier), *Cahiers du cinéma*, 570, pp. 68–71.
Margolick, D. (2002), 'Vivendi's Mr. Universe', *Vanity Fair*, 500, pp. 240–77.
Mazdon, L. (ed.) (2001), *France on Film: Reflections on Popular French Cinema* (London: Wallflower Press).
Miller, T. (1998), 'Hollywood and the world', in J. Hill and P. Church Gibson (eds), *The Oxford Guide to Film Studies* (Oxford: Oxford University Press), pp. 371–81.
Moran, A. (ed.) (1996), *Film Policy: International, National, and Regional Perspectives* (London and New York: Routledge).
Petrie, D. (ed.) (1992), *Screening Europe: Image and Identity in Contemporary European Cinema* (London: BFI).
Polan, D. (2001), 'Auteur desire', *Screening the Past*, 13, *Web Film Journal*, at: www.latrobe.edu.au/screeningthepast/firstrelease/fr0301/dpfr12a.htm, accessed 4 February 2005.
Powrie, P. (2001), *Jean-Jacques Beineix* (Manchester: Manchester University Press).
Puttnam, D. (1997), *The Undeclared War: The Struggle of the World's Film Industry* (London: HarperCollins).
Sarris, A. (1991), Sarris' film column, *New York Observer* (1 April).
Vincendeau, G. (1996), *The Companion to French Cinema* (London: Cassell, 1996).
Vincendeau, G. (1998), 'Issues in European cinema', in J. Hill and P. Church Gibson (eds), *The Oxford Guide to Film Studies* (Oxford: Oxford University Press), pp. 440–8.
Williams, M. (1999), 'French filmmaker of the year', *Variety*, 373 (11–17 January), p. 105.

Notes

1 Besson has managed to maintain personal control over his films even with budgets of the order of 60, 80 and 90 million francs (for *Jeanne d'Arc*, *Léon*, and *Le Cinquième élément* respectively), involving hundreds of technicians and a complex production organisation, the first two films with crews divided between two continents and in various sets and laboratories.
2 All translations from the French are by the author.
3 At least until recently, given his more regular presence at Cannes, also as

jury president in 2000, and the *Prix des Amériques* which he received at the 2002 *Festival des Films du Monde* in Montreal.

4 Ginette Vincendeau regards the upsurge of new approaches on European cinema as an amendment to the traditional, misleading identification of European cinema with 'art cinema', which erases any distinction between films and filmmakers, provides an incomplete account of actual film practices, and reinforces essentialist conceptions of Hollywood as the oppositional norm against which Europe delineates its difference (Vincendeau 1998: 447).

5 Besson was assistant director to Claude Faraldo for *Lions au soleil* (*Two Lions in the Sun*, 1980), Raphaël Delpard for *Les Bidasses aux grandes manœuvres* (1981), and second assistant to Alexandre Arcady for *Le Grand Carnaval* (*The Big Carnival*, 1983).

6 According to Dana Polan, Hayward's reading of Besson constitutes an implicitly auteur-oriented approach, albeit one informed by the intention to contextualise the director as 'one highly significant element in a complex process of film production and reception which includes socioeconomic and political determinants, the work of a large and highly skilled team of artists and technicians, the mechanisms of production and distribution, and the complex and multiply determined responses of spectators' (Polan 2001: 76–7).

7 The momentum of the *cinéma du look* seems to have waned immediately after the international success of Besson's *Nikita* and the failure of Jean-Jacques Beineix's *IP5* (1992). The latter film, despite its potential allure of showcasing Yves Montand's last film performance, passed through the 1992 Cannes film festival without comment, and was a commercial failure in France and abroad. After *IP5*, Beineix made *Otaku* (1994), a short film on Japanese men's hobbies, which was hardly considered at Cannes, and *Mortel transfert* (2001), which had a very poor reception in France (see Powrie, 2001). Carax's next film after almost ten years of silence, *Pola X* (1999), was equally ill-received at Cannes and at the box office.

8 On the consequences that the merging with Vivendi had on Canal+ for France's film production, see Lequeret, 2002.

9 At: www.besson.com, accessed 20 November 2000. The nickname 'J6M' had been coined by Canal+'s satirical puppet show *Les Guignols*, which humorously transformed into an acronym the six Ms in the phrase that the Messier puppet used to refer to itself: 'Jean-Marie Messier, Moi-Même, Maître du Monde' (Jean-Marie Messier, Myself, Master of the World).

10 The film also stars Bridget Fonda and Tcheky Karyo, who play, respectively, the female lead and uncle Bob in the American remake of *Nikita*.

11 In March 2000, Besson faced charges of plagiarism, for having allegedly 'stolen' Kathryn Bigelow's script of *Jeanne d'Arc*. Besson received another accusation of plagiarism in February 2001, from Julien Séri and Philippe Lyon, co-writers of *Yamakasi*. The most serious accusation arrived on 4 June 2002, when Besson was charged with involuntary manslaughter for

the death of cameraman Alain Dutartre, who had been the victim of a car accident while filming a stunt for *Taxi 2*. The charge concerns Besson turning down a trial run that would have tested the stunt that led to Dutartre's death and seriously injured his assistant Jean-Michel Bar and the car's driver. In August 2003, the French press listed Europa among the entertainment companies that make most use of casual work contracts, to avoid having to pay social benefits to its employees.

3

Musical narration in the films of Luc Besson

Gérard Dastugue

It is probably true to say that music plays a significant role in the success of Besson's films where audiences are concerned, despite the fact that reviewers have disparaged the films, and that reviewers have tended to make negative comments about the score as well. The only good thing about such negative comments is that they foreground the score, which rarely gets this level of attention. Part of the reason why music is frequently mentioned is no doubt that the collaboration between Besson and Eric Serra echoes significant film partnerships between directors and composers, to such an extent that the two are often discussed together: Sergio Leone and Ennio Morricone, Federico Fellini and Nino Rota, David Cronenberg and Howard Shore, Steven Spielberg and John Williams, Tim Burton and Danny Elfman all come to mind in the case of Besson and Serra. This is because Besson has consistently called upon Serra for his eight films, although we should perhaps note that Serra has not confined his work to the films of Besson, having scored Martin Campbell's *Goldeneye* (1995) John McTiernan's *Rollerball* (2002) and Danielle Thompson's *Décalage horaire* the same year (these last two films starred Jean Reno, which may be one reason why Serra agreed to do the score). The Besson–Serra collaboration was clearly successful, as the original soundtracks for many of the films have sold well in France: more than 100,000 copies of *Subway*, *Nikita*, *Atlantis* and *Léon*; more than 200,000 copies of *Le Cinquième élément*; more than one million copies of *Le Grand bleu* (which sold four million copies globally).[1]

The two men met in 1979, thanks to Pierre Jolivet, one of Besson's collaborators,[2] who, as a singer, had been looking for a guitar player; they have worked together ever since. Today, the record sales, the awards[3] and the importance given to the music by Besson and by audiences make Serra as much an auteur of Besson's films as Besson himself.

For the public, the composer brings an immediately assimilable personal touch, which may explain why – a fact that is seldom emphasised – he is by the director's side for previews or promotional campaigns, functioning rather like an alter ego:

> I think we complement each other. Luc's the eyes and I'm the ears. Our relationship was difficult in the beginning, because the director and musician are completely different persons. But as we've come to know more about each other, I've been able to tell what Luc's thinking from the way he moves the camera. He's a filmmaker who knows exactly what emotion he wants from the music, and relies on me to express them. So we have developed a musical language that makes our collaborations exciting. (Schweiger 1994: 13)

In what follows, I shall explore the use of musical material in Besson's films and its impact on the viewer. I shall focus on Besson the director rather than the producer, considering the eight films from *Le Dernier combat* to *Jeanne d'Arc* which feature an original score by Eric Serra.[4]

Music to be heard

Generally, the score is composed during the post-production phase when the composer has to write the music in a short space of time (five to six weeks). The average duration of a film score is 45 minutes. It tends to be longer in Besson's films (see Table 3.1). We might argue that this makes his cinema intrinsically musical, something which certain films – *Subway*, *Atlantis*, *Le Cinquième élément* – would confirm. But his films' intrinsic musicality is established well before the post-production phase, at the stage of writing: 'I can't remember a time when I didn't have a walkman on my head after the age of fourteen. I listen to music all the time and obviously, that influences me and speaks to me. I am unable to write without a walkman on my head, I need music to write' (Dastugue 1999).

The story is thus first written to a rhythm which is musical before being cinematic, this being a defining characteristic of the Besson style. On the assumption that music is affect driven rather than programmatically narrative, listening to music creates emotions, and those emotions guide the scriptwriting. The shooting and the editing will then correspond to a *mise-en-scène*, a 'mise en image' of musical emotions and rhythm, the music preceding the image, as it does in a video clip.[5] If audiences hear this music as an integral part of the film, it is precisely because it is given to be heard, just as images are given to be watched. The music is very present throughout the film, and is mixed over the dialogues and the sound effects, whereas the norm is to seek balance: 'Luc gives priority to the music. For example, if there is a problem between the sound effects and the music, usually he will get rid of the sound effects' (Cavanagh 1994: 26).

This primacy of the music over the sound effects reveals the narrative choices made by Besson. A sound effect is the acoustic response of an event visualised on screen whose source belongs to the screen. A slamming door, a gunshot or an explosion, are visual events from which a particular sound emanates, belonging to the diegetic world as well as to its visual source. Film music is extra-diegetic, except in a few cases when the music specifically written for the film is played within the film diegesis, as is the case for *Subway* with the rock band's songs, or the diva sequence in *Le Cinquième élément*. The original score does not belong to the diegesis, it is a bridge between two universes: the universe of the film, and the universe of the spectator. Besson's privileging of extra-diegetic music can therefore be seen as a direct appeal to the audience's emotions. It is also one of the factors leading to what has been called the clip effect.

Mario Litwin gives the following definition of the clip effect: 'The clip effect is caused by an excessive factor of presence and the absence of sound effects and sound environment. It can be accentuated by the intervention of the human voice and, sometimes, by the abundance of the percussion' (Litwin 1992: 64). There are a number of examples in Besson's films, where the interplay between the diegetic and the extra-diegetic plays a significant part.

Le Dernier combat does not feature any dialogue, only a whispered 'hello', the music functioning as a palliative element for the lack of dialogue. The face-to-face between the Man (Pierre Jolivet) and the Brute (Jean Reno) is shot like a clip, the only soundtrack being Serra's pop rock music. Many sequences of *Le Grand bleu* are shot like clips, such as the diving sequences, more particularly Jacques Mayol's first championship dive, where the only sound is the voice of the man counting. The score here is nominally extra-diegetic, not heard by any diegetic character. It does, however, incorporate sounds (whale songs) that belong to the film's diegetic universe, these displaced diegetic sounds (sounds which the protagonist might hear in such a situation) serving as a bridge between the diegetic and the extra-diegetic.

Given that *Subway* is about the creation of a band, there are many opportunities for the kind of effects we might associate with clips. The film opens with a car chase through Paris. Fred (Christophe Lambert) is looking for an audiocassette to play on the car radio when another car strikes him from behind. As soon as the music starts, the rhythm of the images accelerates with the vehicles. The sound effects we might expect from this kind of sequence – cars accelerating, the squealing of tyres – are present, but drowned out by the music. Some visual events are integrated into the score in a Mickey-Mouse effect (the term used to denote close synchronisation between sound and movement), such as the headlights of Fred's car flashing at the jogger before the car shoots over his head. The film also features two songs specifically written for the film, 'It's Only Mystery' (derived from Johnny Nash's 'I Can See Clearly') and 'Guns and People', whose treatment within the film is also clip-like, as we shall now consider.

In the case of the first song, Fred has gathered his musicians together, and the singer (Arthur Simms) is introduced to them. The song 'It's Only Mystery' starts, and while listening to the music, Fred imagines himself sleeping at Héléna's side. In this sequence, the music serves to bring together two discrete spaces. The music starts in a particular place and time (the band playing in the room), and carries on in another time and another place (Fred's dream of Héléna's home).

There is a similar use of parallel editing in the final sequence, when the band gives a concert in the subway, singing 'Guns and People'. During the song several different actions occur: Héléna escapes from the police chief; one of Héléna's bodyguards is ready to shoot Fred; Héléna and Fred are rejoined; Fred is shot; Héléna has an argument with the bodyguards; Fred, lying on the ground, is singing. The music here is diegetic; its source (the band) is present onscreen, and all the characters in the sequence can hear it. But we have here an example of diegetic transgression, the passage from one universe to another, from the diegetic to the extra-diegetic. When Héléna is in the police chief's office (thus a different place than where the band is playing), the mixing of the music would logically have to mark the distance from the source. However, the song is heard everywhere and by everybody (the characters as well as the viewers). The music is therefore both diegetic (the band playing on screen), and extra-diegetic, creating an affective space for the audience, affective precisely because it is both diegetic and extra-diegetic, an 'impossible' space of fantasy, where opposites can coexist: this applies as much to the coexistence of the real and the fantasised, as Fred's apparent resurrection might suggest, as it does to the coexistence of love and hate in Fred and Héléna's relationship, underlined by the song's chorus – 'Guns don't kill people, people kill people'. The sequence thus appears as the clip of the song; its ambiguities and contradictions are explicable through the music. It is a fantasy which to some extent illustrates the preoccupations of the pre-existing song. While there are other sequences with extra-diegetic music and without dialogue – such as the presentation of the drummer and the roller, or the descent into the subway by the police chief and his men – which can also be compared to clip processes, the two pre-existing diegetic songs we have explored are the clearest example of the way in which Besson's style is musical, in this case anchored to a clip effect.

So far, I have concentrated on individual sequences to show how Besson's style is musical. Before moving on to an extended discussion of the scoring of *Léon*, I would like to explore briefly what we could call Besson's 'musical continuum', as part of the way in which music in his films is there to be heard. Table 3.1 shows the approximate percentage proportion of screentime with musical accompaniment in each of his films.

Table 3.1 Music and screentime in Besson's films

Film title	%
Le Dernier combat	30
Subway	50
Le Grand bleu	70
Nikita	50
Atlantis	95
Léon	90
Le Cinquième élément	90
Jeanne d'Arc	90

As we can see, there is almost a doubling of the total time of music onscreen from *Atlantis* onwards, with a wall-to-wall score in the subsequent films. *Atlantis* is a significant break. Presented as a tribute to the underwater world, the film has no dialogue, which explains to some extent the omnipresence of music. Indeed, music prevents *Atlantis* from being a mere documentary, for two reasons. First, music takes the place of a voice-over which might normally have introduced the undersea creatures, or given information about their behaviour, or about their geographical location. Second, the film is divided into themes – love, fear, grace, etc. – which the music supports dramatically, with the kind of redundancy one might expect: threatening music accompanies the shark attack; strings and brass are used to convey the 'nobility' of the dolphins' games; an Arabian-sounding music with a solo flute introduction[6] follows each movement of a snake.

From *Atlantis* onwards, Serra chooses to synchronise his musical score with the events on screen, and to incorporate sound-musical effects in it,[7] creating a musical continuum which covers a significant part of the film, and which is unusual when compared with American cinema. I shall now turn to *Léon* for a more detailed case study.

Léon

The first images of *Léon* open with a familiar trope, also found at the start of *Le Grand bleu*, *Nikita* and *Le Cinquième élément*: a high-angle forward tracking shot, which then tilts up to reveal the title. In this case it is a helicopter shot as we fly over water and trees towards the New York skyline, with the buildings emerging above the trees of Central Park, like the vestiges of a lost civilisation. A sequence of forward tracking shots take us through the streets of Little Italy, and finally to an Italian restaurant. The dynamic camerawork combined with the urban décor might have led us to expect percussive effects, perhaps rap music underlining the 'urban jungle' setting. Alternatively, the district of Little Italy might also have led us to expect a specific kind of music, associated with gangster films such as Nino Rota's score for *The Godfather* (Francis Ford Coppola, 1972), or the compiled pop score for *Goodfellas* (Martin Scorsese, 1990). Eric Serra chooses musical contrast, with faintly oriental music, dominated by chromatic flute music and floating strings, which he called Arabian in interview:

> Every time you see a film that's shot in Manhattan, you hear rap songs. And though I love some rap, that musical relationship has become a cliché. I didn't want to pull that trick in *The Professional*, so I ended up using a lot of Arabian and African percussion . . . I used that music because New York's skyscrapers struck me like Egyptian pyramids. They're very big and old. It's as if they represent an ancient civilization. So the Arabian melodies gave a weird and mysterious feeling. (Schweiger 1994: 13)

New York City is introduced as a jungle where everything is possible, where the strongest is the winner. Here, Léon can live without being noticed by anybody: a worm in the Big Apple.

Léon's first mission, in contrast, is accompanied by all-percussive music, which functions at several levels. First, it imposes a strong rhythm, suturing the rapid and numerous shots of the action sequence. Second, it combines the primitive and the precise, the tribal aspect of the city jungle on the one hand, with the ritual of the hit, and the precision of the professional hitman. There is a third function: the music stops when Léon puts a knife to the fat man's throat, as if the character were hearing these percussive rhythms, as if the rhythms were somehow linked to his body.

A similar contrast and a similar set of connotations occur later when Stansfield (Gary Oldman) visits Mathilda's family. The music we hear adopts the Arabian style (with its connotations of otherness and city-as-jungle), but Stansfield – as if it is music within his head – says that it reminds him of Beethoven. His passion for Beethoven, which as he says to the man he is about to kill, suits 'heavy' work, is a double reference: first to *A Clockwork Orange* (Stanley Kubrick, 1971), and its ultra-violence; second, to the biopic of Beethoven, *Immortal Beloved* (Bernard Rose, 1994), released the same year as *Léon*,[8] in which Oldman plays the role of the composer (and in which there are several references to *A Clockwork Orange*). As in Léon's first mission, the character stops the music (with a click of the finger in this case). Both of these examples again raise the question of the origin of the musical source. Nominally extra-diegetic, the music is manipulated by diegetic characters, creating a space of fantasy where borders are crossed, including the borders of the individual body, which is musicalised. This function of embodied musicality can be seen in my third example of multivalent music.

It is when Léon teaches Mathilda how to shoot, on the top of a tower overlooking Central Park. A right tracking shot reveals a splendid view of New York skyscrapers, to the accompaniment of synthetic strings, panpipes and a multitude of singing and murmuring voices. This musical fusion functions in a variety of ways. First, it is visually an echo of the first shot, with its connotations of New York as a lost civilisation, where musically the panpipes suggest the past, and the primitive forest of the earlier helicopter shot. Second, the fusion of sounds echoes the collaboration of Mathilda and Léon, the lonely killer who becomes her teacher. Finally, the vocal element of the musical mix also serves to suggest what the audience cannot see beyond the cold and motionless aspect of the buildings. The voices, it could be argued, embody the spirits who guide the two killers in their practice; but we could equally well argue that they embody the people of New York, the crowd from which Mathilda selects targets. As we have already seen with *Subway*, the music is diegetised *a posteriori*; the music, which we hear first, subsequently creates possible sources in the visual track. The image is as much an illustration of the music as the other way round.

So far in *Léon*, I have considered individual sequences to pinpoint the features of the Besson–Serra musical system: the music is multivalent and frequently is as determining as the image. Let us now turn to a consideration of the way in which the score for the film as a whole functions.

Eric Serra does not make use of leitmotivs. However, *Léon*'s score is composed of recurring musical themes that build a meaningful network. Table 3.2 charts this network, based on the 108-minute version (rather than the 132 minute version released a few months later). The musical themes column lists only the themes that occur at least twice in the film:

Table 3.2 Musical themes in *Léon*

Sequences	Musical themes	
1	Main titles	
2	Tony and Léon	M
3	Fat man mission	M
4	Léon back home	
5	Stansfield in family apartment	
6	Léon at home	L
7	Morning in the family apartment	D
8	Léon in the cinema	
9	Mathilda shops for Léon while Stansfield murders the family	D
10	Mathilda enters Léon's apartment, Stansfield and his men leave	L
11	Mathilda and Léon	Rm
12	Mathilda and Léon go to a hotel	L
13	Léon and Tony talk about training	
14	Mathilda and Léon on the rooftops	Rf
15	Daily life	
16	Disguise game	L
17	Léon and Tony talk about money	L
18	Mathilda tells Léon she loves him	L
19	Léon on a new mission, while Mathilda tells the hotel receptionist Léon is her lover	D
20	Mathilda enters the family apartment, Stansfield arrives	Rm
21	Mathilda follows Stansfield	M
22	Léon returns with a pink dress for Mathilda	
23	Mathilda and Léon find a new home	Rf
24	Léon tells Tony to give Mathilda his money if he dies	
25	Mathilda tries to kill Stansfield	M
26	Léon saves Mathilda	L, Rm
27	Stansfield at Tony's	
28	Mathilda and Léon shelter in the apartment	L
29	Mathilda leaves through a hole	D
30	Léon escapes wearing a SWAT suit	L, D
31	Léon is killed by Stansfield, followed by explosion	L
32	Mathilda and Tony	L
33	Mathilda goes back to her school	
34	End credits	

Key   L=Léon; D=Death; Rm=Romance; M=Mission; Rf=Rooftop.

The 'Léon theme' comprises four ascending notes followed by four descending notes, and appears several times throughout the film in a variety of orchestrations. It is heard at the beginning of the film (no. 6 in Table 3.2), just after the 'fat man mission', creating an identification and relation between the character and his musical motive. After having been introduced to his warrior's skills, we discover a lonely man, performing his daily routine in his apartment. Léon's theme is first played by a bassoon, as he removes his coat and lets the audience see the weapons; it is then replaced by an oboe, as he is shown ironing, showering, drinking milk and watering his plant. The shift from bassoon to oboe humanises and to some extent feminises the character, as the deeper and darker tones of the bassoon yield to the higher and lighter tones of the oboe. The theme is later reorchestrated in the film's Arabian style when Mathilda comes back from shopping, discovers the slaughter and shelters in Léon's apartment (no. 10) and when they both go to the hotel (no. 12). The oriental style we hear in the main titles influences the score as a whole, underlining not only the Egyptian pyramid-like setting, but also the character's feminine qualities of dissimulation, exemplified in the fat man mission.

The theme, like Léon himself, is Protean; it is played by a bandonion (with synthetic mandolina and rhythm), and thus 'Italianised', when Léon is at Tony's (no. 17). The piece, which Serra entitled 'Tony the IBM'[9] (suggesting that Tony is a kind of computer who controls Léon's missions and money) can be perceived in the sequence as an integral part of the setting, Tony's 'Supreme Macaroni' restaurant. The decorative function of the piece, allied to its title, is potentially misleading, however, in that the audience might hear it purely as Tony's theme. But as a reorchestration of Léon's theme, it constructs Tony as a part of Léon's life, the father substitute, who welcomed him when he came to New York. A similar function is served when the bandonion solo picks up the theme, when Mathilda tells Léon she is falling in love with him (no. 18); the solo emphasises not simply the intimacy of this moment, but the primacy of the moment for Léon as principal protagonist. The emotions generated by this version of the theme will carry over into the final sequences, helping audience identification with the trapped Léon.

What can be called the 'death theme' is mainly heard during the slaughter of the family (no. 9). After a long introduction with synthetic noises and percussions, the camera tracks forward in the corridor to Stansfield's arrival. Then the drums get louder, and the strings come when Stansfield shoots into the door. It is another Arabian-like melody that first appeared when Mathilda, on the phone, pretended to be her mother, and told her headmistress she was dead (no. 7). The final assault features this theme when Léon breaks through the wall with an axe (no. 29), allowing Mathilda, but not himself, to escape, and a little later when Stansfield sees Léon as a SWAT (no. 30), the death theme quite clearly prefiguring Léon's death at the hands of the corrupt cop.

The themes are closely related. If we compare the melodic lines of the Léon theme and the death theme, we find that they have a similar stepped ascending structure, which I have represented graphically rather than with musical notation in Figures 3.1 and 3.2 to help the non-musical reader visualise them:

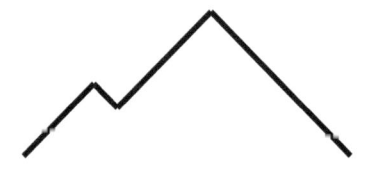

3.1 *Léon's* theme

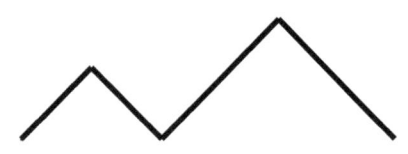

3.2 The death theme in *Léon*

The close parallelism between these two motives creates more than a mere association. On the one hand, Léon is a professional hitman, and so practises death as part of his job. On the other hand, he is also humanised by his relationship with Mathilda, and the musical parallelism marks the character with the burden of tragedy, signalling his end.

If we now compare these two motives with the melodic line of the 'romantic theme', we find that the structure is inverted (Figure 3.3):

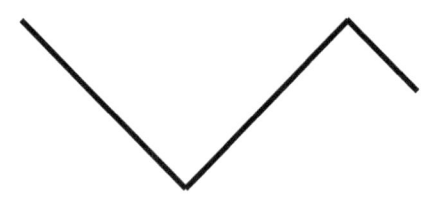

3.3 The romantic theme in *Léon*

The romantic theme thus appears as the reverse value of the Léon and death themes. The romantic theme, embodied by Mathilda, symbolises life, hope, warmth, far from the dark coldness of the death theme. The values are reversed, and this opposition to the Léon theme shows his weakness, i.e. the little girl.

When Léon goes to DEA in order to free Mathilda held by Stansfield's men, the sequence (no. 26) opens with the Léon theme during the action, and ends with the romantic theme as they embrace each other, signalling a turning point for Léon. Up to that point, he refuses Mathilda's love; as if to underline that, it is always the Léon theme that is heard. Now, having rescued her, he is ready for love (as he will tell before leaving her at the end of no. 28), and the romantic theme can appear.

As we can see, the musical score for *Léon* is far more complex than those written by Serra for Besson's previous films. By creating themes and a thematic network, it plays an influential role on the way audiences are likely to interpret the film. It might be objected that most listeners are unlikely to follow the musical structures so closely. But Serra's scores also use intertextual musical references, which audiences are likely to catch in a more obvious way. Thanks to Serra, popular music forms part of the musical patchwork of Besson's films. We find songs by Sting (the end credits 'Shape of My Heart') and Björk ('Venus as a Boy') in *Léon*; and there are songs by Prince, Lionel Richie, Peter Gabriel and the Raï singer Cheb Khaled in *Le Cinquième élément*. Such musical quotations function as recognisable anchors for audiences. Even in *Jeanne d'Arc*, where the choice of symphonic music with choirs is legitimised by the historical context of the subject, some musical quotations allow the viewer to find familiar reference points. Just to take the following example, when Jeanne, who has been hit by an arrow, comes back from the dead at dawn, she leads her sleeping army to fight. There begins a slow breath-like pulse, just like the snoring of the sleeping soldiers. Then a trumpet starts the tune which is repeated again and again, following a crescendo with strings, leading to audience anticipation, as described by Michel Chion: 'In an audiovisual sequence, the audio-viewer consciously or unconsciously recognizes the beginnings of a pattern (e.g., a crescendo or an accelerando) and then verifies whether it evolves as expected' (Chion 1994: 56). The full perception of a piece is thus not possible without taking into account what has already been heard. In this sequence, Eric Serra was influenced by Ravel's *Bolero*. It is likely that most non-music-specialist members of the audience would recognise the reference, and thus anticipate not just the musical crescendo, but also the narrative crescendo to which the music is linked, because, as Chion says, 'one never gets tired of anticipating and of surprising anticipation – it is the very movement of desire' (ibid.). In this sequence, the music influences the perception the audience has of time; it vectorises the sequence towards an inexorable becoming: 'It is the principle of the repetitive construction which increases gradually, whose most beautiful example is indeed Ravel's *Bolero*. It is something inexorable which starts like that, it is a loop' (Dastugue 1999/2000: 19). The music, as we have already seen, is also an embodiment: the slow tempo embodies the awakening of the men both physically (it is dawn), and psychologically (they are convinced they will win as Jeanne has returned from the dead), the repeated trumpet theme functioning as the triumph of military will.

Conclusion

I have tried to show the various types of musical narration in the films of Luc Besson from the point of view of the non-specialist audience, who might well be asking questions such as: why are these images so seductive? why do we feel empathy for this character? Part of the answer lies in the score. The well-known idea that film music is not made to be heard, affirmed by Adorno and Eisler in 1947 (Adorno and Eisler 1994), here collapses. Music in Besson's films is foregrounded, both quantitatively (there is more of it in the later films than in most people's films), and qualitatively, in that even a superficial awareness of its function will demonstrate that it is used playfully, cutting through the boundaries of the diegetic world, to construct spaces of audience fantasy.

References

Adorno, T. and H. Eisler (1994), *Composing for the Films* (London: The Athlone Press).
Cavanagh, D. (1994), 'Eric Serra: essential element', *Music From the Movies*, 16, p. 26.
Chion, M. (1994), *Audio-Vision: Sound on Screen*, ed. and trans. by C. Gorbman (New York: Columbia University Press).
Dastugue, G. (1999), 'Luc Besson ou le cinéma du mélodrame', *Traxzone.com* www.traxzone.com/textes/index.asp?id=1784, 12 December 1999; (accessed 3 January 2005).
Dastugue, G. (1999/2000), 'Eric Serra, le messager de Jeanne d'Arc', *Soundtrack*, 72, p. 19.
Litwin, M. (1992), *Le Film et sa musique: création, montage* (Paris: Romillat).
Schweiger, D. (1994), 'Eric Serra, the professional', *Film Score Monthly*, 52, p. 13.

Notes

1. The commercial success of *Le Grand bleu*'s soundtrack is clearly linked to the success of the film. Reviews of the film have tended to stress the way in which psychological themes (the sea as the mother's womb) work with the new-age sounds of Serra's score (diving deeper into oneself).
2. Pierre Jolivet later became the co-writer and protagonist of *Le Dernier combat*, and worked on the adaptation of *Subway*, before becoming a director in his own right, with rather more intimate films than those of Besson: *Strictement personnel* (1985), *Force majeure* (1989), *Fred* (1997), *Ma petite entreprise* (1999), *Le Frère du guerrier* (2002) and *Filles uniques* (2003).
3. Serra's score for *Le Grand bleu* was awarded a César (the French equivalent of the Oscar), the Victoire de la Musique and Grand Prix de la SACEM for the best score. *Subway* and *Léon* were each awarded a Victoire. All the other films were given nominations.
4. Serra also collaborated on films produced by Besson: Didier Grousset's *Kamikaze* (1986) and Gérard Krawczyk's *Wasabi* (2001).
5. Apart from his nine feature films, Besson has directed clips for artists such as Serge Gainsbourg ('Mon Légionnaire'), Mylène Farmer ('Que mon cœur lâche') and Isabelle Adjani ('Pull Marine'). Indeed, it was after Besson's work with Adjani on this last clip that the actress accepted her role in *Subway*.
6. Inspired from Claude Debussy's *Syrinx for flute*. One of Debussy's more famous orchestral pieces is *La Mer/The Sea*, which is an obvious reference for the *Atlantis* score.
7. I have already mentioned the headlights sound effect in *Subway*. In *Léon*, when Léon puts his glass of milk back onto the table, the score gets a sound-musical response, imparting extraordinary weight to the action, arguably to emphasise the character's power.
8. *Léon* was released 14 September (France) and 18 November (USA) and *Immortal Beloved* on 21 December (USA).
9. According to the credits of the soundtrack CD.

4

Hearing Besson: the music of Eric Serra in the films of Luc Besson

Mark Brownrigg

The purpose of this Chapter is twofold. First, it maps the evolution of Eric Serra's compositional style over the span of his collaboration with Luc Besson. Second, it seeks to mount an argument, by example, for more consideration to be taken of the contribution a long-term composer-director relationship makes to the *œuvre* of an *auteur*.

While some directors habitually use music from a number of sources (Almodóvar, Scorsese, Allen), others work predominantly with just one composer (Spielberg, Lucas, Lynch). Introduced to each other by their mutual friend Pierre Jolivet, Serra and Besson met, aged 18, in a recording studio, and have worked together continually since the director's first short film. The son of a classical guitarist, Serra picked up his first guitar at the age of 5 and added bass to his repertoire as he grew up. During the 1980s to 1990s he evolved into a multi-instrumentalist and record producer, composing and performing scores for films by a number of directors. His relationship with Besson, though, is his most enduring. Besson typically consults Serra once he has an idea for a new project, and Serra then researches possibilities for the score independently before, in the main, coming on board formally at the rough cut stage and composing to the finished images. Their relationship seems to be a close, harmonious and informal one, with Serra in no way contracted to work with Besson.

This chapter takes each of Besson's films in turn, noting both the key elements that make Serra's style unique and tracking developments in his technique as he evolves from a composer of pop scores into a writer of full-blown orchestral film music. In *Le Dernier combat* we find the germ of Serra's style: cues constructed from repeating riffs, more freely improvised material and longline, quasi-song form structures. In *Subway*, Serra expands this last into full-blown pop songs and begins to incorporate a growing number of exotic influences into his style. While *Le Grand bleu* features an increased responsiveness on the part of the music to the action on screen, *Nikita* develops the role of virtuoso percussion writing in his style and *Léon* finds Serra composing for full orchestra for the first time. *Le Cinquième élément* showcases all of Serra's techniques on an epic canvas and *Jeanne d'Arc* marks his final flowering into a composer of conventionally orchestral film music.

The chapter also, however, always seeks to relate this music to image and narrative in order to suggest something of what Serra brings to Besson's films. From the wide variety of directions such analysis can take it will become clear just how rich a component Serra's music is in our experience of Besson's work.

Le Dernier combat

The music for *Le Dernier combat* is modest in terms of instrumentation, built around the core of a funk group (bass, drums, synthesiser, electric guitar, horns), augmented by exotic percussion. The music is generated from three basic musical forms: cues constructed from repeating riffs,[1] around which the musicians improvise, cues comprising more freely improvised material, and cues based on longline, quasi-song-form structures over which, once more, solos are improvised. Conventional, orchestral film music tends to avoid such formal regularity, responding more flexibly to the constantly shifting demands of timing, emotional shading and the rhythms of the images themselves (see Gorbman, 1987).

After a title sequence featuring a soundtrack comprising a blowing wind and the laboured breathing of the Man making love to a blow-up doll that deflates at the crucial moment, a crash edit to the Man pulling a torch-lit trolley through a dark tunnel surprises not just visually (light to dark, open framing to closed), but aurally too, a loud and driving 4:4 beat contrasting dramatically with the organic sounds of before. The rhythm section dominates this first cue, tight, syncopated drums and virtuoso, funky fretless bass punctuated by equally rhythmic figures on horns. The music is constructed around a repeating, rhythmic riff, over which the various instruments add embellishments and variations.

This non-diegetic cue is followed by a second that we assume originates likewise from outside the storyworld of the film. A swelling synth chord evolves into a more relaxed F-major jazz-funk passage using a similar instrumental palette of drums, bass, synth and brass. Again, the cue seems constructed around a repeating riff. Because of the similarities of instrumentation and structure, we are surprised to find that the music this time is in fact diegetic: the Man switches his tape player off, and it abruptly stops. The opening two cues of the film, then, provide us with musical surprises, the first of sonic contrast, the second in the manipulation of the diegetic status of what we are hearing. Furthermore, somewhat unusually, the loneliness of the Man's evidently solitary existence is communicated not by the score, but by the sound of the constant wind, acting as a metonym for the emptiness and anomie of the film's hostile environment. The music functions instead to make him seem cool and quirky in spite of his lack of companions, its lightness preparing us for the picaresque nature of the narrative that follows.

Although written in a jazz-funk style, Serra's music subsequently displays some of the hallmarks of the traditional, orchestral film score. The repetition of the synth note accompanying the Man and the Brute's first duel is a classic suspense technique. Tension is also created as the Man approaches the Captain's camp by jettisoning the rhythmically predictable riff-based approach in favour of a fragmented, out-of-tempo feel, reverbed trumpet and marimba freely improvising over occasional cymbal splashes and drum beats. This comparatively formless, discordant, chromatic music unsettles the viewer just as the similar treatment of an orchestra would. The use of the marimba also hints at an interest in non-Western music that will deepen throughout Serra's collaboration with Besson. Curiously, however, this at heart expressive, improvisatory cue does not really react to the Man's maiming of the Captain in any way, nor to his gruesome discovery of the severed fingers: we hear the trumpet loud and in its upper *tessitura*, but this happens elsewhere in the cue, too. While an orchestral composer might build towards these points to mark them as dramatically important, Serra chooses not to accentuate them unduly.

If the riff idea can be dropped in favour of free improvisation, it can also be fleshed out into a more developed musical structure. Serra often opens the score out into more fully worked through, song-like forms, constructed around evolving, connected sequences of eight-bar musical phrases that comprise, ostensibly, a succession of 'verses'. Such sequences include the maiden microlight flight, scored for cool electric piano, and the bass-dominated cue culminating in a sax solo as the Man ransacks the abandoned bar. These sound more like completed numbers than revolving breaks, and the abandoning of the riff style allows more emotive, affective musical ideas to be voiced (a sense of expansiveness in the former and of hedonism in the latter). More lyrical moments, such as the Man's walk through the deserted city, introducing a guitar to the score, are likewise more song-like in development, and the delicate electric piano first announcing the appearance of the Girl's hand, then, later, of the Man's gift for her, equally sounds like the introduction of a (love?) song.

For *Le Dernier combat*, then, Serra provides a score in the jazz-funk idiom, using a limited instrumental palette. Amplified (electric guitars/basses) and synthesised sound are important elements of this. Many cues are constructed from a sequence of repeating riffs which the various instruments embellish, although other sections feature either free-form sequences of improvisation, or utilise more longline, song-like forms. Continuity is achieved through the limited spectrum of forms, common instrumentation and the reprising of certain cues as the film progresses: the diegetic cue we are surprised with towards the start subsequently reappears in the Man's second abode, again when the Brute breaks the tape player there, and in full over the closing credits. Finally, although writing in a jazz-funk style, Serra is already deploying techniques familiar from the work of orchestral film composers since the studio era, for example, using discord and fragmentation to create unease and upward modulations of key to increase tension.

Subway

Music moves to centre stage in Besson's second film, which begins by quoting Frank Sinatra, and boasts a central character whose first action is to choose what music to listen to in the car, and whose last is to hum a fragment of a song. He assembles a pop group to perform a set of personal importance to him, and having done this can die happy. Here, Serra moves from being behind the camera to being in front of it as well, cameoing as Le Bassiste, a character popping up throughout the film. In the closing title crawl the music credits take precedence over photography, editing and *mise-en-scène*.

Many of the principles defining *Le Dernier combat*'s score are carried forward into *Subway*'s. The basic instrumental palette is again a simple, funky one, and the opening car chase begins with an up-tempo drum-and-slap bass break, reminiscent of the first cue in *Le Dernier combat*; as with the hapless Brute before, the machine eventually devours the tape. *Subway* also shows evidence of play with the diegetic/non-diegetic status of music, as at Youssef's birthday party, where the bass and bongos are revealed to be being played by Le Bassiste and Émile, and, memorably, with the mellow tenor sax solo underscoring the montage depicting Fred and Héléna's separation, and ending with him discovering Le Saxophoniste. As with the gang's assault on the Man's first abode, a simple *accelerando* builds the tension as Gros Bill snaps Fred's handcuffs.

The clearest line of continuity between the scores, however, is the use of the riff technique. With the introduction of Le Batteur and Le Roller, appropriately, drums open, followed by bass, sax and horn section: a typically funky, riff-based cue. Our introduction to Gesberg is also given a riff cue, as is Fred's fluorescent-lit descent ever lower into the subterranean world of the subway: a synth *ostinato* is set up, looping away largely unchanged as he moves through various corridors and hatches. The music is reverbed and industrial, perfect for the echoing concrete spaces, exposed pipes and mysterious vents of the service corridors. When a bridged walkway gives way, and Fred nearly falls into the water below, as with the maiming of the Captain in *Le Dernier combat*, there is no sudden sting on the soundtrack: the volume is merely cranked up a little, only to drop down again for his meeting with Le Roller. The music remains unresponsive to such specific narrative stimuli.

There are, however, two major developments in the score, the first being the increased incorporation of musical exotica. Our introduction to Gros Bill, an enormously pumped-up black man, is scored for two African-style percussion passages using a variety of membraphones and deeply resonant *timbala*-style xylophones. On one level, the music is underlining Bill's ethnicity; on another, Fred is entering a new (under)world, and the soundtrack responds by becoming commensurately 'Other'. This African sound is drawn on frequently in the film and, apart from providing an easygoing rhythmic framework for the film's big song 'It's Only Mystery' – a number that otherwise draws on nostalgic Americana via its intertextual nod to Johnny Nash's 'I Can See Clearly Now' – it reaches its final flowering in the visual image of the band appearing in safari suits and pith helmets for their big gig. Musical influences from outside the Western musical tradition, not just percussive but, later, melodic, will become an increasingly important strand in Serra's work.

The second development is the inclusion of full-blown pop songs. Interestingly, their lyrics are exclusively in English (as, presumably, the *lingua franca* of pop), and the first number sets the scene for what follows. 'Victim of Your Love' mixes the vocabulary of the love song (kisses, subjection) with that of the criminal world (conviction, murder), entirely appropriate to the ensuing narrative. 'Guns and People' rounds the film off in similar style. The narrative effectively grinds to a halt altogether to mark as important the first performance of the discreetly anthemic ballad 'It's Only Mystery', its centrality emphasised by its reprise during the closing credits. As well as providing cross-media synergy and revenues from soundtrack sales (Smith 1998: 2), these diegetic and non-diegetic pop songs, together with Rickie Lee Jones's romantic import 'Lucky Guy', mesh well with the subplot of Fred getting a band together, symbolising the youthful, multi-ethnic, counter-cultural nature of the subway's misfit inhabitants. Riff cues notwithstanding, whether through up-front pop songs or the lyrical, quasi-vocal sound of the dolorous fretless bass underpinning Fred telling Héléna about his childhood, a new melodism is brought to *Subway*'s score.

Like *Le Dernier combat*, the score for *Subway* is conceived in a pop/funk idiom for a limited instrumental palette, consolidating the idea of constructing cues from sequences of repeating riffs and loops. Again, it draws on electronic sound, both amplified and synthesised. Serra experiments more, however, with African as well as Western sounds, and develops the song-form idea of before, allowing full verse and chorus forms to move forward. Vocals make their entrance, replacing the leading instruments of song-like cues in *Le Dernier combat*. Finally, Serra's music for *Subway* moves onto another emotional level, as the music begins to be written not just to sound vibrantly cool, but moving, emotionally affecting. If in *Le Dernier combat* we found a couple of cues reminiscent of the introduction to a love song, in *Subway* we begin to get the love song itself.

Le Grand bleu (long version)

In *Le Grand bleu*, Serra takes over the playing of most of the instruments on the soundtrack, adding his own vocal to personalise his contribution further. While there is much here that is familiar, the music's new-found responsiveness to the images it backs is an important development in Serra's style.

The opening title returns us to the instrumental song-form style, featuring Gilbert Dall'Anese's soprano sax floating effortlessly over Serra multitracking two fretless basses, synths, guitar, drums, sibilant reverb-heavy cymbals, rimshots and tambourine, and an array of exotic tuned and untuned percussion. The tempo is relaxed, the mix as spacious as the views of the sea, the sibilance as brilliant as the Greek sunshine. The high, bent notes of the compressed, distorted electric guitar seem evocative of the singing of whales and dolphin cries.

Unlike before, in this cue the music does respond to the stimulus of danger. As young Jacques dives into the sea, the tempo drops, and a synth pedal note creates suspense, an echoed boom and a cymbal scrape heralding the appearance of a scary-looking fish. While the out-of-tempo, improvisatory feel is similar to the trumpet-marimba duet of *Le Dernier combat*, the various sounds intoned here are more closely choreographed to the edits and images they underscore. Indeed, Serra demonstrates sensitivity to the editing throughout the film, many establishing shots of landscapes, seascapes and cuts to underwater shots likewise being marked percussively.

The music also responds to moments when people dive into water. While one might reasonably expect a sudden, onomatopoeic cymbal splash to mark the moment of entry, intriguingly Serra provides us with extended shakes on tambourine, echoing drum booms and deep, bell-like sonorities. More orthodox is the synth choir that suddenly 'vocalises' as Jacques emerges triumphantly at the end of his first tournament dive, mythologising as epic his rise in the water, intercut grandly with the leaping of dolphins. This choir will sound with more ethereal connotations over the closing image of the film. Elsewhere, the music becomes responsive to the action as a geographical locator through the addition of panpipes as we relocate to Peru, a sound as iconic as the image of a herd of llamas at the railway station. Panpipes return as Joanne reminisces about her trip in New York, and once again much later in the film, making a connection between her visit to an analyst and her love-at-first-sight Peruvian experience. Similarly, place is evoked through a synth allophone of the equally clichéd mandolin as Jacques carries Joanna's luggage to her rooms in Taormina, Italy.

Although the music displays a new responsiveness to the images, Serra still uses his characteristic riff cues. Tellingly, the music, as Jacques and Joanna have sex for the first time, is not lyrical, like a love song, but riff-based. The longline melody is saved for the implied infidelity of his subsequent tumble with the dolphins: the composer, like Joanna, knows where Jacques's heart lies. Their second sex scene is also scored with a riff cue, modulating up as a barometer of their ecstasy, but concluding with an anticlimactic treated sequence of chimes on a bell-tree; the choir of Jacques's triumphant surfacing in the tournament is, in comparison, a far more orgasmic musical moment. Elsewhere, song-like forms abound. As well as the opening title and its reprises, both the panpipe and mandolin music are structured in this way, as is the cheerful diegetic guitar duet at Enzo's pasta party. Serra plays all the instruments on the full-blown pop song, 'My Lady Blue', for the closing credits, a number derived in part from chord sequences taken from the opening title, the lyrics in English again, Serra's vocal reminiscent of Peter Gabriel. Besson is credited as lyricist, emphasising the closeness of their collaboration.

The music for *Le Grand bleu*, then, retains many ideas familiar from previous Serra scores, but marks a further development in his style, primarily through a new-found responsiveness to the images he is scoring, but also through his decision to play most of the instruments himself. The music is further personalised by the addition of his vocals. The mix of prominent fretless bass, idiosyncratic guitar, synth textures, expanded percussion section, funky riffs, song-forms and out-of-tempo, responsive illustrative music, is a highly individual one: this film music does not really sound like anyone else's.

Nikita

In many ways, the score for *Nikita* consolidates the advances made on *Le Grand bleu*. Again Serra plays the lion's share of instruments, the score has a heavily produced, electronic feel, and many trademark gestures appear. What makes this music distinctive is a return to the exotic with a subtly oriental feel, and, developing a strand first heard clearly in *Subway*, a more prominent role being allotted to virtuoso percussion.

Over a speeding travelling shot of streetlights on cobbles, reminiscent of the light-on-water shot that opened *Le Grand bleu*, quietly tintinnabular synth notes sound as various credits pop on and off screen over a synth drone. With Anne Parillaud's name, tempo becomes formalised: a quiet, nervous energy is imparted by a trebly rhythm track comprising hi-hats, finger snaps, cymbals, claves, chime bars and finger drums. As the camera tilts up on the gang, the volume of the music suddenly increases, opening out into a loud, strutting, bass-driven funky riff cue, the cymbals and cowbells of the percussion section still audible behind the pounding drum kit. Quieter percussion then pops and clicks away over a series of synth pedal notes, creating tension as the gang break into a pharmacy, before sneaking out in the lead up to the gun battle. The booming of the gunfire contrasts dramatically with the delicately trebly percussion *ostinato*, sounding more like the loud drums of the riff cue that preceded it.

The score, then, signals its interest in percussion from the start. Another percussion *ostinato* accompanies Nikita's incarceration after the trial, and precedes her attack on Bob before developing into a riff cue on a pedal F# as she takes him hostage. Many of the film's riff cues feature this light percussion overlay, unifying the score: it plays as Nikita is trained to use computers and shoot on a firing range, as Amande encourages her to smile, as Bob takes Nikita out to the duplicitous dinner, as 'Josephine' has her rendezvous in the George V, and as Nikita spies on the ambassador.

Percussion is also important in the scoring of action sequences. In the build-up to the first of these, as Nikita performs her test hit in the restaurant, a rising sequence of synth chords cranks up the tension. An industrial, triplety rhythm *ostinato* starts and is joined by a drum machine, a treated percussion track layered on top. This combo dominates Nikita's flight through the backrooms and kitchens. The move to electronic percussion is a startling one, somewhat alienating and machine-like after the human agency of the trebly pops and clicks we have grown accustomed to. The drum machine returns, augmented with lighter percussion, as Nikita assembles the rifle in the Venetian bathroom, and in the tense build-up to her firing. Similarly, preparations for the ambassador operation are scored for a drum solo and percussive samples of breaking glass. The electronic and sampled percussion from the first restaurant hit return as Nikita flees the ambassador's residence, pleads with Victor not to 'clean' the place, and the two escape by car: this is where the process embarked on at the start has culminated.

Passages of *Nikita* also have a distinctly exotic flavour. After the opening pharmacy battle, as Nikita shoots the cop, a three-note motif sounds on oriental-sounding tuned percussion (F#-A-E). This sound returns as she cries for her mother when she is imprisoned. This, and the pentatonic cast of melodic fragments in cues such as her initial training montage, hint both at the opiates she craves, and at the ruthless, Sun Tzu qualities she develops as an assassin. An inventive piece of chinoiserie is created from bass harmonics, bent into a pentatonic figure by adjusting the tuning pegs, during Amande's first charm lesson. This orientalism will be developed as an index of Léon's Zen-like, samurai qualities in Besson's next film.

Nikita displays continuity, then, and development, too, with the foregrounding of percussion and the sustained return of the exotic. Indeed, the film's song brings the two together, a darkly percussive arrangement featuring pentatonic backing vocals. After the film's closing dedications, Serra's credit is the first to appear on screen, signalling, perhaps, the importance of his contribution both to this film and, cumulatively, to Besson's growing *œuvre*.

Léon

Léon features similar use of riff and song-form cues, and again showcases an elaborate percussion section, acoustic and sampled, pitched a little lower than *Nikita*'s (male versus female protagonist?), but used in much the same way as a rhythmic layer laid over, typically, synth backing. *Léon*, however, marks the first appearance in Serra's Besson scores of an orchestra, and also develops further the interest in non-Western musical traditions.

These two factors combine in the opening title. Again, synth tintinnabulations mark the appearance of names at the start of the credits, the first image (light on water again) greeted with a gong-like sound. A highly expressive, oriental-sounding violin solo begins, the tempo dreamily slow as we helicopter over Central Park. A synth choir vocalises and upper orchestral strings intone fragile, extended high harmonies as a bamboo flute plays. When the camera tilts up on the New York skyline, a bass note underlines this movement with an upward pitch bend. Oriental percussion sounds, along with timpani and an Indian shawm as the title fills the screen. Shawm and bamboo flute duet over the strings until the cue concludes with an enigmatic, disorientating upward modulation. This is an intoxicating opening, sensual, floating, highly eclectic. The orchestra has been immaculately blended into the sound, not just aping the slightly blocky banks of synth strings used in the past, but used in an idiomatic way.

Orchestral strings return, backing Serra's acoustic guitar, as Léon meets Mathilda. The music is relaxed and major key, contrasting with the previous nightmarish riff cue from Léon's storming of the fat man's lair. This music is more organised, both tonally and rhythmically, than the drifting title cue. A slightly stumbling, child-like glockenspiel picks out the theme, a lyrical longline melody, unusually for Serra in lilting waltz time. Strings provide gentle backing for this characteristic song-style cue, our introduction to Mathilda gently pretty with the odd naive hesitation and wrong note thrown in.

These supportive strings are recast in a discordant minor key as Mathilda's dad slaps her around, developing into a lyrical cue featuring solo oboe backing Léon at home washing, doing chores, tending his plant. This sustained passage is written entirely for the orchestra, its poise having an almost Baroque feel with its regular *pizzicato* basses and swelling polyphony: this grace should prepare us for Léon's admiration of Gene Kelly later. This sense of musical order contrasts with the musical ribaldry of Mathilda's life (*Cagney and Lacey* and aerobics music dominate here), and hints at the ascetic balance and repose of Léon's private life, an order about to be upset by Mathilda's arrival.

The orchestra is also given Léon and Mathilda's theme. It first appears on flute backed with soft strings as they sit across from each other in Léon's apartment, and is uncomplicated to the point of being palindromic,[2] lending their relationship a simple innocence, as well as a sense of the complementarily similar. This theme is developed as the film progresses, being given to oboe, expanded to include accompanying harp, *divisi* violins, and a tinkling piano, as Mathilda tells the clerk she is Léon's lover and Léon rescues her from police headquarters. As well as also fleshing out riff-style cues (Léon and Mathilda being thrown out of their hotel), Serra uses the orchestra to provide both an emotional centre for his score (all those warm strings), and to conjure new textures in his work (the opening title).

Another colouristic strategy is his incorporation of musical styles from world music. The orientalism of *Nikita* is given new license in this tale of a warrior asked to take responsibility for one whose life he has saved.

However, multiple influences from world music are felt in the score, reflecting the multi-ethnic, metropolitan backdrop of the film's New York setting. Serra's New York sounds like a crossroads of the world, the archetypal cultural melting pot. The chinoiserie is developed principally through use of percussion and bamboo flute, but the influence of North African/Middle Eastern and Jewish music is also apparent. The oriental violin solo of the title cue can be heard as *klezmer*-like, and the highly chromatic minor key melody played by violins after Mathilda lies about her mother's death to her headmistress displays a similar soulful chromaticism (B/C/B/D/C#/C/B. . .). After Léon tells Mathilda that life is always hard, we hear gong sounds, and the expressive solo violin returns, this time with the chromatic melody above. Here, the *portamento* fiddle sounds very Jewish indeed, despite the swishing oriental percussion. Strings take this figure up once more, as Stansfield demonstrates just how hard life can be by killing Mathilda's family; the theme eventually forms the backbone of the SWAT squad's climactic storming of the apartment at the end. It is unclear whether this crying, bending *klezmer* sound hints at the wandering, rootless Léon's ethnicity, but the solo violin of the score clearly connects with the violin case Léon carries around with him, and Mathilda passes herself off as a child prodigy in the first hotel they move into. The mournful sound of the fiddle's playing, then, links them.

Modal inflections in many of the riff cues (C#/D/B in music in C# major, for example), give a North African/Middle Eastern feel, as do the *andalous*-style unison strings playing the likewise modally inflected melody when Mathilda carries the groceries past the carnage in her parents' apartment, a unison that momentarily erupts into radiant harmony as Léon opens the door for her, bathing her in light. Later as Léon gives Mathilda rooftop target practice, shawm and bamboo flute drift above strings, the tempo again slowed to the floating pace of the opening title. A *qawwali*-esque female vocalise joins as Mathilda takes aim, an Asian flavour echoed in Talvin Singh's string arrangement in Björk's 'Venus as a Boy', needledropped shortly after.

Despite being the first of his scores to feature the addition of an orchestra, this music still sounds distinctively like Serra's. The recourse to riff cues, the intensive use of virtuoso percussion and the developing interest in world music all mark the score as his, and although Sting replaces him for the song over the closing credits, in the penultimate cue, as Mathilde beds out Léon's plant, the acoustic guitar playing over the strings is Serra's.

Le Cinquième élément

The score for *Le Cinquième élément* relies even more heavily on orchestral textures and exotic influences, but blends Serra's characteristic riff and song-form cues with more conventional scoring techniques.

The discreet shading of the strings, slow, gentle, modulating constantly and elusively behind the opening scene in the temple, is more like conventional film music than we are used to. Similarly, as the Professor mentions the Fifth Element we have a hint of the first appearance of a leitmotiv in Serra's work, another technique borrowed from traditional film-scoring (Kalinak 1992: 104). It will develop into F/B-flat/A-flat/G/F/A-flat/F, sounding on high synth, appended with a guitar pitch bend from F to F# and back, giving its F minor the spice of the modally exotic. This watermarks the score as we enter the temple's inner sanctum for the first time, as we see the elemental design on Cornelius's belt, for Leeloo's tattoo, indeed whenever the Fifth Element becomes a point of reference.

Other conventional gestures include the militaristic rattle of snares that develops into a march as the warship prepares to destroy the dark planet and is consumed by it, and the tension-inducing invert pedal stinger as Leeloo growls at Monroe through the glass of her regeneration tube. We hear Mahlerian, funereal timpani as Leeloo learns about war.

The conventional technique of thematic variation and reorchestration (Brown 1994: 43) is also adopted. A major theme of the picture, circling around D/F/G/E-flat/D/F (or their transposition), appears in many guises as the film progresses, in soft underscore as Cornelius advises the president of the disaster scenario facing the Federation, on oboe and strings as the surgeons prepare to regenerate Leeloo, then *pizzicato* as she is reconstructed. The theme is varied rhythmically, notes lengthened, shortened and repeated as the operation progresses, unfolding lyrically on rhapsodic strings for our first view of her, and as she is brought to life. This technique unifies the score in conventional style, the arrangement of this last passage reminiscent of Ryuichi Sakamoto's string work.[3]

Serra returns as provider of the closing song, 'Little Light of Love', showcasing highly melismatic North-African Yemenite backing vocals. The body of the score, too, is highly eclectic. A shawm sounds as the priest pleads with Billy to put his gun down in the Egyptian temple, and again as Leeloo tries to communicate with Dallas after she falls into his cab. Middle-Eastern unison strings are heard over a drum loop of exotic percussion as he subsequently tells her to give herself up, then escapes with her, police in pursuit, a chase sequence backed with an extraordinary blend of *merengue* piano, accordion and Bollywood vocal. A Stalinist–Russian fanfare leads us into the spaceport sequence, and preparations for the flight to Fhloston take place over a Reggae cue, the passengers welcomed with a Hawaiian *hula*.

This score, then, augments Serra's familiar forms with more sophisticated orchestral writing, introduces conventional orchestral scoring techniques, and expands the interest in the eclectic. Serra also takes over the conductor's baton, underlining his confidence in working with the orchestra, a relationship that will be developed further in the final film to be considered.

Jeanne d'Arc

Pastoral oboe, flute and clarinet supported by soft strings, and a Gregorian-style, monophonic chant locate us both in the rural Middle Ages, and within a religious milieu. The music swells to a lyrical *tutti*. After the dark, pounding percussion of the opening, underlining the plight of France, this lush, epic sound completes the evolution of Serra from pop-score writer to orchestral film composer. The sureness of the writing as we get our first good look at adult Joan is also evidence of this, the melody passing seamlessly from clarinet to cello to *vibrato* solo violin. Indeed, the score helps anchor and articulate several aspects of Joan's manifold character as the film progresses: innocent as a child, beautiful as a woman, powerful in the battle sequences, and fragmented and new-age-spiritual in her trance states.

As this might suggest, Serra's handling of the orchestra has become highly responsive to the action on screen. As Yolande tells Charles how well she knows him, the music flits from touching (solo violin over soft strings), to disturbing (a momentary discord as she casts doubts on his parentage; *tremolo* strings as she hints at Joan's possible power), to radiant (*divisi* upper strings for the hope Joan brings). The battle scenes occasion more extensive use of orchestral brass than before, powerful chords connoting the strength of the attackers, and in some cues, such as the battering ram attack on the English, a real choir sings, rather than its synthesised equivalent. Fittingly, given the divine subtext, choral music is often used, evoking both the spiritual (the gently anachronistic coronation vocalising) and the epic (full-throated for the petals in the cathedral). Bells, too, true and sampled, sound throughout the score. This, then, is the largest-scale score Serra has attempted for Besson, occasioning the use of an orchestrator, Geoffrey Alexander, presumably owing to pressure of time, as is the industry norm (Davis 1999: 84). Serra still conducts, and plays percussion parts amongst others.

The score is at once in keeping with a period piece, basking in the temporal non-specificity accorded to orchestral film music written in the neo-romantic idiom, and contemporary: funereal timpani and muffled orchestral bells play over a C# minor chord on strings for the funeral of Joan's mother, but are joined by synth pitch bends. Indeed, synthesisers comprise an important part of the score's palette, as when Joan is incarcerated in Burgundy. Equally, there are some vaguely period touches, such as the lute that plays before Joan's first arrival at the Dauphin's castle, and the use of Gregorian-style plainsong.

Within this framework, much remains familiar. Young Joan, like Mathilda, is given an introduction in 3:4 time, a time signature that follows her around as she travels to her aunt and uncle's and confesses *en route*. Given that Joan describes herself as God's drum, percussion is foregrounded, in particular through a variety of deep-toned, echoing drums evocative of medieval *tambours*, complementing the low contrabass figures that stalk threateningly through the score. A collage of sampled and treated sounds, mixed with a variety of choiral textures, plays over the montage sequence of Joan's early religious ecstasy, and over other trance experiences. An electronic soundscape blends with reverbed sound effects as the English burn her childhood village. As Joan escapes first from her uncle's wagon and races cross country to a church, we even have a riff cue: over a choir a percussion *ostinato* is set up for drum loop and bell sounds; as she takes communion, a solo violin reminiscent of that in *Léon* enters over Gregorian lines. Sleighbells (heard in unorthodox, non-festive context in *Le Grand bleu* and *Léon*) sound over the introduction to the Dauphin's castle, and the arrival of the adult Joan is accompanied by a melody similar to that which introduced Leeloo in *Le Cinquième élément*.

This score, then, marks Serra's final flowering into an orchestral composer, a transition accomplished, generally, with relatively little dilution of the style he has evolved over preceding films. Only on occasion does he sound unlike himself, as with the occasional whiff of Holst's *Mars* in battle scenes, and the somewhat unimaginative paraphrase of Orff's *Carmina Burana* that accompanies the final burning.

Conclusion

As this brief survey has shown, auteur and *compositeur* have embarked on a complementary journey of discovery and development. While Besson's visual and narrative concerns have evolved over the years, yet remained recognisably his, so Serra's style has both changed and remained distinctive. From writing spare, pop-style scores relying heavily on repetition and improvisation, Serra has grown into an orchestral composer with sufficient technique to write music that has become increasingly responsive to the action on screen, more complex and controlled, and displaying growing emotional finesse. In doing so, he has maintained his interest in riff and song-form writing, and developed an increasingly eclectic approach to the soundworld he creates, making percussion and non-Western music important elements in its constitution.

Accordingly, we might do well to remember the contribution a productive director–composer relationship can bring to an auteur's work. Serra's music has become a distinctive and integral part of Besson's work, his writing, performing, arranging and conducting of the music giving him powerful, quasi-authorial control over Besson's soundtracks. As with the Hitchcock–Herrmann, Spielberg–Williams, Lucas–Williams, Coen Brothers–Burwell collaborations, and many others like them, we must remember to listen to auteur cinema as well as watch it.

Glossary of musical terms

accelerando   Getting faster

andalous   A Morroccan musical style using such violin analogues as the *rabab* and the *kamenjah*, the latter being played vertically upon the knee, among other instruments (zither, percussion, Western instruments, etc.).

chromaticism   The interpolation of notes normally foreign to the main key of the music (C major, E minor, etc.). There are eight notes in a simple scale running from Doh-Doh, but chromatic music adds other notes in alongside the Doh-Re-Me... progression, as twelve notes in all are incorporated within the span of an octave. Chromaticism can create a variety of impressions depending on how it is used. It can contribute to an angular or discordant musical style (Bela Bartok, 1881–1945) or be used to broaden the composer's palette and produce music of intoxicating lushness (Richard Strauss, 1864–1949).

divisi   Divided into many parts. It is customary for the violins in an orchestra to be organised into first, second and third violins; *divisi* string writing can call for these sections to be subdivided still further right down to individual desks or players. A *divisi* string sound is one of the hallmarks of the lush, romantic style of film-scoring dominant in Hollywood in the 1930s–1940s.

glissando	A nebulous effect that changes according to the instrument performing it. On piano a *glissando* is created when a finger is run rapidly over the keys in any direction. Similarly, a harp *glissando* is created when the player runs a finger or fingers rapidly across the strings. But on stringed instruments a *glissando* is created by sliding a finger rapidly up or down the string(s), bringing notes that fall outside the customary tones and semitones of the scale (microtones) into play. A trombonist can use the slide to create a *glissando*, while woodwind players can *glissando* from one note to another by increasing lip pressure.
klezmer	Traditional Jewish music emanating from the Eastern European ghettos, often foregrounding solo violin and clarinet.
melismatic	In a melismatic melody many notes are sung to a single text syllable.
merengue	A Latin American ballroom-dance style originating in Dominica and Haiti.
modal inflections	Hints of scales other than those used in standard major key/minor key music. Depending on the mode chosen, the suggestion can range from the exotic to the antiquated.
needledrop	A pre-existing piece of recorded music inserted into the soundtrack. Metaphorically, the needle lands on the record and you have an instant score.
ostinato	A pattern of notes or rhythms that repeats itself over and over.
pedal note	A low note which is sustained unchangingly during a harmonic progression. A high note performing a similar function is an invert pedal note.
pentatonic	Drawing on a scale made up from just five notes. If you run your fingers up the black notes on a piano, you are tracing a pentatonic scale. This pentatonic scale has a markedly Oriental connotation, although folk-music traditions from all over the world build melodies from it: there is more than one pentatonic scale, as the name refers to the number of notes in it rather than which notes are used.
pizzicato	A musical marking asking string players to pluck their instruments rather than bow them.
portamento	An effect used in the performance of vocal or string music where a note is slid up or down to in a brief,

	continuous glide for (occasionally florid) expressive effect.
riff	A short, repeating musical motif in pop, rock or jazz.
stinger	(1) A strident sequence of chords often ending without harmonic resolution, intended to amplify a cliff-hanging sense of shock, peril or revelation; (2) A sudden, loud instrumental crash designed to make the audience jump.
tessitura	The range of notes an instrument/voice is capable of performing. The upper tessitura is the higher part of this range, the lower tessitura the lower part.
tremolo	The rapid, sustained reiteration of a single note, or the equally rapid alternation of two or more notes. Often used to indicate excitement, trepidation, etc.
tutti	All of the performers of the orchestra, or a section of the orchestra, playing at the same time (i.e. *tutti* strings).
vibrato	An expressive technique whereby the player or singer sounds or sings tiny and rapid fluctuations of pitch so a note is not played and sung purely, but inflected by these quick pitch changes.

References

Brown, R. S. (1994), *Overtones and Undertones: Reading Film Music* (Berkeley, California: University of California Press).

Davis, R. (1999), *Complete Guide to Film Scoring: The Art and Business of Writing Music for Films and TV* (Boston, Massachussetts: Berklee Press).

Gorbman, C. (1987), *Unheard Melodies: Narrative Film Music* (London: BFI).

Kalinak, K. (1992), *Settling the Score: Music and the Classical Hollywood Film* (Madison, Wisconsin: University of Wisconsin Press).

Smith, J. (1998), *The Sounds of Commerce: Marketing Popular Film Music* (New York: Columbia University Press).

Notes

1 This and other musical terms are explained in the glossary at the end of this chapter (see pp. 71–3).
2 If a verbal palindrome is a word that reads the same backwards as forwards, a musical palindrome is an equally symmetrical phrase or figure, here: F/E-flat/D-flat/C/D-flat/E-flat/F.
3 Sakamoto is the composer for *Merry Christmas Mr Lawrence* (Nagisa Oshima, 1983), in which he plays a major role, and for many other films, amongst them *The Last Emperor* (Bernardo Bertolucci, 1987), *Tacones lejanos* (*High Heels*, Pedro Almodóvar, 1991), *Little Buddha* (Bernardo Bertolucci, 1993), *Gohatto* (Nagisa Oshima, 1999).

5

Of suits and men in the films of Luc Besson

Phil Powrie

Besson's characters may be marginal, living on the fringes of society, and often at odds with that society; but his cinema is central to an understanding of a variety of relationships. Foremost amongst these is the socio-political relationship of French youth to French society, as Susan Hayward has shown (Hayward, 1998). A decade before *La Haine* (*Hate*, Matthieu Kassovitz, 1995) and the American-inspired *cinéma de banlieue*, the films of Besson, along with those of Beineix and Carax, as explained by Raphaël Bassan in this volume (see pp. 11–21), proposed that alienated young people were driven to the violent margins of society. At a formal level, Besson's films engage, at least apparently, with a postmodern interest in surface and pastiche, as analysed by Fredric Jameson in relation to Beineix's *Diva* (1981). If young people are alienated, it is at least partly, if these films are to be believed, because there is no depth in the postmodern (including the socio-political postmodern of all promise of great reforms and no substance), only surface, and therefore nothing to believe in anymore.

For all that it is central to French cinema, Besson's work is nevertheless eccentric, indeed sufficiently eccentric that it is not as simple as the account given above suggests. Jameson explains how Beineix's *Diva* is pulled between the old and the new. Gorodish is the 'hip new countercultural businessman' (Jameson 1992: 56), who although he meditates like a throwback to the 1960s,[1] also, and more importantly, very actively masters the technological for profit. Jules, on the other hand, is the opposite of Gorodish. He is more passive, and represents the more traditional figure of the *enfant du peuple*, or innocent, tied to a local community by his job as a postman, and tied to the post-war period by his economic and sensible mode of transport, the moped. Broadly speaking then, Jules represents the old, and Gorodish the new, 'post-

Sixties multinational modernity versus a traditional French left populism' (Jameson 1992: 58). Similarly, Besson's work is pulled between the old and the new. Unlike Beineix's film, however, it is not so much the characters who suggest the difficulties of negotiating the transition from the old to the new, as it is the formal characteristics of his films. It has often been said that his narratives are like strip cartoons, the characters broad-brush ciphers, whose motivations are merely sketched out, and put at the service of what have been dismissed as simplistic narratives lines. The implication is that Besson's films are a break with the cinema of the past, 'new' in the worst sense of the word. This is to accord centrality to the New Wave rather than to the popular cinema. Seen in the light of the New Wave, it is true that Besson's work, along with Beineix's, rejects psychological complexities and 'messages', rejects the lack of closure and the ambiguities which are typical of auteur cinema of the 1950s and 1960s. On the other hand, Besson's work is close in flavour to 1960s popular cinema. *Cartouche* (Philippe de Broca, 1962) may be a costume comedy set in the eighteenth century, but its eponymous hero played by Jean-Paul Belmondo, rather like the Fred of *Subway*, robs from the rich, is hated by the police and is romantically involved with an unattainable woman, in this case, the icy Isabelle (Odile Versois), wife of the chief of police.

The comparison with *Cartouche* (which is merely one example amongst many) raises three issues. The first is that Besson's work is anchored in a French cinematic tradition; it is as 'old' as it is 'new', and its moral imperatives are also both 'old' and 'new', in the sense that the values suggested by Besson's films are sentimentally conservative ('true love', the importance of the father and normative heterosexuality), while being attracted to 'new' issues, such as gender instabilities (strong women, cross-dressing, camp) and ecological concerns. The second issue is that Besson's work is pulled between national traditions: it is French, but it is also American, so that it is not always easy to decide whether his films, particularly those from *Nikita* onwards, are Americanised French cinema, or Gallicised American cinema. Third, the comparison with a costume film reminds us of the centrality of costume in Besson's work. While Beineix, arguably, is about postmodern spaces, and Carax is about postmodern use of colour, Besson is about costume. We are unlikely to remember much about Gorodish's (Richard Bohringer) clothes in *Diva*, or Alex's (Denis Lavant) in *Mauvais sang*; we are considerably more likely to remember Héléna's (Isabelle Adjani) punk hairstyle in *Subway*, the diving outfits in *Le Grand bleu*, Nikita's Audrey Hepburn style hat,[2] or, finally and outrageously, Ruby Rhod's (Chris Tucker) catsuit. It is on this combination of inbetweenness – between the old and the new, between the American and the French – and costume, and the violent frictions generated by these binaries, that this chapter will focus. It will rely heavily on the work of one of the more fascinating of the clothes theorists, John Flügel, whose 1930 book *The Psychology of Clothes*, published by The Hogarth Press in their 'International Psycho-analytical Library' series, remains one of the key texts for fashion studies (see, for example, Carter 2003).

This idea of 'inbetweenness' is not new. Both Susan Hayward and Stella Bruzzi in their work on Besson have alluded to different types of 'inbetweenness' in Besson's films. There is generic inbetweenness: Hayward points out how *Subway* is both thriller and musical, how *Léon* is both thriller and family melodrama, for example (Hayward 1998: 128). There is also inbetweenness where the national identity of the films is concerned, as Bruzzi points out when discussing the frequent borrowings between French and American gangster films (Bruzzi 1997: 67–8). Similarly, the issue of violence in Besson's work has been amply explored by Hayward, who sees it as an engagement with and reaction against technology for a youth audience; and both Hayward and Bruzzi have looked at Besson's films from the point of view of gender. This chapter will bring together inbetweenness, violence, gender and costume, starting from an examination of the development of certain key costumes worn by male characters in Besson's feature films. The points to be explored are as follows:

- Besson's sartorial system functions to establish simple Oedipal structures. Based on the suit where men are concerned, it is relatively stable, and ultimately conservative in its establishment of gender roles.
- The diving suit is potentially a site of transformation, but it too is reclaimed for normative purposes.
- The costume's potential for radical transformation is shifted to the cat-suited androgyne Ruby Rhod of *Le Cinquième élément*.

The white suit and the black suit

The suit is the most characteristic male attire in the modern period. Flügel sees in the sartorial simplicity exemplified by the suit what he calls the great masculine renunciation, whereby men gave up beauty for usefulness as a result of egalitarianism (the French Revolution had proclaimed that all men were equal) and the development of the work culture in the nineteenth century, which required simple clothes (Flügel 1930: 111–12). The suit, as the most characteristic element of male clothing, signifies 'devotion to the principles of duty, of renunciation, and of self-control' (Flügel 1930: 113),[3] as well as conformism to the principle of social cohesion; thus 'nonconformity in clothes tends naturally to express nonconformity in social and political thought' (Flügel 1930: 207). It is understandable then that Besson's films, which deal with anomic and marginal characters who do not feel socially integrated, should present us with hated male figures of authority dressed in what Flügel, describing a standard 'social function' calls 'a dull uniformity of black and white' (Flügel 1930: 114). It is with white and black suits that we shall begin.

Men in Besson's films either wear suits or they do not. If they do – and there are a surprising number of suits for films supposed to attract rebellious youth audiences who might associate the suit with a certain type of hegemonic masculinity – they are usually in positions of authority. There is the white suit of the leader (Fritz Wepper) in *Le Dernier combat*, which the hero (Pierre Jolivet) dons at the end of the film as he inherits the leader's woman. In *Le Grand bleu*, Enzo's (Jean Reno) white suit is contrasted with Jacques's (Jean-Marc Barr) black suit at the reception where Joanna (Rosanna Arquette) falls for Jacques, who has to ask the more confident Enzo how to date her; one of the more strikingly surreal scenes of the film is Enzo and Jacques, wearing their suits, sitting at the bottom of the swimming pool drinking champagne. There is Stansfield's beige suit in *Léon*, about which, because it has been stained in the shootout, he is more concerned than any of the family he has just massacred.

Men also wear black suits in Besson, most obviously Fred (Christophe Lambert) in *Subway*, Bob (Tchéky Karyo) in *Nikita* and Korben Dallas (Bruce Willis) in *Le Cinquième élément*. Unlike the white suits, however, associated with men in authority, the black suit generally signifies something less stable, something darker, as was already intimated in the contrast between the supremely self-confident Enzo in his white suit, and the shy Jacques in his contrasting black suit. John Harvey speculates that the black suit in modern European culture combines power and death, 'intensity' and 'effacement'; it suggests 'abandonedness and depth of need', and 'a power claimed over women and the feminine' (Harvey 1995: 257). These are all traits of what we might associate with Jacques, who is intense and self-effacing, and whose diving can be seen as an attempt to possess the feminine represented by the deep blue. Bob's power over Nikita is absolute: he has the power of life and death over her, and he moulds her Pygmalion-like into a tool of death. But by the same token, and because black is associated with mourning, these men are searching for something deeper, particularly Jacques, whose search for depth is a search for death, the self-effacement of 'quasi-neurotic asceticism', as Flügel calls men's dress more generally (Flügel 1930: 213).

In the cases of Fred and Dallas, however, the black suits are much less stable than these comments might suggest; they are transitional, and associated with explosions. Fred blows up a safe while wearing his dinner jacket, and will eventually don an old coat. Dallas is uncomfortable with his dinner jacket denoting social conformity. It will become ripped to a state of unrecognisability as we see him reprising the action tropes and the costume of the *Die Hard* films. In this case, it is almost as if the suit functions as a marker of French style, and its disintegration the mutation of the film towards an 'Americanised' violence, even if the mutation is not as sharply delineated as this might make it sound, given that what Dallas ends up wearing is a stylishly orange (so Gallicised) version of the vest familiar from the *Die Hard* series.

The flapping coat

The white suit connotes power and confidence, while the black suit connotes developing rebelliousness and its correlate, high style, associated with high class, exploding under the pressure of repression into the casual associated with lower class or *lumpen* egalitarianism. The opposite of the suit, both in terms of design and connotation, is the flapping coat, which functions as a sign of marginality and rebellion. It is important that it should be unbuttoned, as it thereby suggests flexibility, circulation through social and urban spaces, and the rejection of formality which attempts to contain social fluidity. In this respect, although it recalls it, it is unlike Jef Costello's (Alain Delon) tightly buttoned trenchcoat in *Le Samouraï* (*The Godson*, Jean-Pierre Melville, 1967). Costello's trenchcoat reflects his attachment to a rigid sense of form (the 'way of the samurai'), and the film's attachment to a coldly alienating sense of style. Bruzzi points out, for example, how Jef deposits his coat and hat in the cloakroom with very precise, ritualised gestures, what she calls an 'ironic theatricality' (Bruzzi 1997: 77). She shows how the coat functions as a 'suit of armour' (Bruzzi 1997: 80), and that the undermining of Jef's impregnable masculinity is signalled by him taking off the coat (Bruzzi 1997: 80–2). Fred, the police chief (Michel Galabru) and Léon, are all loners like Jef, but, unlike him, they all wear open, flapping coats, and are all at ease in their particular underground worlds. The police chief, for example, is contrasted with his deputy (Jean-Pierre Bacri), who wears a jacket, and blunders noisily around the underground with a posse of policemen, unable to catch The Roller (Jean-Hugues Anglade), while the police chief catches him alone and by stealth. The implication is that his flapping coat makes him look 'ordinary', unlike a policeman. Fred too blends into the underground once he exchanges his dinner jacket for the coat. Léon's coat may be 'several sizes too large', functioning as a deconstructive commentary on the stereotype of the gangster (Bruzzi 1997: 92), but when placed within Besson's coat 'system',[4] we can see that its function is also something more specific: it signals the innocence of the child-man, untainted by sordid issues of money, drink or drugs, and who moves invisibly through the city, as the first sequence of the film suggests.

The open coat suggests a fantasy of mobility and invisibility, connected with absolute power; it is almost like the vestigial wings of flying fantasies. The police chief uses this combination to catch criminals; Fred uses it to mount his concert; and Léon uses it to kill. These connotations of freedom and innocence are all the more obvious when we consider how the closed coat functions on the same actor, Jean Reno, as Victor the 'cleaner' in *Nikita*. Like Léon, he is a killer, but with none of the innocence; moreover, it is partly because of his execution of one of the team members that Nikita's mission goes awry. His coat is buttoned up, like Jef Costello's, a sign of repression, coldness and death; indeed, Nikita closes the collar tighter on the embassy steps, telling Victor to 'keep calm', emphasising the coat as a marker of containment.

That innocence extends to issues of national identity. The coat signifies a specifically European innocence ranged against American corruption. In *Léon*, when Léon blows up Stansfield, the issue of national identity is implicit in the contradictions running as an undercurrent: a French actor (playing an Italian hitman) is ranged against a British actor (playing a corrupt American lawman), the pure, because childlike, 'Italian' ranged against the corrupt 'American', in a film which is both French and American. *Léon* is interesting as a film partly for the way in which it plays with the conventions of the American gangster, pitching American identity against a vague Europeanness, as explained by Bruzzi; but it is also because it foregrounds the issue of national identity through its deconstruction and destruction of costume: the stereotypical dandyish American gangster is blown up by the dishevelled anarchic European.[5] The deconstructive/destructive moment of *Léon* is repeated in *Le Cinquième élément*, where once again, it is Gary Oldman as Zorg who is blown up, but this time by a monster, rather than by Jean Reno.

If the open coat functions as a marker of innocence, mobility and fluidity, and the closed coat functions to signal armoured emotionlessness and death, we can now see how astonishingly complex the connotations are for Zorg's coat in *Le Cinquième élément*. It is an extended pin-stripe suit, with all that the suit suggests in terms of repression; it is partly tightly buttoned, and therefore a marker of death. But is also partly flapping open, a marker of mobility and circulation, suggesting his ability to outmanoeuvre his foes, particularly the besuited president; and the fact that it is a spectacularised suit suggests that Zorg is a complex mixture of repression and display. The coat tells us that Zorg is partly a 'father' (the violently authoritarian patriarchal male), but he is also a rebellious 'son'.

At the end of this section, we have seen how white suits are contrasted with black suits and coats, father-figures with sons who revolt against them in one way or another. The sons tend to jettison the problematic black suit, which may be stylish, but is too close to death and destruction, in favour of the casually deconstructed gangster look: they may be gangsterish, but they are at heart innocents at play in a man's world. It is a world that they have renounced, or that they work against, precisely because it is corrupt and blackly repressive. This may make Besson's clothes world sound simplistic, articulated around a binary where things are, almost literally, black and white. But if Besson's white suits are simple, they are paradoxical, in that whiteness generally signifies goodness rather than violent authoritarianism; moreover, as we have seen, the black suit is prone to destruction, and the coat comes to signify the opposite of constraint and repression. Flügel cites Gerald Heard, another 1920s clothes theorist, in some revealing comments about the function of the male coat (Heard, 1924):

> Man's coat, that 'strange compromise between the gravitational and the anatomic'... with its hanging sleeves, its dragging on the armpit and the elbows, is so ill-suited to movement, except of the slowest and most solemn kind, that, by the restrictions imposed, it must – both psychologically and physiologically – reduce the efficiency of the male. (Flügel 1930: 233)

In Besson's films, however, the coat does not function in this way. It is, rather, associated with mobility, flexibility, playfulness; in a word, innocence.

The diving suit

Flügel's comments on the coat do apply, however, to a recurring garment in Besson's films, the diving suit, a term used here to cover a variety of garments and contraptions whose common feature is that they function as armour allowing the character inside to peer out through glass or visor. It is frequently worn by the characters played by Jean Reno in the films; he wears it as the Brute in *Le Dernier combat,* as a diver in *Le Grand bleu* and in *Léon,* when escaping from the apartment dressed as a member of the SWAT team.[6] As the example of *Léon* suggests, where the garment allows Léon to pass unnoticed, its function, like all clothes, is one of protection; but like the suit, it is also, as explained above, a garment which anonymises. The diving suit, more than the suit, turns the character into a cipher, emphasising his maleness, and specifically male competition, at the expense of other traits. For that reason, the diving suit works towards forms of stability, particularly heterosexual normalisation founded in male competition played out over woman-as-possession, in much more obvious ways than the black suit or coat analysed in the previous section. The diving suit may therefore be seen as a garment which reinforces masculinity and patriarchal norms, unlike the black suit and the coat which tend to undermine those norms.

Under the term 'diving suit' we can also include the diving bell, in which Enzo and Jacques are ranged as rebels against the conformist Belgian who berates them for drinking alcohol, and the extension of the diving bell into a variety of similar capsules. In this, we are sanctioned by one of Flügel's more startling passages:

> We have . . . invented a number of objects which are in the nature of transitions between clothes and houses. The roofed-in car or carriage is . . . one type of such an object. The umbrella is another. As regards this little instrument with its emergency roof, it is difficult to say whether it corresponds more to a miniature transportable house or to a temporary outer garment. (Flügel 1930: 83).

Le Cinquième élément is full of capsules where house and garment commingle. There is Dallas's living capsule, and his floating yellow taxi; in both of these our attention is drawn not just to the protective nature of the capsule, but also to the way that the bodies within those capsules interact with the metal or glass, and this is mediated through costume. In the case of Dallas's quarters, its lack of comfort and metallic surfaces, combined with a trap window echoing the visor of the diving suit, the noise and danger outside, and his brightly coloured orange vest, suggest that the capsule is a protective covering in the sense that Flügel outlines in the above quotation. A similar effect of claustrophobic metal capsule and part-nudity occurs when the scantily clad Leeloo drops into the yellow taxi, seeking protection. Whereas in previous films the diving suit and its avatars were closely connected to male competition, the woman being resolutely outside of the suit, in *Le Cinquième élément* the capsule is more obviously connected to the creation and normalisation of heterosexuality; the woman is more often than not inside these capsules, defined as potentially male at the start of the film (Dallas's living quarters and his yellow taxi). Then there is the transformer in which the scientists create Leeloo from a claw (itself originally part of an alien dressed in cumbersome armour, rather like the diving suit), transforming the all-male scientific environment into a place of chaos. Leeloo's birthing capsule returns in the closing sequences of the film where Leeloo and Dallas sink into the same blue which a decade previously in *Le Grand bleu* was reserved for Jacques and his narcissism, and which echoes by its claustrophobia Dallas's woman-free living quarters at the start of the film.

Unlike the suits in the films, whose rebellious connotations remain stable, even if the black suits are in themselves relatively unstable, the diving suits show a development, which we could characterise broadly as a development from the homosocial to the heterosexual. The diving suit, then, is the key garment in Besson's system, as, unlike the stability of the suit, it is *transformative*. Besson has normalised male violence, channelling it into heterosexuality. The suit, marker of male conformity to patriarchal values dependent on the exclusion of women, has been exploded by rebellious sons (Fred and Dallas's black suits), discarded for a coat left flapping open to accommodate women from a position of innocence – for example Héléna in *Subway*, Mathilda in *Léon* – and, finally, expanded into a capsule whose function is heterosexual union. It is important to stress the issue of heterosexuality, because women who go it alone are doomed to fail. As was the case with Nikita, who fails when she cross-dresses, in other words tries to *be* a man rather than *join* a man in his expanded suit-capsule, so too Jeanne (Milla Jovovich) in Jeanne d'Arc is fine as long as she wears armour; but without it she loses her self-confidence and dies.

It is difficult not to see this encapsulated heterosexual closure as just another form of containment, indeed one that is not only contained in a bubble, but fetishised and as a result out of reach. You can look, but you cannot touch what is in the bubble, and the blue tones of the capsule in which Leeloo and Dallas cavort, so reminiscent of the deathly blue void of *Le Grand bleu*, serve to underline its problematic nature. It is almost as if Besson regrets the development described here, from aggressive competition and homosociality to socialised heterosexuality. Seen in this light, we might wish to argue that the development of the homosocial suit into a heterosexual capsule is perhaps less of a transformation than a distortion. The suit is expanded and stretched rather like the morphing faces of the Mangalores.

Le Cinquième élément also transforms the suit in another way: the catsuit worn by Ruby Rhod. The catsuit is, arguably, the unaccommodated excess of the development from one bland stereotype to another, of the homosocial suit into a heterosexual capsule.

The catsuit

It is not that Besson is regressively locked into competition and homosociality; it is more that the heterosexual capsule is not quite what is required by the costume system he sets up in his films. It sidesteps the real issue, which in terms of costume is simple: all would have been fine if it had been Korben Dallas who was dressed in Leeloo's loincloths, if it had been Korben Dallas, rather than Ruby Rhod (Chris Tucker) who had flaunted his musculature campily through this Gallicised pastiche of the American action movie. This would not have been an unusual sight in French culture; Jean Marais, star of films by Jean Cocteau in the 1940s, and in the 1960s one of French cinema's great adventure-film stars, achieved notoriety prior to his film career, partly due to his lifestyle, as Cocteau's openly gay partner, partly by his scandalously stunning Chanel-designed costume in Cocteau's stage version of *Oedipus* in 1937, where he appeared dressed only in loosely wound strips of bandage, much like those we see on Leeloo. The logical corollary of the suit system we find in Besson (the suit as symbol of repressive patriarchal authority) is *for the hero to dress like a woman*, as we can deduce from Flügel.

Flügel explains how there are a number of interlinked 'effects on male psychology' (Flügel 1930: 117) as a result of the great masculine renunciation. Appealing to Freudian notions of repression and displacement, he suggests that men displace exhibitionist tendencies into what he calls 'scoptophilia' (Flügel 1930: 118; it is what we know since Laura Mulvey's work in the 1970s as scopophilia). Second, exhibitionist pleasure is projected onto women (the 'trophy wife' syndrome, although he does not call it that). And third, 'the man may consciously seek to identify himself with a woman by wearing feminine attire' (Flügel 1930: 119). This leads Flügel to consider transvestism, which 'does not necessarily coincide with active homosexuality, or even with a tendency towards the physical characteristics of the opposite sex. Hercules himself . . . spent some time dressed as a woman' (Flügel 1930: 119).

Korben Dallas may well be a modern Hercules in this narrative, fighting absolute evil which threatens to wipe out the human race, but his skills do not extend to cross-dressing, no matter how close he gets to it, as Hayward points out, his orange singlet linking him very directly to Leeloo and her orange hair (Hayward 1998: 177). Besson cannot dress Bruce Willis like a woman, so instead, in his next film, he dresses a woman, Jeanne d'Arc, like a man. But what he does do in *Le Cinquième élément* is to displace the male desire for display onto Ruby Rhod, who is in more ways than one Korben Dallas's 'other', and who fulfils two of the displacements listed by Flügel, cross-dressing in the absence of homosexuality, and scopophilia.

Ruby Rhod is clearly intended to be androgynous, the word used by costume designer Jean-Paul Gaultier of the character, who tells us that Prince, whom he had in mind when designing the costumes, was at one time intended to play the role (Besson 1997: 132). Chris Tucker, the stand-up comic who plays Ruby Rhod, said that the character was for him a mixture of Michael Jackson and Prince, both androgynous stars (Smith, 1997). The name itself suggests androgyny, Ruby being female, and Rhod, in the light of the first hairstyle, being a playful allusion to the penis. He is shown going down on an air-hostess to perform what we assume is cunnilingus, servicing the woman then, rather than the reverse fellatio scenario, which, given his dominance and star persona, we might have more stereotypically expected. Indeed, the woman's pleasure is intercut with the penetration of objects into a variety of cavities, and explosions, stereotypical visual signs more often associated with male orgasm. Chris Tucker himself, who, as a stand-up comic, has occasionally used gay stereotyping in his gags, was at pains to distance himself from any accusations of femininity: 'His reaction when Besson pushed for Ruby Rhod to wear a dress? 'Heyyy-ell no. I wanted to keep my manhood. I didn't want the brothers to think I was going out' (Smith, 1997).[7]

His catsuit is similarly inbetween the masculine and the feminine. On the one hand, it is a parody of blaxploitation film costumes; on the other it positions him in the feminine as nature incarnate, suggesting an animal (the leopard skin), or, more obviously, flowers, since the catsuit's collar is rimmed with flowers, and has a collar which open like a lily, with the penis-like hairpiece reminiscent of a stamen.

He does not just cross-dress. He spends his time looking at everything around him and commenting on it for public consumption. He is the ultimate spectator, looking at and talking about the spectacle we see, combining scopophilia and logorrhea. Because of this, we are more likely to identify ourselves with him than with the more stable parody of the action hero as played by Bruce Willis. 'Korben Dallas is in trouble', Ruby Rhod comments tautologically for us during the battle on Fhlosten, following it up, again tautologically, by what we as spectators are likely to wish, a closer view: 'I'm going to see if I can see something a little closer'. Moreover, like the spectator, Ruby Rhod thinks he controls the show, as is suggested by his comment on escaping from the destruction of Fhlosten: 'That's the best show I ever did'. There is a sense in which he does control the show: the cunnilingus sequence is a parallel syntagma with action elsewhere patterned on his arousal of the hostess (she shrieks as the fuel rod is shoved into its holder, and climaxes as

Zorg blows up his henchman), so that the spectacular action is sexualised, but ambiguously so. And since it is clear during that sequence that Ruby Rhod is not enjoying the arousal as much as the hostess, that it is in effect nothing more than another performance for him, we could say that his character, already inbetween sexes, places the spectator in another inbetween, this time between disbelief and its suspension in a place of ironic displacement. From his perspective, we see a simplistic binary performed without being implicated in it: evil (as represented by the monsters, Mangalores and Zorg) versus good (the heterosexual couple). And at the same time, Ruby Rhod negotiates another inbetween, since he is our anchorman for the spectacular combination of American sci-fi spectacle versus French quirkiness, located in Gaultier's costumes.

He is Korben Dallas's 'other': the black to Dallas's white; the one who talks, while the other one acts; the one who fails – 'Why do I get the one that's broke', he says as he discovers that his stone will not react to his attempts to open it – while Dallas succeeds. But this very fact makes him central to the narrative, reinforcing his function as commentator and voyeur. Indeed, he can be seen as *more central* than the heterosexual couple formed by Dallas and Leeloo, precisely because he combines both male and female, and is the ultimate spectator, as well as (at least partly) controller of the action, thus encouraging us to identify ourselves with him, as much as, if not more than the heterosexual couple.[8]

Conclusion

Ruby Rhod is both the logical corollary of Besson's sartorial system where men are concerned, and its problematic linchpin. Male attire in Besson functions as a discourse that critiques patriarchal power (see Figure 5.1 for an attempt to conceptualise in graphic form what follows), where the suit functions above all, as it does more generally in Western culture, to signify masculine repression, the renunciation of narcissistic display at the service of violent patriarchal law. White suits are worn by powerful father-figures, but whose behaviour is at odds with what is suggested by the colour white. Black suits are worn by son-figures, who revolt against patriarchal power, and as a result remove or destroy their suits to regain their innocence. That innocence is signified by a version of the repressive buttoned-up trenchcoat worn by the tight-lipped gangster, an old coat innocently left open to accommodate what life may bring, and it usually brings a woman in Besson's films. Running parallel to the suit is a special version of the suit, the diving suit. It parallels the white suit in its function as armour against other males in

Le Dernier combat, developing into a less aggressive and more homosocial competitiveness in *Le Grand bleu.* That same film shows that one consequence of male repression is ascetic rejection leading ultimately to death: 'I can't flaunt myself, so I'll kill myself instead'.

Father	Son	
white suit	black suit → coat	androgynous catsuit
aggressive armour →	homosocial diving suit →	heterosexual capsule

5.1 Besson's system of male attire

The way out of this deep/dead end is hysterical morphological distortion, as the suit mutates into more mobile or more transparent objects in which the hero is contained, but is given an illusory sense of freedom – what we have called the 'capsule'. Poised, at last, to mediate desire through display, freed of the constraints of the black and white suit whose primary function is to deny individuality and display at the service of a male community predicated on egalitarianism and the work ethic, poised to allow display to surface, *Le Cinquième élément* steps back from the logic of the system set up by Besson's preceding films. The hero is disappointingly contained within the walls of the capsule, his pleasure in display mediated through the trophy woman who shares the space with him. Male display is displaced onto Leeloo, a vestige of it remaining in the orange singlet, which tries to have it both ways as a marker of 'hard' masculinity, but, also, because of the colour-coding, a link with Leeloo's 'soft' femininity. The happy ending, as hard and soft come together entomologically in cold blue tones under glass, curtails any sense of auto-erotic exhibitionist fun. Besson's sartorial system had been leading us to a different moment, and the continued repression of masculine display at a point when the system was about to reach a logical outcome leads to displacement onto Korben Dallas's 'other', Ruby Rhod, who parades excessively the very display repressed by Dallas. Indeed, because auto-erotic exhibitionist fun is potentially damaging for normative masculinities, Ruby Rhod has to be excessive, comical, camp, so that we accept the contrasting version of masculinity proposed to us by Bruce Willis as the only possible masculinity in the circumstances, complete with a replay of *Die Hard*'s happy end (USA, John McTiernan, 1988).

The repressed always returns, as we know. In *Die Hard,* it is the gun which Sergeant Al Powell (Reginald Veljohnson) is able to shoot once more, overcoming his guilt at having shot an innocent kid, and thus reclaiming his lost 'hard' masculinity. That return is carefully framed; Al can only recover his 'hard' black (and therefore potentially threatening) masculinity with a white man's help. The great merit of Besson's film is that it may not have the courage of its sartorial convictions, but it does not shy away from displaying narcissistic masculinity. The repressed returns not as a hard phallicised gun, but as a soft, blonde, wobbly penis stuck on top of Ruby Rhod's head. True, the film may try to draw our attention away from it by configuring it as the centre of a flower in relation to the catsuit from which it emerges (but flowers are 'feminine'), or by having the character talk incessantly, rather than obeying the law of sobriety and circumspection, of not 'leaking' verbally (but 'chatter' is 'feminine'); it may try to remind us of the object's lack of substance by having it wobble to emphasise the fact that it is only hair; but its 'beehive' structure makes it 'feminine'.[9]

Whatever the film does, it cannot help but make of Ruby's penile hair the logical and central consequence of wearing a suit: hide your desire for display, and it will pop up to embarrass you in ways you did not think possible.

References

Barthes, R. (1983), *The Fashion System* (New York: Hill and Wang).
Besson, L. (1997), *L'Histoire du Cinquième élément* (Paris: Intervista).
Bruzzi, S. (1997), *Undressing Cinema: Clothing and Identity in the Movies* (London and New York: Routledge).
Carter, M. (2003), 'J. C. Flügel and the Nude Future', M. Carter, *Fashion Classics: From Carlyle to Barthes* (OxfordNew York: Berg), pp. 97–120.
Flügel, J. C. (1930), *The Psychology of Clothes* (London: The Hogarth Press and the Institute of Psycho-Analysis).
Harvey, J. (1995), *Men in Black* (London: Reaktion Books).
Hayward, S. (1998) *Luc Besson* (Manchester: Manchester University Press).
Heard, G. (1924), *Narcissus: An Anatomy of Clothes* (London: Kegan Paul Trench Trubner & Co.).
Jameson, F. (1992), '*Diva* and French Socialism', F. Jameson, *Signatures of the Visible* (New York and London: Routledge), pp. 55–62. Originally published in *Social Text*, 6 (1982), pp. 114–19.
Powrie, P. (2005), '*Nikita*', *The Cinema of France* (ed. P. Powrie, London: Wallflower Press).
Smith, S. (1997), 'In his element', *Los Angeles Times*, 5 August 1997, at www.hollywood.com/sites/rushhour/news1.html, accessed 10 March 2000.

Notes

1. In fact Jameson should have said the 1970s, since the 1960s US counter-cultural movement only made inroads into European culture in the early 1970s.
2. See Powrie, 2005 for an analysis of the hat in *Nikita*.
3. Flügel is careful to point out the relativism of such connotations, 'there being no essential connection between, say, a black coat and tight, stiff collar and the due sense of responsibility and duty for which these garments stand' (Flügel 1930: 197).
4. The term 'system' is intended to echo Barthes's 1967 work (Barthes 1983).
5. This sequence of *Léon* is explored in more detail in Chapter 10 in this volume, see pp. 155–7.
6. A narrative trope reprised in *The Negotiator* (USA, F. Gary Gray, 1998), starring Samuel L. Jackson.
7. His role as Detective James Carter in the subsequent *Rush Hour* buddy movies with Jackie Chan emphasises his 'black' heterosexuality; see *Rush Hour* (USA, Brett Ratner, 1998) and *Rush Hour 2* (USA, Brett Ratner, 2001).
8. A small detail pointed out by a contributor to one of the many Besson fan-sites on the internet is revealing in this respect: 'On the periodic table of the elements, on period 5, the first element is Rubidium, then exactly halfway down is Rhodium. Take the endings off and you have Ruby Rhod' ('Richard' on Jason Carlberg's 'The Fifth Element Universe' website, at: www.angelfire.com/ny/UEONews/FifthElementAnswers.html, accessed 7 February 2005. Ruby Rhod, by his very name, is *doubly* the Fifth Element.
9. Unlike the piled hair of Kid (Christopher Reid) in *House Party* (USA, Reginald Hudlin, 1990).

6

From rags to riches:
Le Dernier combat and *Le Cinquième élément*

Susan Hayward

In terms of production, these two science fiction films could not be further apart. The first film was shot on a shoestring (a budget of FF3.5 million; approximately $5 million) and attracted an audience in France of 236,189.[1] The latter film had a massive budget ($90 million) and attracted 7,696,667 spectators (again in France). Yet both unashamedly show their means of production (be it rich or poor). And in terms of content they bear great similarities. Both films lay before us cityscapes of the future: *Le Dernier combat* a post-nuclear Paris, *Le Cinquième élément* a technologised New York of the twenty-third century. In both films the hero goes in search of and successfully gets his woman. He has to undergo various tests of his manhood, but in the end he wins out and regenerates a dying society by procreating with the woman whose body (if not love) he has won. The issue of ecology, another strong theme in Besson's work, runs right through these two films: waste and its recycling, including the recycling of human bodies, point to a world where technology has so enthralled humankind that it willingly and passively would allow it to rule the world were it not for the remaining few who challenge man's (still) modernistic faith in science to explain and 'do' all in his name (for this blind pursuit of science also includes the genetic engineering of humans). But, as we shall see, not even these heroic vestiges of humankind are all they are cut out to seem; they too have vested interests.

As a genre, science fiction films produce a futuristic vision where we are no longer in control either of the world we inhabit (because it is under threat), or the science and technology that we have created (because it has surpassed us, or let us down). Science fiction films, then, act as a counter to the modernist belief in technological progress as a source of social change, and reveal it rather as a threat. However, what this genre significantly does not do, in general, is hold a mirror up to humankind as the one responsible for this very real lack of social progress. Instead, science fiction films show us how technology and aliens are to be feared equally, since both bring with them the threat of imminent death. As such, it works to deresponsibilise us of the very technology we have invented. For both are of our own invention and imaginings; so clearly our fears say a great deal about our socio-psychological pathology and fear of death. Science fiction is, therefore, the *mise-en-scène* of our most irrational fears. It also becomes our way of absolving ourselves from any responsibility for progress in the social order of things. Because we are not in control of technology we are not to blame, and are not therefore responsible for the fact that the system of human relations does not progress. To sum up: modernity says that science and technology (the discourse of science after all) is a source, if not the source, of social change. Science fiction films deny this, not through direct challenge, however, since they mostly sidestep this issue and limit themselves to revealing the life-threatening, almost unnatural power of this technology, and say nothing of our failure to progress. Furthermore, they do this (almost as if not realising the irony of it) through an expository use of the virtuosities of film technology where special effects are in abundance!

Yet, fear it as we may, we are in thrall to technology, particularly because it is 'man'-made. Nonetheless, this cult of technology points to the dysfunctionality of our present social structures which are based on the capitalist order of production, the capitalist imperative to consume, and the refusal to invest in social progress. This point brings us to Besson's work, in particular his two science fiction films. He, for one, is not afraid to hold up the mirror. In terms of capitalism, he sees consumer commodities as signs of death (for example, the graveyard of cars in the Saharan desert, and the floating washing machines in an abandoned car factory in *Le Dernier combat*). In terms of technology, his films consistently reveal a profound ambivalence to its power and fetishistic value (for example, the technological gadgets Zorg relies upon in *Le Cinquième élément*). Indeed, Besson's films investigate the interface between technology and the body, and the various environments we inhabit or pollute (cities, the underground, the sea). In essence then, Besson problematises the relationship between man and technology, although in some regards this confrontation brings with it other sets of problems, as we shall see. But for now let us continue with this idea that he uses the genre as a way of confronting our desire to deresponsibilise our role in this lack of social progress. In the first film, *Le Dernier combat*, there is very little hope for survival in this world laid waste by what, to all appearances, is a nuclear holocaust. In the second, more optimistic film, *Le Cinquième élément*, Besson seems to suggest that despite our rush to destroy each other, somewhere in us there is a grain of humanity and love can, if we persist, bring about an evolution in the social order of things, however small. Thus, the dystopian nature of the first film is spoken back to by the more hopeful (but certainly not utopian) message of the second.

Le Dernier combat is 'an imaginary excursion', says Besson (*Télérama* 1983: 29). He came to the idea of making this film when he was wandering around in the boulevard Barbès in Paris, and discovered an old film theatre all gutted out, but with cinema seats still hanging off the wall. He thought that there must be hundreds of places like that in Paris, and it was then that he put those sights and thoughts together with an earlier suggestion made by friends that he should make a feature-length film of his earlier 1981 short *L'Avant-dernier* (see Hayward 1998: 13, 28). Shot in Paris and in Tunisia (for the desert scenes), *Le Dernier combat* is the tale of an unspecified holocaust where all seems lost. The few survivors of this holocaust have lost the power of their vocal chords as they stumble about in a Paris reduced to ruins and rubble, or attempt to set up camp in the sands of the desert that surround the city. They are constantly on the forage for food and water. Lost then is the power to communicate by voice, the very essence of humanity and what distinguishes us (in our minds) from the animal world. Lost too is the possibility of renewing life since this world is at best sparingly populated by men, but with barely a woman in sight. Shot in black and white and scope, without dialogue, the film documents the desperate attempt of a young man (Pierre Jolivet) to escape a gang of evil-doers, only to find himself locked in mortal combat with an evil marauder (on the rampage for food and sex). He must defeat both the gangleader (Fritz Wepper) and the evil marauder (Jean Reno) in order to establish some kind of social system, and win the privilege of having sex with the (apparently) last remaining woman on earth. He is helped in his quest by the doctor (Jean Bouise), who takes him in when he is wounded, and eventually brings him to meet the woman he keeps (for safety's sake) under lock and key. However, by the time the doctor has decided that the moment of procreation has arrived, it is too late. He dies (killed by a rainstorm of stones), and the woman has been raped and murdered – literally eviscerated – by the evil marauder. The hero eventually kills the marauder, escapes back to his home city, shoots the gang-leader, and is acknowledged as the new leader. In his new capacity, he is introduced to another woman, the dead gangleader's jealously guarded prisoner. She is probably the last woman on earth. They smile at each other in the pre-sexual moment, and the film closes. But all feels far from safe.

Although possibly set in some indefinable future, the *mise-en-scène* and the documentary feel (through the use of black and white film) link us to a very immediate present, and give an aura of realism to this highly improbable tale. This is particularly true of the shots of the underbelly of Paris. The half-gutted buildings, the abandoned multi-storeyed parking lots include a former EDF factory the day before its demolition, and the derelict area around rue Vivienne which at that time had been earmarked for the construction of the new Bibliothèque Nationale. Besson shows us a Paris ravaged by costly reconstruction programmes (so, capitalist greed), begun in the boom years of the 1970s and later abandoned as the economy and thus the construction industry suffered the effects, first, of the oil crises in the mid- and late 1970s and, second, the recession that hit France in the early 1980s.

In *Le Dernier combat*, the first representation of the body is that of a female, but in the form of an inflatable doll which an adult male, the hero, is 'screwing'. This a good metaphor for the interfacing between technology and the human body if ever there was one, especially since he punctures it before climaxing. This display of male sexuality in a vacuum is rapidly followed by the hero's attempt to escape the violent attack of other males as he takes off in a single propelled plane he has built himself. The plane is recycled from waste. The hero's clothing is recycled from waste. He takes off only to crash in the desert – the wasteland *par excellence* (at least in Western mythology) – nearby another derelict city. He has managed to move from one derelict city to another; there is no distinction, as the one could as easily be the other. When he steps outside, it rains fish – tons of dead fish – a consumer product that will only last until it too rots and decays. Waste in excess. Waste, decay, dereliction. This is his environment. The message seems clear, and is deeply ecological as well as moral. To invest technology with the power of signifying as answers to human conflicts means surely that such a process must eventually backfire, turn around on itself, and return the destructive image to man of his refusal to evolve – hence the symbolic value of the loss of voice. And return it as decay, dereliction and waste. The anthropomorphised objects hit back, refusing to act as replacements for human relationships. Thus, violence – the pathology of the repressed – breaks out. The doctor is stoned to death, the marauder is eventually killed by the hero, as is the other evil gang-leader. The hero's trajectory is less to gain supremacy over other males than it is to take the woman and procreate – the alpha-male trajectory in other words. This *flâneur* of dereliction has been forced to resume the basic human instinct: sex. But this is hardly a great *mise-en-scène* of hope. Given the derelict environment which he inhabits, even if he is successful in reproducing, there is little evidence to suppose that there exists a social order of things into which he could reproduce. Despite the fact that both he and the doctor are dedicated to order, symptomatic of a desire to bring back civilisation, there is a deep irony attached to the futility of their gestures. The hero tidily piles up the fish fallen from the sky, keeps his few possessions neatly arranged in a picnic case; the doctor believes in the civility of table manners; both are dedicated to the arts (the hero risks his life to retrieve a painting, the doctor paints frescoes on the hospital walls). But all value systems fall away when the hero is forced to react in a world that has been polarised into good and evil, and he is driven to kill. Humanity, like the city, is laid waste. So, too, is man's future.

There are a number of ironic presences in *Le Dernier combat* pointing to our practice of reproduction and consumption of technological goods, all markers of a moribund society that believes in the principle of consummate and consuming egocentrism. Sex is represented like any other consumer commodity; the hero has to earn his woman (by killing), and the women are ultimately replaceable (rubber doll, woman in hospital, gangster's woman). Sex, like other consumer commodities, lies languishing in death-cells alongside the electronic goods partially submerged under water. And just as sex is used to sell commodities, so the advertising boards for the electrical goods company Darty (which sells using the advertising slogan that its prices cannot be beaten) point ironically to what can no longer be consumed. In this wasteland, all meccas of consumerism have been destroyed (this one is literally underwater). The actual environments Besson chose as his sets are further ironic presences. The disused Citröen factory at Balard points to the end of the motor industry, the derelict EDF factory to the end of light and power. Nothing works, nothing can be made: technology and its objects and our pathological dependence on them has broken down. In Besson's film, we are beyond the fallibility of the object. The object simply is no more. And yet the refusal to take responsibility and work for change is still there as strong as ever before. The doctor, who is arguably the most 'humanitarian' of all the survivors of the holocaust, who draws on walls like a caveman (reproducing the myth of Adam and Eve), and who almost speaks, is the one who comes closest to an embodiment of the earlier social order of things. He believes in life, in procreation; otherwise why would he protect the woman from one type of marauding male and endeavour to find her the ideal partner in the form of the wounded hero? However, he believes in life on his terms. He chooses who will procreate. So he reproduces hierarchies of power, albeit in a vacuum. He also suggests the idea of genetic selection; he will only present the female with a suitable male (he checks out the hero's genitals and reproductive engine, for example).

The derelict city is a threatening space, but hierarchies of power are reproduced, suggesting that human beings have no other knowledge. Predators scavenge and kill, survivors (good and evil) privatise space for the rare commodities that still exist (water). The doctor has the 'hospital', the gang leader the sewage pipes. Ideology is recycling itself to death. The city is beyond dystopia. It is beyond belief – no hope for utopia here. It too is the sphere of death.

Le Dernier combat is a metaphor for the death of ideology. It is also a metaphor for our living death. The film shows us what we already know, but refuse to acknowledge, preferring instead to transmogrify death by projecting it onto technology, and subsequently willing its death. And the film shows us how we deny that knowledge through social, cultural and sexual regression, which leads, ultimately, to the death of the sexual, social and political body. In this regard Besson's film is a science fiction film with a strong moral message.

If *Le Dernier combat* shows us the paucity of its means of production, but provides a political edge, not so *Le Cinquième élément* – a visually resplendent film and far less politicised. It is a film which spectacularises costume, set design, sexuality and technology. But it is a conscious spectacularisation. In *Le Cinquième élément*, Besson brings together Jean-Paul Gaultier's intellectually transgressive costume design, Moebius-inspired surrealist set designs – both of which help him to play with sexuality in a new way, and free his narrative from the heterosexual constraints of his first film – Cinemascope (his favourite filming format), and digital technology for the computer-generated images of twenty-third-century New York.

To take this last point first, Besson consciously experiments in this film with photographic imagery and digital (post-photographic) imagery. Special effects have always been an ethical preoccupation of Besson's since *Le Dernier combat*.[2] His question has always been how not to cheat with special effects. It is not accidental, therefore, that he chose to work with Digital Domain in California rather than any of the other digital effects companies in the USA.[3] James Cameron, one of the co-founders of Digital Domain, was the special effects man for his own films *Aliens* (1986) and *Terminator 2* (1991). Cameron's guiding principle, which he took with him to Digital Domain, was to make special effects an integrated and integral part of the movie, and not to fetishise special effects by flagging them up, priming the spectator for them, as occurs in Spielberg's *Jurassic Park* (1993) say, with its computer-generated dinosaurs. In other words, Besson turned to Cameron because the challenge for him in his film was to make the photographic image and the post-photographic image make sense together, rather than aiming to obtain the maximum of extraordinary effects (as so often occurs when new technology comes on to the scene/screen). In this respect, Besson is following the tradition first set by George Lucas in 1977 with his *Star Wars* where the 'natural' of his hyper-space contrasted markedly with what had preceded in sci-fi cinema (particularly that of the 1950s).[4]

The New York of *Le Cinquième élément* was created from images shot of a scaled model of the city (Manhattan) that were subsequently digitally manipulated. The special effects, then, are not entirely digital, but a combination of old film practices (scale models) and new technology (digital). The whole thing could have been digitally pulled out of a bank of prefabricated images in a computer, a hyper-realisation of special effects that Besson chose against, clearly for aesthetic purposes. His choice is for a degree of naturalism compounded by the camera work. Here is what the film critic Nigel Floyd tells us about these images:

> The film's extraordinary cityscapes and flying vehicles were created by cutting edge SFX company Digital Domain. Besson himself provided more than 8000 drawings, created by a nine-strong team in the 12 months before shooting. The director and special visual effects supervisor Mark Stetson then worked on the detailed miniatures and computer-generated effects, blending them with the director's photo-realistic cinematic style. 'I tried to stay totally anonymous with my camera; as if I were shooting in the street,' says Besson. 'I think it gives the film a sense of reality; the camera doesn't suddenly shift speed or change style to suit a special effect. A shot of the New York skyline with 400 flying cars is enough.' (Floyd, 1997)

This aesthetic sensibility is described by one of Digital Domain's representatives, Valérie Delahaye, as a European approach to special effects, which refuses to privilege the technical over the artistic (quoted in Canteloube 1997: 84). Thus, the effects themselves tell part of the story. In *Le Cinquième élément*, they are a force driving the narrative and constitute therefore, as with the fashion designs, a strongly motivating sign of the narrative. This detaches Besson's film from accusations that it is poor Hollywood pastiche. He is trying out other ideas with the technology available, making an actualisable world of the future-present which it is unlikely Hollywood would attempt. The point with Hollywood sci-fi films is not just the scarcely hidden political agendas, but the happy ending which tells us that we need not fear we will end up in such an imaginary world because the hero will disable the technology that makes such a world possible. In Besson's film, the opposite occurs; the hero prevents twenty-third-century New York, the futuristic new world, from being destroyed. In fact, Besson's world has today's technology (radio, cellphones) alongside that of the future (Zorg's magnificent multipurpose weapon of mass destruction, the space stations, the flying taxis). The past floats in as well, quite comfortably, in the form of reference to other sci-fi films (most obviously *Blade Runner*, Ridley Scott, 1982); food is parodied in a past–present tension with the Chinese junk carrying exotic memories of Los Angeles (*Blade Runner* again), and McDonald's gratuitously going up in smoke (a counter-cocacolanisation the French audiences must surely have enjoyed). Besson's future-present world is *not* necessarily a world we might want to live in, but it is *not* one in which the city itself is a menacing presence. It is fast, potentially dangerous, heavily surveilled, and the lower regions of the city are dirty and smog-ridden. We already live in cities such as this one. We cannot therefore reject it from our consciousness as easily as we might other imagined cities in the sci-fi genre. As we saw, a similar effect of realism was created by Besson in *Le Dernier combat*, which portrayed a derelict post-atomic holocaust Paris, location shooting this time in abandoned factories and warehouses in the city and its environs giving a great deal of verisimilitude to the potentially unrealistic narrative.

There are ways in which Besson's *Le Cinquième élément* can be read as a postmodern nightmare, however. In many regards, it is a film that takes on board the effects of cyberspace and technology on human consciousness. The world it presents is one where the modernist world is crumbling in the face of a virtual world that is post-narrative, post-photography and post-biological. The paradox of Besson's movie is that Leeloo, the supreme being, embodies or – better put – is the site where these two worlds collide. The love story, which is one of the core narratives, is bound up with the race against time (indeed, even back in time). This traditional narrative is under constant threat from a techno-erotics (technology as a projection/displacement of the erotic body) in which the technology to delete the body (the evil careening towards New York) looks seriously like outsmarting more conventional ways of resolving the crisis (through love and intelligence). As a result, the classical narrative of man making his break from the tribe, proving his manhood, overthrowing the malevolent forces and killing the chief, finally to reap his rewards of security and marriage, almost does not happen. Leeloo, the virtual embodiment of woman, only relents at the eleventh hour to Korben's entreaties to love him, that is to assert his subjectivity, and help him fulfil his Oedipal trajectory. The classical narrative is under numerous threats, not just from the aliens (the Mangalores) and Zorg (two different aspects of techno-erotics), but also from the pure (but apparently forgettable) embodiment of techno-erotics itself, Leeloo. In other words, the narrative is saved only if we forget that Leeloo is not human. We know for a fact that she is a cyborg (at best); however, the Oedipal narrative works very hard to make us forget this. The outcome, man having intercourse with a cyborg, is far from a classical one. Thus the narrative ends up in a postmodern capsule. Literally, we are on the verge of the post-narrative.

As for the other issues of the postmodern nightmare (post-photography and post-biological), here too we are almost already there. We are already in an age of post-photography, where images – including images of the human form – can be digitally invoked on the computer screen. The material body need no longer figure, since it can be seen and experienced virtually. The recreation of Leeloo in the film makes this clear, as does the scientist's blissful reaction ('perfect') to her digitalised reconstruction. Indeed, the ethics of reconstructing Leeloo come down to a degree zero; the question becomes whether it is safe to do so, *not* whether it is morally a good idea. Leeloo is also post-biological in that she may well be a DNA sample, but she is not meat; effectively, she is reconstructed as the body without meat (muscles and 'covering' are bio-technically imaged onto her frame which itself has been bio-technically rebuilt). A positive reading of this could lead us to say that whilst man seeks to delete the body (through his pursuit of techno-erotics – investing his subjectivity in technology), he cannot actually allow himself to let it happen. To the question 'can thought go on without a body?', the answer is, presently, 'no'. A less positive reading brings us to an analysis of the characterisation of Leeloo herself, who to all intents and purposes is the font of all knowledge, and yet we see very little manifestation of this. If anything, she is merely the crucial element of the puzzle, and men have to find out where she fits. As we see, it is the men who resolve the enigma. She, meantime, spends a great deal of her intellectual energy absorbing man's past (off digitally created images on the computer). 'Can thought go on without a male body?' might be a better way of rephrasing the question.

A crucial problem is posed by the embodied presence of Leeloo. The question is not who, but what is she? This was a question which did not arise with *Le Dernier combat*, where it was the last vestiges of humankind we were watching. Here, with Leeloo, we are not sure what she is. Is she a cyborg? an alien? an android even? Perhaps we can assume she is not an android, since androids are robots masquerading as humans (like the replicants in *Blade Runner*). Nor indeed would she be an alien, although she comes close, since these are extra-terrestrial beings; whilst Leeloo seems to come to us from outerspace, she is in fact very clearly a recreation – genetically engineered – from a mummified body which we presume had a terrestrial past since it appeared to originate from Egypt (from where it was taken to a place of safety). So we must perhaps think of her as a cybernetic organism, a techno-body maybe. What she is not massively (*en masse*, as matter) is her original self. That got burned up, only the charred remains of one hand/claw remain. Anne Balsamo and Claudia Springer offer some useful definitions and distinctions between different types of cyborgs which can help our analysis here. The two most common types as represented in popular culture are, first, the cyborg which 'combines the human organic body, which either preexisted as a person or was genetically engineered, with non-organic mechanical or electronic implants or protheses' (Springer 1996: 19). The second type 'has no organic form but consists of the human mind preserved on computer software' (Springer: 19–20). In respect of this second type, one thinks immediately of Hal in Kubrick's *2001: A Space Odyssey* (1968). Humans who download software directly into their electronically wired brains are also cyborgs, as for example in Kathryn Bigelow's (*Strange Days*, 1995). In a sense, Leeloo crosses both types. She is the result of a human-machine coupling, and, thanks to her massively overendowed DNA structure, she can download at the rate of cyber-knots the entire history of man into her memory.

Balsamo's definitions concur with Springer's. She goes on to say, however, and this is interesting in the context of Leeloo's identity, that:

> Cyborgs are hybrid entities that are neither wholly technological nor completely organic, which means that the cyborg has the potential not only to disrupt persistent dualisms that set the natural body in opposition to the technologically recrafted body, but also to fashion our thinking about the theoretical construction of the body as both a material entity and a discursive process . . . Cyborg bodies are definitionally transgressive of a dominant culture order, not so much because of their 'constructed' nature, but rather because of the indeterminancy of their hybrid design. The cyborg provides a framework for studying gender identity as it is technologically crafted simultaneously from the matter of material bodies and cultural fictions. (Balsamo 1997: 11)

In other words, because cyborgs are like us and yet not like us and because their identity is 'predicated on transgressed boundaries' (Balsamo 1997: 32), they foreground 'the constructedness of otherness' (Balsamo 1997: 33). Cyborgs show that gender identity is socially and ideologically predicated, because the cyborg body is not a 'natural' body, and yet it appears in popular culture (film and fiction for example) as gendered (for example, RoboCop is definitely male). But how can this be so since definitions of gender rely upon 'appeals to the natural body' (Balsamo 1997: 25)? This is the point of exposure: the actuality of the cyborg (as human/machine) means it is 'other' than natural; and yet it passes as natural, as human, and becomes engrained/enchained in the ideology of the gender divide. Through its transgressiveness (as a technologically recrafted body), it exposes the ideological constructedness of otherness that is based in the (psychoanalytical) principle of difference. Freud and Lacan explain that male subjectivity (sexual identity) is dependent on and affirmed by the female other (she who is sexually marked as different from the male). Since we cannot in truth impute a sexual identity to a cyborg, how can it be possible to inscribe it within the concept of gender?

Because we do impute gender identity to cyborgs, it becomes clear, then, that gender is an ideological concept that emanates not from the 'natural' body itself, but from the exchange between the physical body and the social body (alternatively known as the social order of things, patriarchal law, the symbolic). In other words, gender is not something your body intrinsically is. Gender is not your sex, but how you socially act or perform your sex. The social body requires, for example, that heterosexuality prevail in order for the social order of things to be perpetuated through procreation. Clearly, a transgressive body will cause problems for the social body; indeed, it will expose the anxieties felt by ideology (patriarchy) about the social body and its securedness (see Balsamo 1997: 17–28). If we consider the still very real hostility towards an everyday transgressive body, that of the homosexual or lesbian, we can see how the reaction says more about fear for the securedness and legitimacy of the social body than it does about the transgressive body itself, about which so little can be known. How does one control a body that is not entirely knowable? If we impute a gender to cyborgs, it is because the cyborg body, the techno-body is in fact an unruly body – one that disrupts because it is not of the centre, is obscene in its uncentredness, potentially exposing the fragility of the social body.

If we accept this reading of transgressiveness, why then does man spend so much of his scientific energies trying to reproduce the human in robotic or cyborg form, the very essence of the transgressive body? Why does the military invest massively in artificial intelligence (AI)? Why does man make transgressive, unknowable forms of simulated life? Why does he seek his own obsolescence? There are two obvious answers: to avoid investment in the improvement of social relations (which would eventually dispense with power relations), and to overcome, through displacement, man's deep-rooted fear of his own sexuality.[5] If we are at the dawn of a new revolutionary age (of life 'in silico'),[6] then we are at the dusk of the sexed body – possibly man's greatest ambition. And the way to get to it is by dissolving the distinction between technology and humanity. Genetic engineering, cloning (begun a century ago with frogs), templating the human brain onto computers (AI) are but the latest manifestations of man's desire to 'not be'.[7] They are also part of man's ongoing desire to remove that which, to his own mind, most threatens his subjectivity/sexuality: woman (because her presence reminds him of it all the time). Equally, these manifestations represent the desire to replace, through bio-technological reproduction, the female's function of reproduction. The paradox, as always, is that man seeks to perfect (the scientist's term in *Le Cinquième élément*) the very thing that will expose what he most wants to hide. Cyborgs and robots are the projections of what man fears most: fear of his own sexuality (including its precarious security dependent as it is on the female other), progress in the system of human relations (an end to hierarchies of power), and of course fear of his own death. These techno-bodies, then, are simultaneously a containment and a displacement of those fears, and so they are always already transgressive in that they stand for what the social body (patriarchal law) most desperately wants not to be or not to happen.

Let us return to Leeloo. As a cyborg body, she is an extremely complex set of hybridisations. And yet we never really get to read her body as transgressive. Indeed, it is the Mangalores who, as a group, are the most fulsomely transgressive bodies, switching their identities from alien to human, from male to female, cross-dressing even. In fact, Leeloo reads as a throwback to earlier, nineteenth-century science fiction writing, where woman is constructed as the one who retains moral purity (there is much insistence on her virginity); she is the one who will redeem the capitalist (now post-capitalist) world and save it from its worst excesses (such as total annihilation). Leeloo seems to fit all of these descriptions, and yet she is a cyborg. Inside the supposedly transgressive but gendered cyborg body lurks a fulsomely conservative set of values, therefore. This begins to answer the question why, in Besson's film, the fifth element is a woman. We recall that the explorer in Egypt explains that it is the fifth element alone that can save the world in the twenty-third century. The assumption made all along is that this supreme being will be a male. Yet it is female. In the film narrative, rather than transgress the social body, Leeloo helps to restore it, to make it secure, much as the nineteenth-century science-fiction characterisation of woman before her. She is the (male) scientist's dream cyborg: truly contained and not threatening to man. Remember the scientist who has reconstructed her calls her 'perfect'; Korben also calls her 'perfect'. In fact she becomes very much a cypher (to complement her waif-like body), much like the women in *Le Dernier combat* before her; it is mostly Korben Dallas who does all the figuring out. Agreed, she almost refuses at the end of the film to 'save humanity', but finally she succumbs, and succumbs to that other exigency of the social body: the heterosexual imperative. She has sex with Korben in the very capsule that made her. 'In vitro' meets 'in silico' 'in camera', giving a completely new meaning to safe sex, to say nothing of the imaginary and the Oedipal complex: man having sex in a genetic-engineering capsule with a cyborg, whatever next! In other words, Leeloo is the very last 'person' to foreground the constructedness of otherness. Her body only transgresses as an idea, not as a fact. We are led to believe that she is amazingly strong, as her hand to gun combat on the paradise planet/space-hotel Fhloston demonstrates, but she has none of the muscularity and vigorous health we associate with techno-bodies. Cyborg bodies are supposedly hyper-built, not just DNA structures in excess. Leeloo is never the opposite of what she appears to be. She is never allowed to look or be transgressive. To have had the muscularity of the techno-body would have meant that she would have to have recrafted *herself* the body that emerges from the capsule (through body-building); but it is the scientists (the masters of technology) who have made her. We note she has an enormous appetite, but it does not get transformed into any change of matter. But we do know that techno-bodies are, as in those of female body-builders, 'delegitimated as cultural markers of proper femininity' (Balsamo 1997: 47). There can, it would appear, be no improper female masculinity for Leeloo; she is made to make man feel safe and not under threat. She comes to represent a false maternal body, a concept echoed by the Diva, whose womb is used to conceal the four elemental stones (for which she will die). In fact all of Leeloo's cyborgness is suppressed; this is perhaps why we get none of the male rage and aggression we normally see directed against the female (cyborg) in American sci-fi movies, as for example, *Alien* (Ridley Scott, 1979), *Aliens* (James Cameron, 1986) and *Alien 3* (David Fincher, 1992). In the final analysis, Leeloo challenges nothing. She is the mere (sartorial) mirror to Korben Dallas. As Jean-Paul Gaultier made clear, 'her braces are orange, the same colour as Bruce Willis's T-shirt, to suggest they are made for each other' (*Evening Standard* 1997). And in case we had missed that point, her hair is orange too.

The inherent paradoxes of the social body, or the realities of 'forbidden' fantasies, may be repressed, then; but as we all know they reappear elsewhere, often in the form of pathologies, or as displaced excess. This is particularly true where film diegesis is concerned; in melodrama, for example, the excess in décor acts as a *mise-en-scène* for the suppressed contradictions in marriage and for repressed desire. What is so very interesting about Besson's film is that the challenge to the social body does not occur through the presence of the cyborg body at all (Leeloo), but rather through the transgressive male body. The Mangalores are a first hint of this, and act as foils to the two central and truly transgressive male bodies: Zorg and Ruby Rhod. Both, in different ways, embody improper masculine femininity. They ultimately become, visually at least, more interesting (to look at) than Leeloo, for sure, and almost Korben Dallas who, thanks to his sexy latex trousers and T-shirt – rubber was used to make Willis sweat for his vanity, Gaultier naughtily tells us (*Daily Telegraph* 1997) – saves the day for proper masculine masculinity. Clothes design becomes the play arena for questions of male sexuality in this film. We should not forget that, back in the 1980s, Gaultier designed the male skirt. Zorg's skirted coats with their nipped-in waistlines recall the earlier design. Gaultier explains that he pulls from past designs – not just his own – to create his effect (*Evening Standard* 1997). Zorg is, of course, a reimagined Hitler of the twenty-third century, as Besson explained to Gaultier (*Evening Standard* 1997). But, more significantly, he is a putative cyborg because of his Plexiglas skull. He is also a body that visibly leaks, and as such transgresses boundaries of the skin (when his forehead haemorrhages). He wears his transgression (doubly so, skull and clothes) on his body and is surrounded by robotic domestic knick-knacks that serve only to undermine his 'hard' image, particularly when they are thrown out of control as he nearly chokes to death on a cherry stone. Indeed, in the final analysis, none of his fancy technics work for him; they end up by blowing him up. He falls victim to his own desire to delete humanity, to obsolesce the body. Zorg, the techno-body, mechanical man and arms dealer, confirms his impotence. He can no more hide behind the multi-functional arms he sells than he can behind the skirt of his coat. Thus Besson uses Zorg to attack the scientists mentioned above who associate technology with perfection and the obsolescence of man.

If Zorg is the 'bad' side of the coin of transgression, the same is not true of Ruby Rhod. S/he crosses every line possible, and helps to save the day. Ruby performs all the sexes, in dress and implicitly in action; and s/he camps up all the generic roles s/he can muster. One critic describes Ruby as swathed in leopard-skin with Cruella de Vil collars (*Daily Telegraph* 1997). S/he also drips with ostentatious (costume?) jewellery. Ruby's dress-code is a pot-pourri of the blaxploitation-look movies of the 1970s, and the black hip-hop style of the 1980s, both of which in their own right derive their style from parodies of other earlier styles. The former 1970s clothes-chic of flares, tight polyester tops and platform shoes is derived from the dress-codes of black pimps and prostitutes. The latter 1980s city-slicker cool suits (often with high necks) and masses of thick gold chains, chokers and rings come from Coco Chanel's use of ostentatious fake jewellery to adorn her classic cut suits. Rhod becomes a hero despite herself. It is s/he who complements the masculine Korben Dallas: s/he is the ultra-feminine black body to his ultra-masculine white body. Both are in excess, but Rhod is more visibly transgressive; her/his body manifests an ability to play with sexuality in a way that the very white Korben cannot.

The challenges around sexuality and gender performativity that *Le Cinquième élément* puts on display (or at the very least the *mise-en-scène* of these excessive and transgressive bodies) mark the film as contestatory of dominant ideology to a degree, and demarcate it strongly from the earlier Bessonian sci-fi prototype *Le Dernier combat*. It parodies genre and stereotypes, whereas *Le Dernier combat* was merely playful. It also raises issues around male sexuality which the first film did not even begin to touch upon. However, it stops short of a resistance to the social order of things through its misogynistic representation of Leeloo, and through committing her (as indeed her foresisters in *Le Dernier combat*) to the heterosexual imperative of the Oedipal trajectory. Thus, both of Besson's forays into the sci-fi genre are models of the conservative and the radical. *Le Dernier combat* is radical through its means of production and its ecological and anti-capitalist positioning. Similarly, Besson's challenge to our fascination with technology distinguishes *Le Cinquième élément* from many of the Hollywood sci-fi films of the 1990s, as indeed does his daring play with camp and the queer. However, there are problems which cannot be glossed over. Misogyny aside, there is the question of the problematic representation of blackness. It could be argued that blackness is either neutralised, aestheticised, or in excess. The black president is an ineffectual puppet of the white military; the leader of the Mangalores can transform himself from the monstrous ugly into the beautifully black (as indeed the camera makes clear when it circles around him in medium close-up). And, finally, the outrageously camp compère Ruby Rhod, who at one point sports a displaced white phallus on his/her forehead, is uncomfortably caricatural of black singers such as Little Richard and Prince. The excess of camp s/he embodies renders him beyond sexuality. In a sense he is far too queer, just as, in the opposite direction, Leeloo is merely a cypher of her promise, and remains a weak and rather meaningless characterisation. In both instances, these regressive representations point to a film which despite its look is, in many respects, far less challenging than any of his previous films. But then, Besson's purpose has always been to please his audience, to offer a spectacular respite from the everyday social unease, not to cure it. As he says, his work is 'Mission Elastoplast' (Frodon 1997: 18) – with all the imperfections that connotes.

References

Balsamo, A. (1997), *Technologies of the Gendered Body: Reading Cyborg Women* (Durham/London: Duke University Press).
Besson, L. (1993), *L'Histoire du Dernier combat* (Paris: Bordas).
Baudrillard, J. (1996), *The System of Objects* (London/New York: Verso).
Buckland, W. (1999), 'Between science fact and science fiction: Spielberg's digital dinosaurs, possible worlds, and the new aesthetic realism', *Screen*, 40, pp. 177–92.
Cantaloube, T. (1997), 'La Magie digitale', *Cahiers du cinéma*, 513, pp. 81–4.
Daily Telegraph (1997), Interview with J.-P. Gaultier, *Daily Telegraph*, 6 January 1997.
Evening Standard (1997), Interview with J.-P. Gaultier, *Evening Standard*, 5 June 1997.
Floyd, F. (1997), Review of *Le Cinquième élément*, *Time Out*, 11 June 1997.
Frodon, J. L. (1997), 'Je connais bien ce monde du XXIIIe siècle, j'y ai longtemps habité', *Le Monde*, 9 May 1997, p. 18.
Hayward, S. (1998), *Luc Besson* (Manchester: Manchester University Press).
Springer, C. (1996), *Electronic Eros: Bodies and Desire in the Postindustrial Age* (London: Athlone Press).
Télérama (1983), *Télérama* 1734, p. 29.

Notes

1 He presented the film at the Alvoriaz Science Fiction Film Festival (1983) and it won the two major awards (Critics and Special Jury).
2 Not surprisingly, given this ethos, ever since his first film, Besson has always been very explicit as to how he has achieved his difficult shots and published these details in his books of the films; see, for example, Besson 1993.
3 For example, he chose not to work with Pixar (linked with Disney) and PDI (with Dreamworks) precisely because they are attached to the majors in the industry and have formulaic ways of making their special effects felt. Interestingly, Besson did not choose Industrial Light and Magic (ILM) either. This company was founded by George Lucas and is the only other independent company in California. However, ILM did make the special effects for *Jurassic Park* and *The Lost World: Jurassic Park* (Steven Spielberg, 1997). It could be that Besson, in his concern not to flag up the special effects imagery in the ostentatious way they are signalled in *Jurassic Park*, decided to opt for Digital Domain. Warren Buckland would probably disagree with this reading of Spielberg's use of special effects. He argues that there is a seamlessness between the digital and photographic images in both Spielberg films (Buckland, 1999).
4 On this question, see Canteloube, 1997.
5 For a more developed discussion of this idea of obsolescence and robotics, see Baudrillard 1996: 109–33; for a more detailed analysis of Besson's films and technology, see Hayward 1998, 94–118.

6   Which, according to Claudia Springer (1996: 21) is a dream of A-life scientists (artificial life computer scientists and biologists).
7   For a film example of this templating see Kathryn Bigelow's *Strange Days* (1995); one of the co-authors was James Cameron (the other author was Jay Cocks).

7

The sinking of the self: Freudian hydraulic patterns in *Le Grand bleu*

Laurent Jullier

> There I will not hear
> The empty sound of the world any more
> (Sainte Thérèse de L'Enfant Jésus 2004: 645).

If *Le Grand bleu* were analysed in the terms of a classical narrative, we would probably say something like this. This is the slow-developing story of a young man who wastes his youth and who dives into water holding onto a cable. He looks like an expressionless top model, and aspires only to be a dolphin. Because he cannot be a dolphin, he is the curse of those who love him. For over two hours, ethnic, advertising and sexist stereotypes follow one another to a soundtrack composed of easy-listening electronic music, until the hero finally decides to go and live with the dolphins. This is more or less how French critics viewed the film, as Besson himself recalls to us, quoting a range of critical comments in the book he wrote about the film: 'an abdication of thought', 'slow and heavy', 'cheap philosophy as a pretext to make images', 'we watch but we do not learn anything', 'overwhelmed with music', 'this week's must-miss movie', and so on (Besson 1994: 104–7). 'I watched the newspapers make mincemeat of the film, tear it to pieces with the dirtiest words', Besson remembers (Besson 1994: 98). But the problem is that *Le Grand bleu* is *not* a classical narrative; it is a postmodern film. More than that, it is a social phenomenon, a symptom, which focuses on a number of contemporary issues. In Besson's book, comments by critics who did not understand this are cleverly contrasted with raw and very telling data: a 187–week exclusive run in Paris, 9,066,835 spectators in France. 'Of course', Besson writes ironically, 'the media then changed sides, and discussed at length this "cult-movie"' (Besson 1994: 98).

Now that the postmodern is a more familiar discourse in critical analysis, now that Luc Besson is a French cinema tycoon, now that *Le Grand bleu* is out of fashion, it may be easier to talk about the film more dispassionately, even if the complexities remain. The first problem is the range of the film's possible meanings. Contrary to the classical Hollywood cinema – organised in such a way as to restrict overly variable readings – here we have a polysemic artefact. If multiple readings are possible, indeed, if it is difficult in the circumstances to conceive of misreadings, why bother analysing this film, why work towards something which is bound to be restrictive to some extent? The answer is very simple. This film has had very little serious critical attention in France, despite Susan Hayward's groundbreaking work in the UK (Hayward, 1998). Two years after its release, Olivier Mongin was already wondering why the film had generated so few comments when it was so obviously a 'contemporary mythology' (Mongin 1991: 95).

Le Grand bleu is one of these postmodern narratives which is incoherent in its coherence. Logic and structure are at odds with each other. For example, its hero seems to be disgusted by the entire humankind – he prefers dolphins – but the choices he makes play a major part in feeding the misanthropy which will eventually kill him. To start with, Jacques suffers from Enzo's attitude. His best friend struggles to push the diving challenge ever further, when he should accept his defeat. That being the case, why does Jacques not put an end to it? Why does he not let Enzo delude himself with the idea he is the number one? Is it that important to win the race when the animal kingdom is set up as a model of social organisation? Jacques kills Enzo because he, Jacques, wants to be the strongest. When it comes to women, the same incoherence can be seen. Jacques does not really love Johana; he finds sex boring, something of a chore, especially compared to dolphin-riding. As for becoming a father, we are left in little doubt that such a misanthropic and infantile youth would not have much to hand down to a child. So why in this case get Johana pregnant? It is perhaps logical that a character so close to nature would resist using artificial contraception; but how could Jacques afford the risk of an unwanted pregnancy? For the capable athlete that he is, would it be that difficult, like a yogi controls his breath, for Jacques to control ejaculation? A part answer, coming from a Freudian perspective, could be that it is his parting gift to Johanna. It was only on that condition that she would 'let him go'; she therefore carries the phallus that he abandons (as irrelevant).

And then the narrative organisation is incoherent. From the classical cinema it takes the quest; from modernist cinema it takes the ambiguities of its characters, which make of it an open work. *Le Grand bleu* is a self-service where meaning is concerned; everyone takes from it what they want. Rather like Harpo Marx's coat, you will find everything you need. If we restrict ourselves just to French critics, Olivier Mongin sees the film as a mirror of the times, Daniel Sibony as a metaphor for drug addiction, Serge Daney as the essence of what he calls the audiovisual contrasting the cinema of the look against the cinema of being and message.

It follows then that a purely internal analysis, divorced from the film's social context, is unlikely to lead to much. We would end up in the interpretative trap discussed by David Bordwell in *Making Meaning*: because the postmodern narrative is polysemic, anything goes, and theorists feel free to construct their own reading. But where an external analysis is concerned, it too carries risks, as has been underlined by Jacques Aumont in *À quoi pensent les films* (Aumont, 1997): the film works as the mechanical exemplification of a big theory which exists without it.

To minimise both risks, our starting point will be *Le Grand bleu*'s success: millions of cinemagoers and videotape buyers cannot be wrong. The theoretical problem then becomes how to account for this infatuation. There are at least three possible approaches. First, the film can be located in what Aloïs Riegel calls the *Kunstwollen* of the social and historical context (Riegl, 2003). It is successful because it is the first to encapsulate artistic forms corresponding to the times. Second, the film crystallises socio-cultural specificities, engendering a mirror-effect where some of the more publicly visible social groups can see themselves narcissistically. Third, there is another mirror-effect, but outside of the realm of history: the film explores an unusual aspect of human psychology. Here the problem is to decide to what extent the behaviour explored is widespread in the viewing public, or whether it is more likely to be seen as specific to the hero, as a psychopathological feature.

I shall reject the first of these approaches. Many people commented on the fact that film's undersea shots are no better than the most ordinary sequences of Jacques Cousteau's cinema. Framing and cutting are not that original either, no matter what the director says: 'Young directors tell a story differently than older ones. We prefer flashes and shocks to narrative explanations' (Besson 1993, cited in Sojcher 2002: 142). Jacques's story from diving to death is explained at length, in a linear fashion; the 'metric' game (who can go deepest, i.e. who has got the biggest penis) could be understood by a 7-year-old child. A similar contradiction can be found in Besson's 1985 conception of the 'filmic modernity' he is supposed to exemplify: 'Placing the camera and moving it straight to the target' (cited in Sojcher 2002: 142). However, many mobile shots do not go straight to the point in his films: *Le Grand bleu*'s first shot, a fast track forwards, has not even something in the shot which it is approaching; we are just rushing forwards, and that's it. Music videos and commercials have accustomed us to this kind of wandering camera, a camera that veers away, turns around, or flies over the subject. No doubt the music is partly responsible for the film's public success, but here again we have heard all this before: Mickey-Mousing, compiled pop scores and Serra's standard Akaï S-900 sampled sounds do not leave a great deal to the imagination. We need to look elsewhere for an explanation. Let us turn away, then, from the purely formal aspects of the film, to those arguments which focus on the film as a mirror.

Jacques feels *blue*, as the title of the film might well lead us to understand. But his ailment is not in any sense specific to the 1980s. In 1820 Esquirol wrote: 'All epochs have been characterised by a cluster of monomanias coloured by the intellectual and moral feature of the times', while Michel Foucault reminds us in *Folie et déraison* that 'humour' was a preoccupation of the eighteenth century. To have humour consisted in being the 'victim of all the calls made on body and soul at the surface of the world' (both cited in Huguet 1997: 12). Monomania and humour are ancient words; today we would say Jacques suffers from melancholia; but Foucault's formula fits perfectly here because the hero finds an unlikely salvation *beneath* this unbearable *surface* of the world.

Jacques is in *internal exile*. His 'passion for an unreachable Elsewhere' (Huguet 1997: 13) sets him apart. The deeps where he protects himself symbolically from the *Umwelt* can be likened to the convent in which the mystics lock themselves up, changing their 'inability to feel the presence of the Other' into 'pure experience of (their) own lack' (Huguet 1997: 19). Deep under the sea, emphatically underlined by the sounds of Serra and their cathedral-like reverberations, St Theresa's 'empty sound of the world' from the epigraph to this chapter can no more enter than in a convent. It is worth recalling, given that this formula is Saint Theresa's, that in Alain Cavalier's film devoted to her, released two years before *Le Grand bleu* (*Thérèse*, 1986), the nuns seem in a literally suicidal hurry to join their Maker, as one of them swallows Theresa's infected saliva at the tombside (although of course it is not clear whether this is to incorporate a little of Theresa's holiness, or to reach the sweet Hereafter faster). Just like Jacques at the end of *Le Grand bleu*, Theresa knowingly decided to 'run away from the Earth's grove' (Thérèse de l'Enfant Jésus 2004: 675): 'I saw that everything here is ephemeral/I saw my happiness fade, die' (Thérèse de l'Enfant Jésus 2004: 676). Theresa successively saw her mother and her father die; Jacques saw his father and his best friend die, and his mother leave.

It is true, as Mongin points out, that *Le Grand bleu* does not try to set up a religious metaphor, which was clearer in the first versions of the script, but then left out (Mongin 1991: 103). Nonetheless, Besson will return to mystical problems, indirectly in *Le Cinquième élément*, then directly in *Jeanne d'Arc*. It is striking to say the least that it is Dustin Hoffman who plays Joan's confessor: Benjamin, the character he played twenty-two years earlier in *The Graduate* (Mike Nichols, 1967), bears some resemblance to Jacques, as he daydreams in front of his aquarium, or at the bottom of his pool. *The Graduate*'s first shot shows him in the middle of seaweed and fish; opening and end credits are overlaid by Simon and Garfunkel's resonant line, 'Hello darkness, my old friend'. 'The Sound of Silence', the song from which these lines are taken, closes with the wish to live in a *world of silence* – words which themselves resonate with Commandant Cousteau's *World of Silence* (Jacques-Yves Cousteau and Louis Malle, 1956). Moreover, *The Graduate*'s last scene shows Benjamin fighting with a sacred cross in guise of a sword, without wounding anyone, exactly like Jeanne in Besson's *Jeanne d'Arc*. This network of quotations confirms the extent to which the film is postmodern. But one must acknowledge that Jacques is the direct descendant of *modern* heroes, at odds with society and desperately seeking a return to their natural roots. Antoine (François Truffaut, *Les 400 coups*, 1959) runs away from the detention centre where he is being held just so that he can see the sea, even though he cannot swim.[1] Guy (Jacques Demy, *Les Parapluies de Cherbourg*, 1964) spends his youth dreaming of going to sea while watching a model ship; and when life disappoints him, he consoles himself by regressing to a childish, wilder and more natural world (the film's last shot shows him crouching and playing Indians with his son). The sea is barely less present in Bergman's *Sommaren med Monika* (*Summer with Monika*, 1952), a 'pre-modernist' work which might well have influenced Truffaut and Demy's, as far as we can judge from a trope they both take up, Harriett Andersson as Monika looking at the camera, 'the saddest shot in cinema history', as Godard wrote (Godard 1985: 137). Antoine Doinel (*Les 400 coups*) steals a publicity picture of Harriett Anderson from outside the cinema; Geneviève (*Les Parapluies de Cherbourg*) will have the same straight-to-camera look for the same diegetic reasons, through her wedding veil. Monika 'calls the spectator to witness the scorn she feels for herself' (Godard 1985: 137) because she agrees to a compromise, and because – like Antoine and Guy – she does not take her disgust in the face of human society to its logical conclusion.

Jacques will be the only one to go to the bitter end of this disgust. Of course, he is not the first modern hero to commit suicide. To take an example from a post-1968 road-movie, the main character of *Vanishing Point* (Richard C. Sarafian, 1971), drives his car straight into a police road-block. Much earlier, the French Surrealist Jacques Rigaut (who took his life at the age of 30 in 1929), laid the foundations of a 'General Suicide Agency, an agency recognised as a public utility' (Rigaut 1970: 39). Nevertheless, these suicidal heroes appealed to a limited audience and readership.

Two issues need to be considered where the meanings of Jacques's suicide are concerned: the ambiguity of *Le Grand bleu*'s last scene, and the reasons Jacques has to commit suicide. The last scene places death off-screen; no one knows if Jacques changes his mind at the very last minute, or if he realises he is able, once more, to breathe underwater, or if – as happens at the end of *The Abyss* (James Cameron, 1989) and *Artificial Intelligence: A.I.* (Steven Spielberg, 2001) – a last-minute rescue is performed by aliens. Maybe the whole final dive is a dream – there was a dream sequence earlier in the film. Spectators are invited to imagine what they want, from the darkest dystopian end to the lightest and most fantastical utopia; inconclusive narrative closure is one of the tropes that the postmodern narrative borrows from narratives of modernity. What about his reasons to have done with it all? What are they exactly? If it is Jacques's idiosyncratic circumstances – remorse at being the cause of Enzo's death, sorrow that he lost his father when young – that motivate his suicide, we probably need to look for *Le Grand bleu*'s success elsewhere. But that changes if the suicide is motivated by experiences that many people could share. This would be Besson's view, who said that the nine million spectators who ensured the film's success 'experienced, either as children or teenagers, great pain, irretrievable pain – the loss of a parent, of a relative, a divorce, difficulties in expressing themselves, loneliness, an existential crisis' (Besson 1999: 50).

Let us tread with care and explore the extent to which Jacques can be seen as an archetype, and the reasons for his imbalance. He suffers, as I said above, from melancholia; but what is striking in this character, given that he is no longer a child, is the persistence of what Freud calls *Hilflosigkeit*, the feeling of being forsaken, originally present in the baby who cannot fulfil its desires without grown-up help: 'The infant needs external help to maintain homeostasis' (Janah 1997: 154), homeostasis being the situation where the infant regulates change so as to maintain stability. We can make two assumptions in this respect. First, Jacques's imbalance is *internalised*, it comes from the *Innenwelt*, our own world of thoughts and emotions, in that a drive forces Jacques backwards in evolutionary terms, to the animal, and beyond that to the uterine ocean, the 'gynesis'). Second, Jacques's imbalance is also *externalised*, it comes from the *Umwelt*, the material, external world, in that Jacques is abandoned successively by his mother, his father and his best friend; and nobody understands the passion he feels for dolphins.

Le Grand bleu **115**

The internalisation argument is not a strong one. What is so exciting about dolphins? Their struggle for life is at least as cold and violent as it is for humans: injured, aged or lonely animals do not survive a long time. The easiest solution is to put this new contradiction of the character down to the polyvalence of postmodernism, where contradictions can be accommodated in theoretical terms. But another way of looking at it is to see in it proof that Jacques practises denial. He simply refuses to see anything which disturbs him. His denial combines *projection* and *magical thinking*. 'Projection is the defense of denying unacceptable aspects of the self and simultaneously attributing them to others' (Nesse and Lloyd 1991: 611). Jacques attributes to Enzo the compulsion to win, and if not to Enzo, to society which turns this compulsion into a value, when he is in fact propelled by it himself. Magical thinking consists in believing that every problem can be resolved deep in the ocean, among dolphins, and in the denial that a human being simply cannot breathe there. By dint of denial, 'the melancholic does not know what he [sic] has lost any more (and it perhaps himself that he loses)' (Richard 2001: 64). We could even suggest – especially when we consider the way in which some scenes are filmed like music videos – that Jacques is just striking a neoromantic pose, where 'great pain is contrived at the service of a narcissistic aesthetics' (Richard 2001: 64), or adopting the behaviour of the poet, whose lies, according to Freud, effect a transformation of reality more in line with the poet's desires (see Freud, 1957). Jacques would be like Goethe's Werther, who has no particular reason to commit suicide, but whose *Weltschmerz* is incurable.

What then of the externalisation argument? This is related to the teenage crisis, and is all the stronger in postmodern societies where family, civic responsibility and country are exhausted grand narratives, especially when seen through a teenager's eyes:

> The predisposition to negative melancholic narcissism is strengthened by social and cultural alienation which diminishes coherence and the attraction of external objects. As a result the teenager insists on making the Other the source of the problem, when in fact he [sic] suffers because of his inability to inscribe his individuality within a social arena which is greater than him and which includes him. (Richard 2001: 197)

Jacques clearly fits this diagnosis: he is literally unable to *situate* himself, to such an extent that we can see traces of autism in his behaviour.

If autism means 'the highest degree of narcissistic return to a cell where mother and child are one' (Richard 2001: 30), then the answer is yes. Jacques's final vanishing in an amniotic nirvana definitively settles the question of homeostasis, referred to above, since substance and pressure now become the same inside and outside the body (the same equality can be found in the human foetus, as in *The Abyss*'s main character when slipping on the experimental diving-suit). If autism is what the cognitivists think it is – that is the inability to stand in the Other's place so as to imagine what the Other has in mind – maybe the answer is yes again. If Jacques had been capable of standing in Enzo's shoes, he would have foreseen the hubris which drives Enzo to overestimate his physical abilities, and he would have put an end to the competition. But there is a big step between autism as metaphor and autism as a clinical condition. Jacques is not totally turned in on himself. Moreover, what he searches for deep in the water remains ambiguous. Is it the autistic fusion with the mother's body? Or the lost father within for a son engulfed in what Freud calls the *Vatersehnsucht*, the nostalgia for the father? (see Freud 1961a and 1961b). French allows the pun *mer/mère* (*mother* and *sea* are homophones); German allows *Water/Vater*. . . Daniel Sibony tried to combine both in a review of the film: 'Jacques cherche le père que la mèr(e) lui a fait perdre' ('Jacques searches for the father the mother/sea took away from him') (Sibony 1988: 2).

To continue with the external causes of Jacques's maladjustment, let us turn from the teenage crisis and its corollary of autistic behaviour to the well-worn argument of the battle of the sexes. At the end of the 1980s, 'men are losing the historical social attributes, which defined their role as leaders where kinship and family are concerned; but this loss has not been accompanied by a fundamental questioning of the traditional family order' (Neyraud 2000: 250). This order consists of 'a private female power corresponding symmetrically to male domination (which) is very clear in the public sphere, but which is anchored in the private sphere. Sexuality is predicated on two opposing spheres of power, one masculine (the sexual act), the other feminine (before and after this act, i.e. seduction and children)' (Neyraud 2000: 317). In other words, men do not recoup in the private sphere what they left in the public sphere, and so they experience doubts. This fairly stereotypical view seems at first sight to match *Le Grand bleu*. But Jacques could be said to transcend the commonality of the public sphere because he is a professional sportsman, in a sport where the male, because of lung size, and so on, will always do better than the female. There is nothing he need fear, figuratively or literally, from the women's movement. This genetic 'superiority' means that he can let Johana deal with the before-and-after of their relationship, and even with the ritual of the sexual act. It is Johana who nets him (after all he is a dolphin), and, as Mongin writes, 'imposes a progeny on him' (Mongin 1991: 106). In this perspective, reading *Le Grand bleu* as a typical symptom of troubled *fin-de-siècle* masculinity does not make much sense.

Neither a focus on arguments of internalisation, nor on those of externalisation seem conclusive. It would clearly be more productive to combine them. To continue with the psychological tools we have been using, Jacques seems to perform a particular form of *coping*. Psychologists call 'coping' our way to respond both to inside and outside dangers, a 'way of adapting our behaviour both to the *Innenwelt* and the *Umwelt*' (Janah 1997: 148). It is a concept familiar in the somatics of pathology, for example when dealing with the onset of cancer in reply to a hostile environment. The latter point has been famously illustrated by Fritz Zorn's *Mars*. The Swiss hero of this dark autobiographic novel lives in a society which does not even *notice* him, leading to a cancer which kills Fritz when he is about the same age as Jacques at the time of Jacques's suicidal dive. Could it be, then, that the technocratic and individualistic 1980s are equivalent to bored Swiss bourgeois society at the beginning of the twentieth century; in other words, do the 1980s kill Jacques?

There are many indications that teenagers in late capitalist societies are frequently disposed to *vertigo behaviour*; *Rebel Without a Cause* (Nicholas Ray, 1955), with its eloquent title and its fatal car challenge, is a case in point. Such behaviour can have purely internal causes: 'Highrisk behaviour is related to what happens in religious ordeals [when the individual submits to divine judgement], in which we can see a phantasy of omnipotence. It shows a diffuse but massive castration anxiety' (Richard 2001: 200). Vertigo behaviour 'begins with narcissistic display of power and turns into self-destruction, paradoxically with a subject who believes he is immortal' (Richard 2001: 204). We can discern such behaviour in Jacques.

But there are equally external causes of a socio-historical nature. In the richest and oldest postmodern societies, 'you constantly have to prove your own existence; castration anxiety seems to apply to the entirety of the self' (Richard 2001: 205). However, once castration anxiety is displaced, it is difficult to locate, which is why the rebel is 'without a cause'. In what sense might there be a meaning attached to the desire to dive deeper and deeper into the depths of the ocean? *Le Grand bleu* does not give us any clues. Jacques is used as a guinea pig, but nothing is said about what discoveries might emerge from his prowess. The doctor seems to be there mainly to check that everything is all right, or to measure Jacques's heartbeat in the hope of discovering why he is different from ordinary mortals. Unlike his father, who was diving for something (for his living), Jacques dives *for nothing*; or perhaps for himself. It is a perfect example of the transformation of an industrial society into a society of the spectacle. First the father engages in *telic* behaviour, driven by material motives, followed by his son who engages in *paratelic*[2] behaviour, driven by immaterial and non-causal motives (*what is he really diving for?*). This shift is also symptomatic of the collapse of the grand narratives in postmodernity, in that the quest is problematised; as Johana wisely says, 'there is *nothing* in the depths; everything is black'.

Is this a version of punk's 'no future' tailored for a wide public twelve years after it had been proclaimed? If dolphins, medical experiments and sporting competition are value-free pretexts, then we might be inclined to say yes. Or is it rather an appeal for the *return of the Father*, one of these reactionary themes modernist critics often accuse postmodernism of harbouring? If Jacques put his *Weltschmerz* down to the *Vatersehnsucht*, surely he would not commit suicide when hearing that Johana is pregnant, since this would mean that despair would be passed on to the next generation. Maybe he thinks that way but still decides to drown himself; maybe he doesn't. In the end, the result comes to the same thing. From a political perspective, beyond punk agitation, the 'revolutionary suicide' hypothesis remains. Jacques dies in the same spirit as some Buddhist monks might have done, to signal that the values of the society which surrounds them are not good ones. But here again, positing this meaning is fraught with difficulties, since it would mean that the film is denouncing aggressive competitive individualism with a hero who seems to subscribe to those values.

More simply, then, perhaps *Le Grand bleu* simply proffers a mirror to us. This is Mongin's position: '*Le Grand bleu* reflects our own image, the image of times without passion, unless the only passion still remaining is out of all proportion and necessarily brings death' (Mongin 1991: 95). We could propose a somewhat more prosaic version of this position: if you set aside the film's handsome actors and CinemaScope sunsets, the film quietly describes a self-destructive society, whose members knowingly decide to make fewer children than necessary to keep the population number at the same level. In France, the birth-rate dropped below the fatal number of two per family during 1975. *Le Grand bleu*'s release corresponds to a particular set of spectators who could not be unaware, given the importance of demography in France, that fewer than two children per family means, in the long run, *no future*. As Baudrillard wrote in the fourth volume of his *Cool Memories*, 'maybe the human race is actually planning, albeit obliquely, the same extermination it slowly but surely intends for other species' (Baudrillard 2000: 95). No doubt the shortage of children is one of those oblique means. If we feel threatened by this hypothesis, we could remind ourselves that it is only one of many possible interpretations this typically postmodern narrative allows; and we could also remind ourselves that the birth-rate may well climb again.[3]

References

Aumont, J. (1997), *À quoi pensent les films* (Paris: Séguier).
Baudrillard, J. (2000), *Cool memories IV* (Paris: Galilée).
Besson, L. (1994), *L'Histoire du Grand bleu* (Paris: Intervista).
Besson, L. (1999), 'Mes années 90, propos recueillis par Jean-Pierre Lavoignat', *Studio*, hors-série 'Les années 90' (December), pp. 48–54.
Freud, S. (1957), 'Five lectures on psycho-analysis', *The Standard Edition of the Complete Psychological Works of Sigmund Freud*, Vol. 11 (London: Hogarth), pp. 3–55.
Freud, S. (1961a), 'A seventeenth-century demonological neurosis', *The Standard Edition of the Complete Psychological Works of Sigmund Freud*, vol. 19 (London: Hogarth), pp. 72–105.
Freud, S. (1961b), *Civilization and its Discontents, The Standard Edition of the Complete Psychological Works of Sigmund Freud*, vol. 21 (London: Hogarth), pp. 64–145.
Godard, J.-L. (1985), *Jean-Luc Godard par Jean-Luc Godard* (Paris: Cahiers du Cinéma-L'Étoile).
Grodal, T. (1997), *Moving Pictures: A New Theory of Film Genres, Feelings, and Cognition* (Oxford: Clarendon Press).
Hayward, S. (1998), *Luc Besson* (Manchester: Manchester University Press).
Huguet, M. (1997), 'Exil intérieur et ennui', *Psychologie clinique*, 4, pp. 11–23.
Janah T. (1997), 'Le *coping*, une logique de survie', *Psychologie clinique*, 4, pp. 147–63.
Jullier, L. (2001), 'De la Nouvelle Vague à l'immersion', in J. Cléder and G. Mouëllic (eds), *Nouvelle Vague, nouveaux ravages* (Rennes: Presses Universitaires de Rennes), pp. 59–75.
Mongin, O. (1991), *La Peur du vide: essai sur les passions démocratiques* (Paris: Seuil).
Nesse, R. M. and A. T. Lloyd (1992), 'The evolution of psychodynamic mechanisms', in J. H. Barkow, L. Cosmides and J. Tooby (eds), *The Adapted Mind: Evolutionary Psychology and the Generation of Culture* (Oxford/New York: Oxford University Press), pp. 601–24.
Neyraud, G. (2000), *L'Enfant, la mère et la question du père* (Paris: Presses Universitaires de France).
Richard, F. (2001), *Le Processus de subjectivation à l'adolescence* (Paris: Dunod).
Riegl, A. (2003), *Le Culte moderne des monuments*, trans. J. Boulet (Paris: L'Harmattan).
Rigaut, J. (1970), *Écrits* (Paris: Gallimard).
Sibony, D. (1988), 'Le Grand bleu de nos malaises', *Libération* (10 August 1988), p. 2.
Sojcher, F. (2002), 'Luc Besson ou les contradictions du cinéma français face à Hollywood', *CinémAction*, hors série 'Quelle diversité face à Hollywood', pp. 142–56.
Thérèse de l'Enfant Jésus (2004), *Œuvres complètes/Textes et dernières paroles*

(Paris: Le Cerf/Desclée de Brouwer; website available at: http://bibliotheque.editionsducerf.fr/).

Notes

1 For an extended discussion of the links between *Le Grand bleu* and *Les 400 coups*, see Jullier, 2001.
2 For the contrast between telic and paratelic activities, see Grodal 1997: 101–2. Telic means 'goal-seeking', and paratelic 'means-oriented'.
3 I am grateful to Phil Powrie, Susan Hayward and Dolly Masson for help with the English version.

8

Imprisoned freedoms: space and identity in *Subway* and *Nikita*

Mark Orme

In his seminal study *L'Espace au cinéma*, André Gardies argues that space is not simply the agent of a film's physical or geographical dimensions, but is as important as the characters, with a key role to play in narrative unity (Gardies, 1993).[1] Drawing on Saussure's distinction between *parole* and *langue*, Gardies posits that *le lieu* in film is determined by *l'espace*, so that just as one understands the French *language* by interpreting individual *words*, so one understands *space* in film by interpreting individual *places*.[2] Space, Gardies writes, 'must be constructed' (Gardies 1993: 72), with *le lieu* being seen as 'the "text" of space' (Gardies 1993: 71). Pivotal to this process of spatial understanding, and underpinning the diegesis, is the association between the film's characters and the space they occupy, since 'space is only understandable when it is apprehended by a subject' (Gardies 1993: 115).[3] In this chapter, it is precisely this relationship between subjects and their spatial situation that I wish to explore with reference to *Subway* and *Nikita*, with particular emphasis being placed on the two principal protagonists of each film, Fred and Nikita. In keeping with Besson's interest in depicting characters who possess a socially regressive nature (see Hayward 1998: 82), both Fred and Nikita similarly reject the standards of conventional society and establish alternative lifestyles to the norm. They are both social deviants. My aim in what follows is to examine how Besson exploits the films' settings in revealing the emotional state of these two seemingly equivalent characters, and to explore how space is used as a vehicle for communicating a sense of 'imprisoned freedom' on which each film pivots. As I hope to demonstrate, the link between physical environment and personal psychology in the construction of gender and identity differs markedly in the two films at issue.

By its very title, *Subway* is spatially delimited. The opening sequence showing Fred's high-speed car chase (played out against a rebellious, rock music soundtrack) ends with him crashing his vehicle into an entrance of the Parisian Métro, his 'home' for the entire film (and, one might add, for the rest of his life). From the unconfined space and sense of freedom of the open road, the film immediately descends, then, into the depths of a labyrinthine enclosed space, where danger and confusion merge in a topos of claustrophobia.[4] This contained setting lends visual intensity to *Subway*'s décor. Yet despite its imprisoned dimensions, the Métro depicted in Besson's film – essentially a male space, with Héléna the only substantive female character to gain access to this male-dominated environment – is a source of liberation and revolt for its eccentric inhabitants: the individuals living in the bowels of the Métro complex all live outside the law and exploit their subterranean space to create an alternative community. Indeed, theirs is a perfectly self-sufficient, if unorthodox living environment, which, as well as providing a sense of neighbourhood – with some areas more welcoming than others, as Jean-Louis is keen to point out to Fred – and a ready supply of material goods (via theft), also furnishes its residents with makeshift amenities such as a gymnasium (a show-case for Gros Bill's physical prowess), a dance hall (providing a romantic setting for nocturnal entertainment), a party venue (enabling Fred to make acquaintance with his fellow subterranean dwellers) and, ultimately, a concert hall. A travelling shot at the start of the film (4″),[5] showing a train entering the Métro network, heralds the arrival of the title *Subway* on the screen, and thereby announces the underground's alternative social space where day suddenly turns into night.

An early sequence showing Fred wandering his way through the depths of the Métro (16″) highlights the dark, threatening and dangerous nature of this incarcerated environment, although, even at this stage, the distinctive-looking hero (dressed in tuxedo and sporting bleached blond hair) already shows signs of spontaneity and revolt. He blows open a safe he happens to come across ('I don't like safes', he reveals to Héléna, whose husband's safe he also breaks into during her birthday party), and jokes with the roller-skater Jean-Louis, whom he meets that he, Fred, is there 'on holiday'. To the trembling skater, moreover, Fred appears calm and confident in this initial confrontation. What needs to be emphasised here is that, from the outset, as he begins to explore his subterranean situation, Fred's behaviour indicates that he is easily able to adapt to his new underground surroundings. 'Nice place', is his observation of the inhabitants' underground hideaway, which, in spite of – or perhaps because of – its uninviting atmosphere and seemingly threatening characters, quickly becomes a source of enchantment for Fred. Or, to use Susan Hayward's terminology, '[t]he métro becomes a labyrinth that fascinates in its familiar unfamiliarity' (Hayward 1998: 40). For Fred, as for his fellow subterranean inhabitants, physical enclosure is not psychologically repressive; on the contrary, it provides a vehicle for asserting personal identity in the quest for independence from the shackles of conventional society. Indeed, as David Berry points out, when Gros Bill tears off Fred's handcuffs, 'the last vestige of social restriction is removed' (Berry 2000: 16). Each of the individuals comprising the band of misfits living in the Métro is defined by virtue of his underground (criminal) activity; while for Fred himself, as we shall presently discover, the confined setting of the Métro is actually a site of personal rejuvenation and realisation of ambition.

The significance of *Subway*'s underground setting is further confirmed by Besson himself in an interview granted to *Film Français* in 1985: 'I had a strong idea, the métro. But I couldn't find a story strong enough to match the décor' (quoted in Hayward 1998: 35).[6] This quotation confirms the status of the Métro as the motor for the film's diegesis and confirms Besson's oft-cited predilection for atmosphere over narrative (see for example Hayward 1998: 19). Closed off from the conventional world with its own customs and procedures,[7] *Subway*'s underground location is the perfect instrument for communicating a sense of 'imprisoned freedom' since, as Berry observes:

> [O]n the one hand, the Métro, as a dark subterranean space, suggests associations of entombment, encapsulation, the horrors of sewers and catacombs or speleological engulfment . . . On the other hand, paradoxically, this tomb can become a womb; it can then represent a place of safety and protection . . . it becomes a refuge and a means to freedom. (Berry 2000: 9)

These remarks rightly point up the binary opposition of *Subway*'s spatial situation, serving as both a setting of intimidation and personal security. As such, it perfectly reflects the complex duality of Fred's own persona. A social misfit who does not respect conventional law and order (and whose distinctive appearance similarly suggests defiance of conformity), Fred represents, on the one hand, a threat to the status quo. He does not question his actions, preferring instead to act on impulse, and follows his instincts even if this means breaking society's laws (by stealing and blackmailing), or putting himself in danger (as is the case in the final sequence of the film, as we shall see below). Yet, on the other hand, Fred's personal integrity is beyond dispute. He is both sensitive (notably towards Héléna, with whom he falls in love), and 'honest', in that he does not intentionally set out to deceive (unlike Héléna's husband and group of associates, whose underhand schemes betray their unscrupulous and superficial motives merely to make money.) A scene showing close-up shots of Jean-Louis and Fred in a *tête-à-tête* discussing the possibility of an armed raid on a Métro train (30″) indicates that, while the means may justify the end for the former, the latter is not naturally predisposed to violence. Indeed, the money obtained from the armed robbery in which Fred himself later partakes (81″) is quickly given away to further his musical dream, rather than hoarded for his own private use.

It is in the physical space of the Métro that Fred's revolt against conventional society and the manifestation of his own individuality converge, thus forging an important link between physical environment and personal psychology in the film. Retreating into the alternative realm of the Métro both confirms Fred's divorce from the real world, and provides opportunities which are denied him on the outside. Just as Jacques Mayol in *Le Grand bleu* finds his *raison d'être* below the surface of everyday reality – the champion free-diver feels more at home underwater than above ground, and favours the companionship of dolphins over that of human beings – so Fred in *Subway* secures a sense of personal authenticity in his underground prison.[8] By making friends with the Métro's band of unusual inhabitants, Fred learns how to exploit the underground network, and thereby consolidates his own alternative lifestyle. Hijacking the topography of imprisonment in his subterranean environment, he reroutes it as an alternative space which, while enclosed, assumes the magical qualities of a haven liberated from the constraints of conventionality. The incarcerated space of the Métro is thus accorded exotic appeal, a point seized upon by Berry when he observes that '[t]he desire to gain access to a foreign, exotic environment, to an exciting state of other worldliness is implicit from the very title of the film. The word "subway" immediately evokes the New World, the glamour of New York. The Métro has become "Americanised"' (Berry 2000: 16).

Further confirmation of *Subway*'s exotic attraction is provided by Héléna's growing fixation with Fred and his alternative lifestyle underground. This point owes much to critics such as Berry and Hayward (Hayward 1998: 35), who usefully highlight the Orphic overtones of Héléna's descent into the depths to find Fred, whose independence and spontaneity contrast markedly with her hollow and unscrupulous husband and group of associates, all of whom are defined by deceit. The suffocation Héléna experiences at her superficial life *above ground* – brought into particularly sharp focus in the dinner party scene (62″), where pretentious bourgeois respectability is sacrificed on the altar of spontaneous human instinct – throws into relief the sense of liberation derived from the night she spends dancing and watching fireworks in the Métro with Fred and his fellow eccentrics. The underground here takes on a curative function, providing Héléna with a means by which to escape the disillusionment of conventional life, thus rehabilitating her mindset. It is indeed no coincidence that just as 'Batman' had earlier been the butt of Fred's joke following the theft (by Jean-Louis) of the unnamed female passenger's handbag, so the reborn Héléna now vents her spleen on the same inane officer with her yarn about losing her passport. What all of this demonstrates is that far from a claustrophobic setting, the Métro comes to represent a site of personal liberation, a claim which can be further verified with reference to an energetic tracking shot late in the film (75″), structurally similar to the opening car chase sequence, showing how Fred takes advantage of his physical environment to effect his escape from the Métro police, who are left stumbling in pursuit. Thus, while the bumbling officers, seeking to uphold the norms of law and order in the underground, are seen to be frustrated by their confusing surroundings – as Inspector Gesberg himself points out, 'It's big here; we get lost ourselves sometimes'[9] – Fred increasingly takes advantage of his circumstances, outwitting his adversaries in dazzling displays of dexterity. As Berry comments:

> [T]he progress of the hero . . . through this underworld is like a rite of passage in which his identity is transformed and through which he seems to be increasingly imbued with magic powers. He becomes able to perform several vanishing tricks and to practise the art of escapology: at the beginning he escapes his pursuers by jumping under the wheels of the train and crawling along the tracks of the métro; he begins a science-fiction style journey down a series of corridors, armed with a tubular glass light, as if both a sword and a wand, like the famous laser weapon in *Star Wars*; he falls through a grill in the floor and, unharmed, dangles in space; much later he disappears mysteriously from inside a lift. (Berry 2000: 15–16)

The key point here is that Fred is able to manipulate successfully his physical surroundings to meet his own ends, thereby enabling him to affirm his individuality. Rather than stifling creativity, *Subway*'s physical enclosure becomes a liberating force for Fred, whose real sense of imprisonment is that of the imposed structure of conventional society's laws and customs for which he has little time, a claim supported by the rejection of received wisdom announced by the film's epigraph: '"To be is to do" – Socrates; "To do is to be" – Sartre; "Do be do be do" – Sinatra'. Inasmuch as it provides Fred with the means by which to achieve his lifelong ambition – forming and managing a rock group – the Métro itself becomes a vehicle for Fred's creativity, equipping him with the miscellaneous musicians he needs to realise his dream, a dream denied him on the outside following a serious automobile accident which had severed his vocal chords as a child. A scene showing the group rehearsing (70″) bears witness to its hypnotic effect on Fred, who finds himself fantasising about Héléna – his other fixation – as he listens. Rejecting the cosy reassurances of conventional society, the lyrics of the song performed during this rendition, highlighting life as 'totally mystery', perfectly reflect Fred's own alternative mentality. In the final sequence, moreover, we see how Fred's musical creation is able to transcend differences of class and ethnicity in the audience as a testimony to his personal idealism. As Phil Powrie observes: '[T]hrough music the film constructs a rejection of existing heterogeneous social formations; the creation of the band is both a marginal, counter-cultural activity, as well as a very personal project for Fred. The final sequence substitutes simple and magical solutions for the complexity of urban existence' (Powrie 1997: 125–6; see also Hayward 1998: 129). In as much as it supplies him with the musical experience he craves, the Métro here assumes a therapeutic role for Fred, helping him to rediscover his lost voice. Indeed, while Susan Hayward is right to highlight that his fascination for the band ultimately leads to Fred's downfall,[10] it should be stressed that he dies in rapture, shrouded in song (the principal lyric of which is, poignantly, 'people kill people'), and even momentarily conquers death to forge a final communion with the music he has created in his very own 'imprisoned freedom'.

In *Subway*, then, far from representing an impediment to Fred's predisposition to freedom and revolt, the physical enclosure of the Métro becomes a vehicle for liberation and self-discovery. For Fred, as for Héléna, the underground setting is a catalyst for personal fulfilment, enabling the former to realise a lifelong dream and the latter to purge herself of her bourgeois pretensions, via the precedent set by Fred. For Fred, moreover, the Métro takes on magical properties, empowering him to outsmart the upholders of conventional law and order who are portrayed as inept and weak by comparison. Confirming his status as social rebel, and fuelling the film's diegesis, the Métro thus assumes a key role in the construction of Fred's persona, in keeping with Gardies's view that space and identity are intricately entwined.

Like *Subway*, *Nikita* is set in a labyrinthine environment below the surface of conventional reality – an underground organisation forming part of the French Secret Service. And, as in *Subway*, the décor of *Nikita* has a key role to play in the film's diegetic structure. Hayward is telling in this matter when she comments that *Nikita*'s 'décor had to work to substantiate the totally unsubstantiable storyline. Hence the mixture of the baroque and the modern in terms of architecture and design to provide a real but menacing atmosphere for this narrative on State terrorism' (Hayward 1998: 19). Yet if the enclosed space of *Subway*'s subterranean setting positively reinforces Fred's persona, for the protagonist of *Nikita*, by contrast, the physical enclosure in which she finds herself incarcerated (both literally and figuratively) is inextricably linked to her sense of psychological imprisonment, from which she finds it impossible to escape. A drug addict living on the margins of society, the Nikita we initially witness cuts a desperate figure who is totally alienated from the norms of conventional society. With neither friends nor family to support her,[11] she is socially excluded, drifting in a world that has abandoned her. From the outset, she is represented as a mental captive, conditioned by her physical situation. Throughout the opening raid sequence, while her fellow bandits Rico and Zap revel in the violent confrontation with the police, Nikita remains passive and detached, blending in with the background as a seemingly helpless victim desperately awaiting her next fix. Just as she cannot evade her cravings – 'I want some, I want some' is Nikita's repeated appeal – so she is unable to escape from her physical confinement: her psychological situation is reflected in her physical situation throughout this opening scene. Furthermore, following her cold-blooded murder of the policeman and subsequent sentencing, we again witness a Nikita whose state of mind is mirrored by her physical circumstances. Awaking to a bright light in a bleached-white room symbolising her own stripped identity (12″), Nikita's dazed and confused psychological state is conveyed in the harsh physical environment in which she now finds herself interned. A shot showing her bare feet momentarily touching the bare tiles reveals the cold, uncomfortable setting of her cell, which poignantly reflects Nikita's emotional insecurity as she desperately questions whether she has died and gone to heaven.

Not unlike Fred in *Subway*, Nikita is, on the one hand, a social deviant rebelling against conventional society. Early scenes in the film showing her violently attacking the inspector during her police interview (8″) and being dragged literally kicking and screaming from the courtroom (10″) vividly illustrate Nikita's defiance of, and revolt against, patriarchy. Yet, on the other hand, she is portrayed as a victim of society. In the opening raid sequence, surrounded by gunfire, she adopts a foetal posture (2″) – a trait later reiterated in the violent exchange in the Train Bleu kitchen, following Nikita's first assassination mission (43″), and during her final, failed mission, following the intervention of the volatile Victor (92″) – which points up her inherent vulnerability, while during the administering of her injection (11″), she desperately calls out for her mother as further confirmation of Nikita's defencelessness in the face of the state monolith. Nikita's first encounter with Bob (13″) bears testimony to this dual persona which once again finds concrete expression in her spatial situation. At the start of this sequence, Nikita is depicted as a defenceless individual, insecure in her new and confusing environment. Dressed in white, she is indistinguishable from the barren background of her physical space. The arrival of Bob – wearing a smart black suit to illustrate by contrast both his power over Nikita and his domination over his physical circumstances – acts as a catalyst for Nikita's act of revolt: in her eyes, he is a figure of authority against which she is naturally programmed to rebel. It is surely significant that Bob makes a conscious effort to put Nikita at ease by physically moving his desk closer to her in an attempt to surmount the psychological and physical barrier separating them. A gesture of his immediate fascination for Nikita? Perhaps. Whatever the truth of this, it is clear that in the following scene (16″), once she has been briefed on her situation, Nikita's vulnerability makes way for her instinctive rebelliousness which comes strongly to the fore as she desperately tries to seize control, firstly by attacking Bob and subsequently by holding him at gunpoint as she attempts to make her escape. Yet this act of revolt is soon defeated by Bob who remains in control throughout and, in the next scene (19″), Nikita – shot in the leg for her act of defiance – returns to the submissive and subdued character she assumed at the start of their initial interview. It is the impregnability of the physical surroundings and protective state apparatus that thwarts Nikita's reckless attempt to break free in this early sequence, thus establishing the film's spatial parameters in the construction of Nikita's subservient persona. While physical enclosure in *Subway* neither prevents Fred from realising his ambitions, nor obstructs the development of his identity, Nikita's quest for freedom and revolt is unable to transcend the limitations of her physical environment, so that her identity remains the property of the state. As her graffitied cell walls, sporting statements such as 'No Visitor' and 'Get Out' (30″) testify, Nikita is in revolt against, but is ultimately unable to overcome, the confines of her incarcerated space.

The truth of the matter is that Nikita is both physically and psychologically enslaved. Imprisoned in her compound where she is recreated by the machinery of the state, she becomes, in Bob's terminology, 'an element of the centre'. Her physical environment and personal identity are equally determined by the state. Under constant surveillance and awarded the new name 'Marie' and the code name 'Joséphine', Nikita is 'institutionalised in all senses of the word' (Hayward 1998: 160).[12] A scene showing Nikita, hermaphrodite and clown-like, searching for a countenance in front of Amande's theatrical mirror (33″), bears eloquent witness to her quest for identity in this state of emotional and physical servitude. It is also important to recognise that the debt she owes to society for having killed a policeman, coupled with the fact that she has been given a second chance – to serve her country – consolidate Nikita's sense of mental captivity vis-à-vis her state superiors, a mindset which is in turn reflected in the sense of claustrophobia conditioning her physical confinement throughout the film. Thus, from the prison of social exclusion which defines her character at the start of the film, Nikita subsequently finds herself contained in an alternative incarcerated space, where she will be equally unable to assume a real identity. In other words, she is invited to leave one underworld only to enter another.

Moreover, even when she is released from her physical detainment, Nikita's sense of freedom remains an imprisoned one. Indeed, in the film's social and open spaces such as the Train Bleu restaurant and Venice, Nikita's persona continues to be conditioned by, and filtered through, a repressive mental apparatus. The Train Bleu sequence (39″) is particularly telling here, in that it represents the site of Nikita's 'liberation' from her state enclosure. An analysis of this pivotal scene confirms that Nikita's state of mind is still inextricably bound up with her physical situation. Supposedly a treat to celebrate her twenty-third birthday, this excursion to the plush Parisian restaurant marks a radical departure from the enclosed spaces comprising the film hitherto. Red velvet curtains unveil a deeply majestic setting, and wide-angle shots reveal a rich décor far removed from Nikita's (former) graffitied cell inside the compound. Yet even before the true motives of Bob's invitation to dinner become clear, Nikita appears imprisoned in her new-found freedom. She is bewildered and ill-at-ease in her luxurious environment, and is apprehensive in marked contrast to Bob's calm self-assurance. Throughout, power and authority remain with Bob, who offers first verbal encouragement to the insecure Nikita, before presenting her with the gift which, seemingly reassured, she embraces with childlike delight. The point of view shot showing Nikita opening her present – not a token of love, but a 'Desert Eagle' gun – produces a sudden change in atmosphere, however, and Bob's rapid explanation of the mission which Nikita must now execute has a disorientating effect on his companion. In the preceding scene (37′), we witness Amande offering Nikita a pair of black velvet gloves (an emblem of what Amande calls 'the pleasure of a woman') and now, dazed with confusion, Nikita carefully takes them off, thus removing the veneer of femininity in her (male) role of assassin. It is no coincidence that, having successfully carried out Bob's assassination orders, Nikita finds herself confined to the gents toilets, with the anticipated escape route literally blocked up. Her desperate desire to escape is once again frustrated by her physical environment – which here has clear patriarchal connotations – and she has to rely on her own resourcefulness to survive. Survive she may, outmanoeuvring her male adversaries in an energetic exchange of gunfire in the restaurant's kitchen, but the fact that Nikita ends this sequence in a rubbish heap suggests that she has not achieved any substantive sense of freedom in this, her first night in the real world for several years. As this and her subsequent missions reveal, she remains a pawn of the state, incarcerated in a male-dominated space.

Indeed, while her success in the Train Bleu mission results in Nikita's liberation from her state internment, she remains unable to purge herself of her patriarchal fetters as she attempts to readjust to the outside world. In the apparent freedom she has been granted, Nikita continues to be psychologically imprisoned. Open spaces such as the street (51″) and the supermarket (52″) appear as threatening and alien environments to her, while her refusal to answer questions about her past means that even her domestic space with Marco is psychologically repressive. (It is interesting to note in passing that the spontaneous way in which she picks up Marco in the supermarket, before taking him home for dinner and sex (53″), provides an emotional release for Nikita after her years of physical and emotional incarceration.) Nowhere is the link between Nikita's psychological and physical imprisonment more evident than in Venice, ironically the setting for her honeymoon with Marco (69″). It is here that the tension between Nikita's private life with Marco and her public duty towards Bob and the state – a tension which is already well to the fore in the preceding dinner party sequence (65″) – reaches new heights, as her two worlds collide in telling fashion. As the sequence opens, we see the newly-weds enjoying Venice's open spaces, and the accompanying soundtrack is both diverting and uplifting, marking an apparent liberation from the film's claustrophobic intensity hitherto. Moreover, once back in the hotel bedroom, Nikita's sense of freedom continues to find eloquent expression; her dynamism in this scene lies in stark contrast to Marco's fatigue. However, the telephone call announcing Nikita's next mission transforms the bedroom from an intimate space for lovers into an enclosed and suffocating prison for Nikita, a transformation which is reflected in her own movement from carefree to subservient individual as the scene progresses. Entering the enclosure of the bathroom to prepare for her assignment, Nikita finds herself boxed in, both physically and psychologically. Just as she cannot escape her state of physical incarceration, so she is unable to avoid the confrontation between her private and public worlds, caught between on the one hand Marco's emotional declaration, and on the other her superior's cold orders to kill. The idea that Nikita is particularly vulnerable throughout this scene is confirmed by the fact that she is dressed only in her underwear, and that she is forced to handle a gun, the size of which dwarfs her. She is also unable to contain her feelings as she awaits news of her target: listening to Marco, Nikita's emotional insecurity is once again clearly apparent. To this it should be added that her target on this occasion is a fellow female, thus heightening the tension between Nikita the public assassin and Nikita the private woman, who is here ordered by her patriarchal superior to dispatch 'one of her own'. A shot using a telescopic lens showing Nikita's eye looking at her intended target poignantly captures the intensity of the conflict between woman as creator and (here) woman as eliminator of life. The mission duly completed, Nikita ends the scene psychologically torn and physically contained. Unable to open up emotionally to Marco and confined to the bathroom, she is emphatically imprisoned, both mentally and physically.

It should be clear from the above that, throughout, Nikita is unable to break free from the patriarchal orbit into which her sense of self falls. She is a character in search of an identity, since both at the start of the film, when she appears as a social pariah, and subsequently, when she is recreated by the state, her own individuality is consistently and manifestly denied. Or, to put the matter differently, Nikita's psychological imprisonment remains unable to overcome the confines of her physical environment, a point leading us to the film's dénouement, where the space Nikita occupies is one of lack, of absence. The failure of her final mission (84″) confirms Nikita as a character in crisis. Forced to assume the identity of the (male) ambassador following Victor's 'cleaning', she is once again psychologically dominated, suffocating in her mental prison as she watches the assignment which she had been planning for six months implode into violence and chaos. Unable to escape from her sense of physical and psychological incarceration, which finds potent expression throughout this sequence, Nikita's only choice, ultimately, is to disappear. Correspondingly, she elects absence in the pursuit of personal identity, a decision which, on the one hand, attests to Nikita's inability to effect change in her life while she remains a prisoner of the state and which, as such, may be deemed an admission of defeat on her part. Yet, on the other hand, as Hayward submits of the Nikita at the close of the film:

> [A]bsence becomes a form of resistance: no one can teach or reach her now. Her power is to become the unembodied body without power. Paradoxically, there is considerable power in Nikita's disembodied powerlessness

because she no longer functions as an assertion of male power – she marks through her absence. (Hayward 1998: 157)

That Nikita 'marks through her absence' both Bob and Marco is clear by their shared avowal at the very end of the film that '*we* will miss her'. It is unclear, however, how far Nikita herself will be able to exploit this new state of 'non-being' finally to assert her own identity.

To conclude, both *Subway* and *Nikita* are set in underground environments, each defined by a sense of 'imprisoned freedom'; but, as I have demonstrated, the interaction of space and identity differs significantly in the two films. On the one hand, for Fred, physical enclosure does not impede his quest for freedom: liberated from the fetters of conventional society, the protagonist of *Subway* finds meaning in the alternative realm of the Métro by transforming its topos of danger and claustrophobia into an alternative space which enables him to attain self-fulfilment in the midst of death. On the other hand, for Nikita, physical incarceration is inextricably bound up with a sense of psychological imprisonment, so that any sense of freedom she has remains conditioned by a repressive mental apparatus, controlled by her patriarchal superiors. Furthermore, while *Subway*'s subterranean setting becomes a vehicle for the development of Fred's identity, manipulating as he does his physical environment to meet his own ends, Nikita remains defined by her incapacity to escape from her physical situation, thereby suppressing any sense of self. It follows that, while Fred projects an image of masculinity which is active and achieving – he dies with a song on his lips, having realised his lifelong ambition in his state of incarceration – Nikita projects an alienated and restrictive image of femininity, since she is unable to assume her real identity in her patriarchal prison and leaves the film defined by absence.[13] In the final analysis, then, while in *Subway* physical enclosure is not a serious impediment to (male) freedom and revolt, in *Nikita* (female) psychological imprisonment is seen to be intricately linked to physical enclosure. In both films, moreover, it is Besson's use of space which lends density and resonance to his characters, while also serving as a vehicle for the diegesis, in accordance with Gardies's view that 'Space undoubtedly constitutes one of the active forces of the narrative' (Gardies 1993: 150).

References

Berry, D. (2000), 'Underground cinema: French visions of the Metro', in M. Konstantarakos (ed.), *Spaces in European Cinema* (Exeter: Intellect), pp. 8–22.
Brown, J. A. (1996), 'Gender and the action heroine: hardbodies and the *Point*

of No Return', *Cinema Journal*, 35:3, pp. 52–71.
Gardies, A. (1993), *L'Espace au cinéma* (Paris: Méridiens Klincksieck).
Hayward, S. (1998), *Luc Besson* (Manchester: Manchester University Press).
Konstantarakos, M. (ed.) (2000), *Spaces in European Cinema* (Exeter: Intellect).
Powrie, P. (1997), '*Subway*: identity and inarticulacy', in P. Powrie, *French Cinema in the 1980s: Nostalgia and the Crisis of Masculinity* (Oxford: Clarendon, 1997), pp. 121–9.
Reader, K. A. (2000), 'Subtext: Paris of Alexandre Trauner', in M. Konstantarakos (ed.), *Spaces in European Cinema* (Exeter: Intellect), pp. 35–41.

Notes

1 In the words of the blurb, 'cinema is above all and fundamentally an art of space'. For an interesting European perspective on what, until recently, has been a largely neglected aspect of cinema studies, see Konstantarakos (2000).
2 As 'master(s) of space' (Gardies 1993: 67), spectators engage in a 'spectatorial contract' (Gardies 1993: 65) with the film by which to interpret the images they see on the screen, thus enabling them to regulate the film's narrative structure.
3 As Gardies goes on to observe, 'all narratives, whatever the medium, tell the story, either explicitly or implicitly, openly or between the lines, of humanity's relationship to space' (Gardies 1993: 142–3). The relationship between characters and setting is particularly resonant in Besson's films, which, shot in Cinemascope, point up tensions between individuals and their spatial situation; see Hayward 1998: 17.
4 'In the metro we discover the amalgamation of two topographical inventions, the collision of two disturbing phenomenological creations: the tunnel and the maze. The maze is normally a complex network of pathways above the surface and often open to the skies, like the maze at Hampton Court. Enclosed and enveloped by the tunnel and buried underground, the maze is transformed into the labyrinth, a topos of mental confusion, oneiric terror and claustrophobia' (Berry 2000: 8).
5 Signifies the number of minutes into the film.
6 *Subway*'s sets were designed by Alexandre Trauner who, as Keith Reader reminds us, is also credited for the set designs of films as diverse as Carné's *Les Enfants du paradis* (1945) and Welles's *Othello* (1959) (Reader 2000: 35–41). As Reader perceptively remarks, the scrutiny of space in cinema studies can usefully embrace the role played by set designers like Trauner, whose work reinforces the visual impact of film. Nowhere is the importance of visual impact more evident than in *Subway*, where décor is intricately linked to the film's spatial intensity.
7 It is worth noting that Besson deliberately wanted to avoid direct realism in his recreation of the Métro in *Subway*, preferring instead the look of the

underground space-station – a choice which was not always well received by critics, however (see Hayward 1998: 39–40).

8   As Hayward rightly points out, a core theme of all of Besson's films is that of escape from the constraints of the social world: 'Hence the presence in his films of the underworld (literal and figurative) as a major attraction' (Hayward 1998: 19).

9   This remark lies in stark contrast to the lawbreaker roller-skater Jean-Louis, who 'knows the corridors inside out', thus highlighting the resourcefulness of the Métro-dwellers as against the ineptitude of the Métro police, led by the comical 'Batman' and 'Robin' (ironically deemed 'the best' by the inspector). Another of the film's high-energy chase sequences showing Jean-Louis successfully evading his police pursuers through the maze of the Métro (36″) tellingly illustrates this disparity. Although, by the end of the film, Fred will be dead and Jean-Louis captured – singlehandedly by Inspector Gesberg (73″) – Héléna's ultimate rejection of the standards of conventional society indicates that the balance between law and order and social deviancy remains at odds as the film reaches its climax.

10 Fred's 'transgressive behaviour (his voyeuristically watching the band, his own fetish, and not the woman, the traditional object of the gaze) puts him on display to the predatory, surveilling and phallic eye. He is unintentionally, unwittingly hiding in the light' (Hayward 1998: 105–6).

11 For an informed discussion of the death of the family in Besson's films generally, see Hayward 1998: 127–68.

12 As Hayward also reminds us, 'Nikita' is actually a Russian name for a boy, thus heightening still further the confused question of identity in the film (Hayward 1998: 115). The ambivalent question of gender representation in *Nikita* (or, more specifically, the American remake) is explored by Brown (1996).

13 For an elaboration of the question of male subjectivity and female otherness in *Nikita*, see Hayward 1998: 110–18.

9

Nikita: consumer culture's killer instinct and the imperial imperative

Hilary Ann Radner

In a widely cited examination of French culture, Kristin Ross isolates a number of themes that she sees as characterising post-Second World War France in the 1950s and 1960s (Ross, 1996). These include: the new centrality of the consumer durable, in particular the automobile, but also the refrigerator; the focus on hygiene, 'nettoyage' (cleaning), as a vehicle for product usage and consumption; the creation of a new middle-class couple; the re-articulation of the social body as quantifiable and anonymous, as opposed to a collectivity of individuals with specific rights; and, finally, the suppression of France's imperial past in favour of the new demographic state. Though these same themes (preserved through the 1970s and 1980s) are reiterated in *Nikita* (Besson, 1990), indicating the continued relevance of Ross's analysis, the film highlights an issue ignored by Ross, the problem of the single woman and her importance to consumer culture.

The Single Girl is, nonetheless, present in French New Wave culture as exemplified by roles such as that incarnated by the cult French actress of the period, Françoise Dorléac, in the 1964 film, *La Peau douce* (*Soft Skin*), directed by François Truffaut. The film recounts the disintegration of the main character's marriage as a result of his affair with Dorléac who plays a stewardess. This relationship is predicated on Dorléac's beauty as an object that can be consumed, most strikingly in the photographs that her lover (an obvious stand-in for Truffaut himself) takes of her. He is routinely depicted as observing Nicole: her well-turned ankles as she changes shoes on the job, her hands, her hair. He disapproves of her jeans, and she changes into the skirt that he prefers. He buys her stockings (she requests DIM), and while she sleeps he gently caresses her legs sheathed in the 'Scandale sable' stockings he bought her instead.

Dorléac as the stewardess incarnates the model of consumer femininity associated with Bardot, an anti-high-fashion youth-oriented ideal. Her skinny runway-model image belies her intimate connection with the obvious 'sexiness' of Bardot, a connection manifested through the consumer culture affinities of both stars. Vincendeau comments: 'New Wave women's looks . . . fitted the surface modernity of the new Fifth Republic, in love with the consumer goods of American-identified modernity such as cars' (Vincendeau 2000: 119). With her blue jeans, her nude DIM stockings, her taste for nightclubs and dancing, Dorléac's character represents the New Wave as it was understood in its time: as a wider cultural phenomenon that extended to all aspects of life, especially among the young. Economically independent but not rich, beautiful but also adept in the arts of feminine adornment, she is always meticulously dressed and coiffed, her make-up impeccable. She exercises, but does not read. She is trilingual, but without any intellectual curiosity. She is apparently frigid, and only enjoyed sex with a man she claimed more or less raped her. Her seeming promiscuity is without compulsion. It is the result of her desire to please, rather than to please herself. She is brutally frank and, as she comments, makes no demands. Her apparent docility suggests that she represents an ideal of femininity that stands in contradistinction to that represented by Anne Parillaud in Luc Besson's 1990 film, *Nikita*. Though there are real differences, many differences are more apparent than profound. Nikita, and killer-*femmes* like her, seemingly invoke a femininity grounded in autonomy and action that refuses the passive role of object-to-be-looked-at associated with consumer culture. In fact, I shall argue that the killer-*femme* is yet another means of circulating feminine consumer culture at a global level as part of the youth culture movement.

Ross's analysis undervalues the implications of this new femininity represented by Dorléac's role in *La Peau douce*, and fashioned for a global youth culture in the late 1950s and 1960s. Though her study cites a number of significant French women who make their lives outside the home, notably Françoise Sagan and her coterie, Ross's focus on the feminine role in the home perhaps justifies the lack of attention afforded the French single girl. In Ross's analysis, there is no discussion of the new feminine star emblematised by Brigitte Bardot, who discards high fashion in favour of ready-to-wear, and evokes a culture of consumer non-durables, as opposed to consumer durables. Vincendeau remarks: 'Bardot's championing of new fashion coincided with important changes in the clothing industry . . . The fashion industry was also waking up to the power of the young consumer' (Vincendeau 2000: 89). Bardot and her contemporaries establish a significant tradition in French culture which equates this new consumer femininity with youth and availability, a tradition continued in the image of woman offered by *Nikita*.[1]

The link between the New Wave and the present in *Nikita*, its feminine genealogy, is provided by Jeanne Moreau in her role as Amande, who literally gives Parillaud, as Nikita, the instruction necessary for her transformation within the film's narrative. *Nikita* recounts the rehabilitation of a drug addict, who becomes an assassin for the state, but it is also a 'transformation film' like *Pretty Woman* (Garry Marshall, 1990).[2] Jeanne Moreau as Amande is part of a team that trains Nikita in her development from drug addict to killer. Moreau as Amande adds to Nikita's arsenal the weapons of seduction and vulnerability. Moreau's history as a legendary star of the New Wave generation adds another dimension to her role as Amande and that of Nikita, locating the two characters in a tradition of 'Frenchness'. Parillaud's articulation of a child woman, a sex kitten à la Bardot (albeit a kitten with claws), who becomes a deadly agent, highlights the contradictions of the new feminine, in which youth and its implications of vulnerability and dependence must be reconciled with the ideals of autonomy and self-determination. This new feminine does not break with the past and is explicitly linked to the New Wave iconic actress, Jeanne Moreau. Vincendeau comments: 'Moreau plays godmother to young killer Nikita (Anne Parillaud) by giving her lessons in femininity, translated as seduction' (Vincendeau 2000: 129). In many ways, then, Nikita learns to be 'feminine', or at least to exploit her femininity as well as her propensity for violence. The combination of seduction and violence as a peculiarly 1990s reconciliation of the contradictory demands placed upon women may in part explain the popularity of this figure, which I call for want of a better term, the killer-*femme*.

Susan Hayward quite rightly points out that Besson's work in this period is marked by the social position of youth in France that resulted from the Mitterrand years. The character Nikita commences at the beginning of the film as an exemplar of disaffected youth, of the 'new poor' (Hayward 1998: 52). However, as a petty criminal, though guilty of homicide, she is not fatal enough. The state offers to rehabilitate her as a state assassin. A deal is struck: she will be taught not only how to be fatally fatal, but also how to be a feminine consumer, a single girl in consumer culture terms. This is an improbable narrative that combines the makeover film and the thriller. Guy Austin aptly sums up the film: 'The resultant narrative is divided almost exactly into two halves: the first relating Nikita's transformation during three years in a secure training centre; the second her life outside her subsequent mission and eventual desertion' (Austin 1996: 130). Once Nikita proves herself by successfully completing an assassination assignment, she is let free on the world, no longer an unkempt juvenile delinquent, but a snappy single girl in a stylish little suit.

The characteristics of the single girl are defined above all by Helen Gurley Brown in *Cosmopolitan Magazine*, which she edited from the 1960s into the 1990s.[3] Dorléac as Nicole in *La Peau douce* incarnates the ideal of the single girl as initially defined in the 1960s by Gurley Brown. I argue elsewhere that this ideal continues to dominate feminine consumer culture (Radner, 1995). For example, in *Legally Blonde* (Robert Luketic, 2001), *Cosmopolitan* magazine is cited as the bible of consumer culture and is shown as imparting the knowledge that enables the heroine of the film to win her case in court. One might say that in *Legally Blonde*, as in *Nikita*, the heroine (played by Reese Witherspoon) also deploys her knowledge of consumer culture in order to be legally fatal as well as blonde (she is not naturally blonde). Nikita is not blonde, and though she changes her hair colour at will, she is never blonde, but rather true to the original Musidora/Theda Bara type of the dark *femme fatale*. The television version, *La Femme Nikita* (USA Network, 1997–2001), re-enacts the transformation of its heroine (who is naturally blonde) in its credit sequence, just in case the viewers might forget that good grooming is a crucial tool in the secret agent's arsenal. Nikita and her fellow television killer-*femmes* are expensively and sublimely dressed – 'fashion divas' (Tung 2004: 97). Certainly, the show served as a vehicle for Costume National, a European Italian-based designer shoes and clothing line; however, more importantly, the television show underlines the ways in which the context of this macha killerette figure creates an environment that is conducive to the cultivation of consumer culture in particular, a consumer culture directed at the feminine consumer.

Hayward argues convincingly that, from the perspective of a masculine spectator, Nikita, the character and her image, offers up a specular fetish that serves to deny masculine anxiety about castration (Hayward 1998: 116–17). But what about the feminine spectator? A convincing argument is that the macha killerette satisfies feminine desires for autonomy and agency, while allaying masculine fears and feeding masculine desires. Ultimately, the macha killerette is not dangerous – at least not to those men capable of sexually fascinating her – yet she appears to offer the fantasy of being 'transgressive and obtaining freedom' to a female spectatorship (Hayward 1998: 110). In this sense, she is the result of the condensation of two contradictory forces, of a deliberate ambiguity that attempts to resolve the irresolvable conflict between new feminine ideals of autonomy and agency, and masculine needs for possession, in particular sexual possession.

The macha killerette is a figure that answers both to an identificatory and to a possessive mode of desire, in which to be and to have are equally important. She is a cross-over figure, not only in terms of the desires that she mobilises, but also in terms of the roles that she plays. Nikita cross-dresses from drug addict to single girl to lethal killer. In so doing she mobilises a number of contradictory fantasies within a single figure. Her mastery of the feminine arts is one sign of her ability to cross-dress. Hayward remarks that 'Nikita crosses gender boundaries', suggesting the importance of the external signs of her transformations, such as lipstick (Hayward 1998: 112). From a cinematic perspective, Nikita 'cross-dresses', in Yvonne Tasker's terms, between genres as well as gender. She literally cross-dresses when she behaves and dresses like a teenage male at the beginning of the film, and when she dresses like a man near the end of the film in the course of an operation as an agent for the state. She also cross-dresses as part of the transformation process inherent in her makeover.[4] She crosses over from androgynous childhood to seductive femininity, from feral cat to sex kitten.

Why do killer-femmes need lipstick? Why do killers cross over into femmes? Certainly the femininity of the killerette functions as a 'cover' that deceives those around her who, distracted by her femininity, do not see her as potentially violent, or, in more mundane terms, capable of decisive and potentially disruptive action. Though female spectators as a rule will not be called upon to kill, women are increasingly required to assume roles, leadership roles for example, traditionally reserved for men. In this sense there is a very real invitation here in the figure of the killerette, or in her more benign 'legally blonde' counterpart to 'act' – to cross gender boundaries. This invitation is, however, accompanied by an equally strong invitation to construct the feminine body as a visible presence that conforms to the codes of consumer culture (as signified through such practices as wearing lipstick) in a manner that ultimately confirms the significance of masculine desire as the sign of approval. Finally, the feminine position is never a stable position, though its appearance can be fixed, as it were, through the deployment of consumer culture.

The connection between consumer culture, the makeover and what I call the killer-*femme* is usually maintained in the reproduction of the stereotype, despite the fact that, initially at least, the relationship between consumer culture and the killer seems counter-intuitive. *G.I. Jane* (Ridley Scott, 1997), in which Demi Moore strips herself back and reconstructs herself as a terminator-like killing machine, echoing the transformation of Linda Hamilton in *Terminator 2: Judgement Day* (James Cameron, 1991), at least makes sense. Triceps and biceps, muscles in general, come in handy when performing feats of violence; lipstick seems less useful. Both Moore and Hamilton detailed the process whereby the new killer body was 'produced' in the popular press and in women's magazines more particularly.[5] Their extra-textual transformations were reiterated within the film, lending narrative weight to the 'new' bodies that they offered up to the film spectator's gaze – bodies that were ready for action.

Nikita initially seems to have reversed the makeover process portrayed in these films. Rather, the makeover in *Nikita* is the classic transformation advocated by Helen Gurley Brown from 'mouseburger' to 'glamour puss',[6] only in this case more accurately from drug addict to starlette. The makeover as portrayed by the film corresponds very closely to its historical definition in popular culture (Fraser, 2003). Outside the film, in terms of the lead actress's preparation, it is a different matter. Thus, Anne Parillaud describes the manner in which she trains for the film in the same terms as those described by Hamilton in preparing for her role in *Terminator 2*, as an arduous challenge that is 'unnatural' to her.[7]

As a film actress, Parillaud is already the seductive starlette that Nikita becomes, but she does not have the strength to portray a killer convincingly, and it is precisely this strength – or this musculature – that she must acquire under the film director's tutelage as preparation for taking on the role. Hayward describes her transformation as a star persona: 'With the release of the film, Parillaud went from bimbo-starlette to ferocious androgyne to lethally armed female' (Hayward 1998: 55). Within the film, Nikita 'naturally' has the strength and particularly the stamina to 'represent' violence – literally, to kill. These are skills that she refines at the training centre. 'Femininity', however, it would appear, is not 'natural' (at least to Nikita as a character in the film, if not to Parillaud in real life), and is something that she must learn at the training centre where she undergoes a complete makeover, a transformation of which Helen Gurley Brown would approve.

Nikita is ultimately, and paradoxically, a free agent, like Helen Gurley Brown's Single Girl, even if one must argue that her agency is limited. She is outside the law and family structure. She is not tied to the family. In particular, her identity as a woman is defined outside marriage. In the film, her father is never mentioned. Though she calls for her mother at the moment when she believes she is going to be put to death, she is told that her mother believes her dead. She has no responsibilities, no ties except to herself and the imperatives of her own survival. At the same time, as a figure, as the image of an idealised feminine, embodied by the single girl, she must enable, or at least represent, the possibility of marriage, and, certainly, at the very least, of seduction. To be fatally fatal, a woman must be duplicitous; she must hide her lethal capacity beneath her femininity. Part of Nikita's training, then, consists of transforming herself into the sort of woman whom a man might marry – or at least whose appearance might suggest, however erroneously, that possibility. In this sense the film offers a perverse rewriting of the marriage plot, associated with the romance, in which disappearance takes the place of marriage as the ultimate conclusion of the film.[8] Ironically, the film is unable to resolve the problem of the single woman as a feminine ideal. Within the world of *Nikita*, femininity is both necessary and fatal to the single girl.

Hayward quite rightly underlines the ambivalence of the film's ending in which Nikita disappears (Hayward 1998: 110–18). In one sense, we might see Nikita's rehabilitation as complete. From being an asocial, amoral agent of her own most immediate desires, she becomes transformed, humanised and able to recognise the other as human, as like herself. She rejects the Cleaner (Jean Reno), the agent sent to help her on her last mission, and in so doing rejects her previous self, the violent delinquent, but also ensures that she must disappear. She becomes feminine, capable of empathy as a sign of her humanness, and also of her femininity; this femininity proves fatal to her.[9]

By acknowledging and foregrounding the impossibility of the feminine position (in its irresolvable contradictions), the film clearly continues a certain tradition within French cinema in which the woman serves to represent masculine desire while gesturing towards a new tradition inaugurated by the single girl in which a woman performs according to her desires. *Et Dieu créa la femme/And God Created Woman* (Vadim, 1957), the film that propelled Brigitte Bardot to international stardom, was already informed by this contradiction between appearance and performance. In the stereotype of the killer-*femme*, this contradiction is rendered in bold, marked out as contradiction, highlighted through the problem of violence. The boldness with which this contradiction is announced is an important facet of this post-feminist icon, that of the macha killerette.

Though Ross fails to recognize the importance of the Single Girl to the new culture of consumerism that continues to mark the France of the 1970s and 1980s, she does observe that it was the feminine role to carry out the demands of the reconfiguration of everyday life in French post-World War II culture (Ross 1996: 77). The feminine ideal thus moved from homemaker to consumer-oriented housewife. This movement suggests why the Single Girl emerged as a privileged consumer, initially embodied by Brigitte Bardot, who technically was married more often than not, or involved in high-profile relationships, all of which ended disastrously (Rihoit, 1986). Brigitte Bardot was in this sense a transitional figure, both single girl dashing from nightclubs to the beach, as well the bourgeois housewife. The ideal exemplified by the character Nikita is far more violent than her more innocent predecessors.

Though marked by violence, when not in her role as state assassin, as a character Nikita is first and foremost a consumer; she exhibits no vestiges of the pre-consumer culture housewife. Her first act as a homemaker is to purchase canned ravioli, a gesture that supports the new ideology of consumption of ready-made goods. It is also a gesture that directly affronts the French tradition of *haute cuisine*. Outside the centre, Nikita's life is defined by consumer culture, in particular by the middle-class aspirations of the consumer couple. Marco (Nikita's lover), in spite of his activities as a craftsman, desperately attempts to create a relationship with Nikita that corresponds to that of an ideal middle-class couple with its intimate dinner parties, champagne, flowers, family and familial histories. The sanity and sanctity of this relationship is assured by the newly cleaned and renovated apartment that appears to emerge as a magical result (because of the marked ellipsis in time) of the couple's lovemaking. Marco aspires to move into the middle class, leaving his job as a cashier in a supermarket with the hope of founding his own company and moving to a bigger apartment, more suited to his consumer-renovated 'princess', Nikita.

Typically, then, the film embodies the aspects of consumer culture in France that Ross describes as emerging in post-Second World War France, and which is also represented in *La Peau douce*. By the 1980s, this consumer culture had become firmly entrenched within the French home, supported by the rise of privately owned television stations, pay television and cable television. French cinema, in particular, found itself under threat; at the same time, it was indebted to television as the source of its economic salvation (Jeancolas 1995: 89–111).

Nikita underlines the way in which French culture maintains a highly ambivalent relationship with consumer culture. It is not then merely a coincidence that initially Nikita must be cleaned up. The trope of cleaning – the cleaning of Nikita herself, so that she is free of her addiction, and made hygienically 'feminine', and finally in the figure of 'Le Nettoyeur', the Cleaner – is another significant strand within *Nikita*, one that Ross identified as endemic to the development of consumer culture in France in terms of its association with decolonisation. Ross remarks that in the context of post-Second World War France a certain logic was at work upholding consumer culture as part of national movement to cleanse France, thus ridding it of its colonial past. Ross explains:

An efficient well-run harmonious home is a national asset; the quality of the domestic environment has a major influence on the physique and health of the nation. A chain of equivalence is at work here; the prevailing logic runs something like this: If the woman is clean, the family is clean, the nation is clean. If the French woman is dirty, then France is dirty and backward. But France can't be dirty and backward, because that is the role played by the colonies . . . France must so to speak, clean house; reinventing the home is reinventing the nation. (Ross 1996: 78)

The character of the Cleaner, the agent sent to help Nikita on her last mission, is seized upon by critics in general, even Serge Daney, as an important image, one that reveals the time – the history – of the film (Daney 1993: 237). Austin points to the Cleaner's relations with 'advertising's obsessions with images of cleaning' (Austin 1996: 131).[10] The Cleaner's role is to erase the evidence that might lead back to the state in the event that a mission is aborted or goes awry. The use of consumer durables in the form of cars, gadgets of all sorts, computers, etc., is foregrounded as necessary to the functioning of the centre, and above all to the Cleaner himself, who ultimately dies in his car. The image of the Cleaner suggests the association between the need on the part of France to clean up its image internally as a former colonial power and consumer culture.

More obviously, in *Nikita*, the state is an anonymous apparatus that functions in terms of a pure instrumentality without an ethics of individual rights. In this sense, the state has been 'cleansed'. This is a sinister cleansing, however, very much in keeping with the figure of the Cleaner himself. *Nikita* offers a world in which the exigencies of bureaucracy triumph over the eighteenth-century tradition of individual rights, in which the individual is subjected to the relentless erosion of his or her identity in the face of the demands of an anonymous state. As Susan Hayward remarks: 'Nikita is the mise-en-scène of the death of the individual' (Hayward 2000: 307). Nikita is, so to speak, cleansed of the marks of her identity, her ties to friends and family, by her training at the centre. This cleansing effect is also the work of the genre itself.

The hybrid genre of the film – that of the fantasy thriller, somewhere between action film and science fantasy, overlaid with the romance and the coming-of-age narrative as melodrama – obscures the very real threat of state-sponsored terrorism in France during the 1980s, and thus has a cleansing effect in the terms defined by Ross above. The genre of the film, its stylistic and emotional excess, by making this terror so obvious, serves as a decoy that draws the viewer's attention away from the notorious incidents of state terrorism perpetrated specifically by France in this period. The propagation of the macha killerette and her relations to consumer culture further serve to distract the viewer. The fact is that France did engage in acts of state-sponsored terrorism during the 1980s, in exploits that severely damaged its reputation in various areas of the world, most notably Australasia. These exploits served to underline France's continued attachment to its colonial heritage. For example, in 1985 a team of French agents penetrated Auckland harbour in New Zealand and blew up *Rainbow Warrior*, a 'peace boat' destined for Mororoa Atoll where it intended to protest upcoming nuclear tests. It is generally assumed that these actions by the DGSE (Direction Générale de la Sécurité Extérieure) sprang from concerns about the status of French Polynesia. Apparently five agents were involved; two were apprehended by the New Zealand authorities, Dominique Prieur and Henri Mafart, a woman and a man. They served two years of a ten-year term. Following initial denials, the French government admitted responsibility and paid indemnities to the family of the New Zealand photographer killed in the incident and to the New Zealand state (Porch 1995: 592–5.)

In the context of the *Rainbow Warrior* incident, *Nikita* takes on a different resonance, a resonance that is effectively silenced through the reproduction of the macha killerette as a phenomenon of global consumer culture. It seems appropriate to conclude an analysis of *Nikita* with the story of Dominique Prieur as a means of emphasising the effectiveness of this film in both expressing and displacing the concerns of the 1980s. *Nikita* looks back at the three decades of French culture that preceded it, decades marked very obviously by the triumph of a global consumer culture, but also by the spectre of state-sponsored terrorism, France's imperial legacy. The continued proliferation of the macha killerette as an icon and vehicle for consumer culture throughout the 1990s testifies to the vitality of the issues that *Nikita* both expresses and elides.

References

Austin, G. (1996), *Contemporary French Cinema: An Introduction* (Manchester: Manchester University Press).
Baron-Cohen, S. (2003), *The Essential Difference: Men, Women and the Extreme Male Brain* (London: Allen Lane Press).
Brunsdon, C. (1997), *Screen Tastes: Soap Opera to Satellite Disks* (London: Routledge).
Daney, S. (1993), *L'Exercise a été profitable, Monsieur* (Paris: POL).
Fraser, K. (2003), 'The makeover and its consumer narratives', unpublished Ph.D. dissertation, McGill University.
Hayward, S. (1998), *Luc Besson* (Manchester: Manchester University Press).

Hayward, S. (2000), 'Recycled woman and the postmodern aesthetic: Luc Besson's *Nikita* (1990)', in S. Hayward and G. Vincendeau (eds), *French Film: Texts and Contexts* (London: Routledge), pp. 297–309.

Jeancolas, J.-P. (1995), *Histoire du cinéma français* (Paris: Nathan).

Porch, D. (1995), *The French Secret Services: From the Dreyfus Affair to the Gulf War* (New York: Farrar, Straus and Giroux).

Radner, H. (1993), '"Pretty is as pretty does": free enterprise and the marriage plot', in J. Collins, H. Radner and A. Preacher (eds), *Film Theory Goes to the Movies* (New York: Routledge), pp. 56–76.

Radner, H. (1995), *Shopping Around: Feminine Culture and the Pursuit of Pleasure* (New York: Routledge).

Radner, H. (1998), 'New Hollywood's new woman: murder in mind: Sarah and Margie', in S. Neale and M. Smith (eds), *Contemporary Hollywood Cinema* (London: Routledge), pp. 247–62.

Radner, H. (1999) 'Queering the girl', in H. Radner and M. Luckett (eds), *Swinging Single: Representing Sexuality* (Minneapolis: University of Minnesota Press), pp. 1–35.

Radner, H. (2002), 'Migration and immigration: French fashion and American film', in. M. Barnier and R. Moine (eds), *France–Hollywood: échanges cinématographiques et identités nationales* (Paris: L'Harmattan), pp. 203–23.

Rihoit, C. (1986), *Brigitte Bardot: un mythe français* (Paris: Livre de Poche).

Ross, K. (1996), *Fast Cars, Clean Bodies: Decolonisation and the Reordering of French Culture* (Cambridge, MA: MIT Press).

Tasker, Y. (1998), *Working Girls: Gender and Sexuality in Popular Cinema* (London: Routledge).

Tung, C. (2004), 'Embodying an image: gender, race and sexuality in *La Femme Nikita*', in S. Inness (ed.), *Action Chicks: New Images of Tough Women in Popular Culture* (London: Palgrave), pp. 95–118.

Vincendeau, G. (2000), *Stars and Stardom in French Cinema* (London: Continuum).

Notes

1 The significance of Bardot as a fashion icon is explored at greater length in Radner, 2002.
2 For an elaboration of the social significance of the makeover, and 'the transformation or makeover film,' see Fraser, 2003, in particular chapter 4, 'Transformation films: happily ever after'. Charlotte Brunsdon refers to these films as 'Shopping Films' (Brunsdon 1997: 81–104).
3 For a more developed discussion of the importance of Helen Gurley Brown's single girl, see Radner, 1999.
4 See Tasker, 1998 for a discussion of cross-dressing and transformation in contemporary Hollywood film.
5 See Radner, 1998 for discussion of the transformation of these two stars.
6 See Radner 1995: xi–xiv for discussion of the issue of transformation and Helen Gurley.

7 See Hayward 1998: 55–6 for a discussion of Parillaud's description of her preparation.
8 See Radner 1993: 56–76 for a discussion of *Pretty Woman* and an elaboration of relations between the marriage plot and the ways in which women are exchanged between men.
9 Regardless of its validity, the popularity of the thesis expounded by Simon Baron-Cohen indicates the importance of empathy in social constructions of gender (Baron-Cohen, 2003).
10 As Austin points out, it is difficult not to view Léon, also played by Jean Reno, as an avatar of the Cleaner (Austin 1996: 131).

10

Léon and the cloacal labyrinth

Phil Powrie

As Susan Hayward points out, the public view of *Léon* particularly in the USA is that it is potentially a troublingly paedophilic film (Hayward 1998: 64–5). In reviews of the film, whether positive, but even more so when they are negative, Mathilda is described as a Lolita figure, and concern is frequently expressed at the relationship between a 40-year-old man and an 11-year-old girl. The purpose of this chapter is to shift the focus away from the 'father–daughter' relationship, which has been identified by Ginette Vincendeau as a familiar trope of French cinema (Vincendeau, 1992),[1] to an exploration of homoerotic relationships, and the way in which masculine identity is problematised by the film.

The film is in this respect tellingly framed. It begins with a vertiginous set of tracking-in shots over water, Central Park, the streets of 'Little Italy', and into an Italian restaurant where Léon and Tony are planning the next hit. Not quite at the end of the film, Léon and Stansfield talk together before Léon blows them both up. This latter scene reverses the vertiginous tracking-in movement, as Stansfield is ejected from the corridor by the explosion. The two sequences are linked not just by the way they echo each other (movement in/movement out), but because in both cases two men are locked into a 'special relationship'. The final sequence, Mathilda's 'coming of age', is almost bolted on as a sentimental coda to the real matter of the film, which is, arguably, less the relationship between Léon and Mathilda, or the recovery of innocence through the female muse, as an anxious exploration of what it means to be a 'man'. As Tony says to Mathilda as she tries to persuade him to take her on, 'the game's over, Léon's dead'. The game in question is the game of being a man.

The chapter will therefore take up where Susan Hayward leaves off in her analysis of the film. She argues against the issue of paedophilia by showing how both Mathilda and Léon are fragmented in terms of their identities. This is partly because they take the place of Mathilda's dystopian family, massacred by Stansfield and his men at the start of the film. Her biological family eliminated, Mathilda becomes, in relation to Léon, 'daughter, mother, lover' (Hayward 1998: 139), and correlatively, Léon becomes 'father, son, lover' (Hayward 1998: 141). Hayward also devotes considerable attention to the explosion scene which will form the focus of this chapter, suggesting two complementary readings. In the first, she suggests that Léon must die because he represents a threat as an inhuman 'robot'. In the course of that discussion, she points out how Léon is a 'feminised phallus', by which she means that, as a child-man, he is deprived of his masculinity, and that the weapons of destruction which he carries are oddly unconnected with his childlike character: 'He stands as a feminised phallus, who has to strap the guns onto his body, like a prosthesis. His body is ornamented by the phallus, is not the phallic itself' (Hayward 1998: 100). Her second reading brings together the issue of the fragmented family and the phallic. She points out how the multiple family roles the two characters are obliged to play lead to destructive fragmentation, and that (the shadow of paedophilia reappears here) social pressure makes it impossible for him to become Mathilda's lover, requiring immolation and de-phallicisation: 'Having acknowledged his love for Mathilda, the only way that love can be sublimated is through death, that is, through a de-phallicising of the masculine body' (Hayward 1998: 141). Finally, Hayward suggests that Besson's men show 'the male body as hystericised from within even though it is disciplined from without' (Hayward 1998: 161–2).

Suggestive though these readings are, this chapter will turn away from the phallic, and the focus on the father which it implies; it will turn away from the questioning of the phallic through feminisation and hystericisation, and the heteronormative binaries which these structures imply. Instead, it will question the phallic economy by reference to the cloacal, the maternal and the homoerotic, with reference to what Calvin Thomas calls 'scatontological anxiety' (Thomas 1996). Before we explore what Thomas means by this neologism, we need to return to the issue of *Léon*'s spatial organisation, where the focus will be on hybrid labyrinthine structures, and their association with toilets and food.

Lavatorial space and 'scatontological anxiety'

The labyrinth, or maze,[2] particularly the underground labyrinth, is a favourite trope of Besson's films. In *Le Dernier combat*, the old hospital is a complex set of passageways, at the centre of which is the 'last woman'. In *Subway*, the labyrinth is underground and even more maze-like, with, again, at its centre, a woman. In *Le Grand bleu*, the sea, arguably, takes on the function of the previous films' labyrinths. In *Nikita*, there are several labyrinths: the Centre where Nikita receives her training, the restaurant with its dead end in the men's toilets, and the Embassy, with the monstrous dog at its centre. *Léon* reprises the multiple labyrinths of *Nikita*: Léon's hit at the start corresponds to *Nikita*'s restaurant sequence; then there are the police headquarters, where, as in *Nikita*, the main part of the action takes place in the men's toilets; and, finally, Léon's apartment, from which both he and Mathilda manage to escape.

Labyrinths are traditionally seen as feminine in so far as they are uterine and associated with rituals of rebirth: 'Entering the labyrinth or the underworld is returning to the womb of the Earth Mother for new birth' (Purce 1974: 104). The presence of women at the heart of the labyrinths Besson creates in his films seems to concur with this general view. There is the woman of *Le Dernier combat*, Héléna, Nikita, Mathilda; and there are also Leeloo and Jeanne, to the extent that the spaces and the narratives in those two films depend on their centrality as protagonists, and on their 'monstrosity' (the cyborg Leeloo, the cross-dressing Jeanne). The labyrinth is not just a metaphor for uterine femininity, however. The 'intestinal labyrinth' is a phrase found both in medicine, and in texts describing concrete topographies, as well as abstract concepts, such as in this meditation on Socratic rhetoric: 'The labyrinth is static, fixed, and its geometry, folded like an intestine, is consistent with the production of parasitic and excremental matter because it is deprived of the vitality, of the quest and the dynamism of a route guided by the exploratory instinct' (Battistini 2002: 3). The labyrinth is therefore as intestinal as it is uterine, and this is particularly true of Besson's labyrinths, filled with 'parasitic and excremental matter', such as the oddballs and heteroclite objects of *Subway*, the mess in the flat belonging to Mathilda's family (before and even more so after they have been massacred), or the detritus at the end of *Nikita*'s kitchen chute.

Léon's spaces are generally connected with food: Tony's birthday cake, the pizza eaten by Stansfield's man before Léon kills him, the milk which Léon and Mathilda drink throughout the film. On at least two occasions, the most labyrinthine space (the labyrinth as dangerous initiatory space) is specifically connected with food and toilets. Nikita goes straight from the toilets to the kitchen, and manages to escape by going down the rubbish chute. In *Léon*, Mathilda follows Stansfield into the toilets with her pizza, and in the ensuing conversation, Stansfield refers to 'shit' ('what filthy piece of shit did I do now?'). In both of these cases

– *Nikita*, *Léon* – the intestinal labyrinth as operative narrative space is blocked, compacted ('compacted' is the meaning of the Greek word, *stiphros*, which gives our 'constipated' via Latin, as well as 'stiff' via German); only a violent explosion can expel the protagonists, as if they were embodiments of their profession as assassins, human cannonballs shot from the barrel of a gun.

Following Robyn Longhurst's work in social geography, we could call these labyrinths 'corporeal spaces' (Longhurst 2001: 125). Longhurst points out how geographers tend to avoid discussion of closet spaces (toilets, bathrooms), still less discussion of 'the messiness of bodies' (Longhurst 2001: 23). She also points out how interdisciplinary work on the body has tended to avoid the exploration of heterosexual white men. Part of her research focuses on the combination of these two categories (heterosexual white men's talk about bathrooms), with the aim of showing how these spaces 'are often experienced as sites/sights of abjection', and exposing the male body so that such men 'can no longer pass themselves off as solid and hard' (Longhurst 2001: 66). Bathrooms were seen by her respondents 'to be places inhabited by bodies that are at the mercy of (Mother) Nature, bodies that are potentially both seductive (including seducing oneself to sexual pleasure) and repulsive' (Longhurst 2001: 82). Reviewing the possible names one could give to such a space – Homi Bhabha's 'Third Space', constituted by hybridity (Bhabha, 1994), or Kristeva's *chora*, which is coterminous with the abject (see Kristeva 1982: 13–14) – she settles, following Moss and Dyck (1999: 389) on the rather more useful term 'corporeal space':

> Corporeal space consists of context, discursive inscriptions, material–economic and matter-based–inscriptions, the biological, and the physiological . . . These spaces are fluid, congealing from time to time around the body, only to be destabilized with new boundaries forming when any part of the context, the discourse, or the materiality shifts. (Moss and Dyke 1999: 389 quoted in Longhurst 2001: 125)

If we are evoking Longhurst's work, it is because in both *Nikita* and *Léon* the scene in the toilets functions as a pivotal event. For Nikita, it is the final part of her training; for Léon, it is the event which will lead to his death. Crucially, in both films, the toilets are male toilets invaded by a female protagonist intent on violence, but who is in both cases prevented from escaping. The toilets in both films are therefore places of anxiety, where masculinity is threatened in its most intimate corporeality. That anxiety has been called 'scatontological anxiety' by Calvin Thomas.

Thomas brings together Freud's account of the *fort/da* game, and his theory of cloacal birth: 'It is a universal conviction amongst children that babies are born from the bowel like a piece of faeces: daefecation is a model of the act of birth' (Freud quoted in Thomas 1996: 85). He suggests that the *fort/da* game 'is implicated not only with the boy's phantasy of having been produced through his mother's bowels, and his foreclosure of that phantasy, but also with his own struggles to secure identity through the control of his bowels' (Thomas 1999: 29). Those struggles, Thomas suggests, are never really successful, and all modes of representation are haunted by scatontological anxiety: 'The image of "unimpaired masculinity", the self-produced, self-representational image of the actively "self-made man", is haunted by the earlier phantasmatic image of having been a passively and cloacally (m)other-made child' (Thomas 1999: 29). Cinema, like all representational practices, suggests Thomas, transforms the subject into a representation, and this can be experienced as trauma. He relates this trauma to cloacal activity:

> Identity cannot be secured without recourse to modes of representation – speech, writing, image-production, including photography and cinema – that inevitably transform the representing subject *back* into a represented object. And this production, this transforming *back*, can be a phantasmatic *falling back*, a dissolution of ego boundaries, a traumatising *Durchfall* (a German word that means failure, falling through, and the involuntary emptying of the bowels) . . . The *image* of unimpaired masculinity through which the dominant fiction supposedly guarantees itself is ultimately unable to overcome historical trauma, and it fails to do so precisely by virtue of *being* a produced image. (Thomas 2004: 229)

The anxiety generated by *Léon* is directly related at a narrative level to the way in which his identity is taken over by Mathilda, as for example when she wears the same dark glasses and skull cap as he does, when she goes for her first real hit. Stella Bruzzi in her work on costume points out the 'constructedness' of the gangster's image, and the way in which this points to a crisis of masculine identity:

> Through the transferral of himself and his ideal to Matilda [*sic*], Léon reveals his essential lack. Gangsterism, if it can be so quickly learnt by Matilda, is no longer related to 'essence' or 'content' or even to masculinity, because masculinity itself is a collection of mementoes to be discarded or assumed by whoever chooses to pick them up. (Bruzzi 1997: 93)

The fact that Mathilda takes the same sartorial elements which constitute Léon's image, and throughout the film tries to take over his functions as a hitman, even invading male toilets in dogged pursuit of her brother's killer, suggests only too clearly the encroachment of the female other on masculine identity, the expulsion of the male from his private spaces.

In this section, we have seen how *Léon* establishes a shifting, hybrid space which is more intestinal than labyrinthine. As in *Nikita*, that space is not just intestinal in form, but is also associated with the lavatorial, in two senses of the word. First, the space established is abject, associated with violence and detritus, 'mess' in its most general sense; second, and to some extent paradoxically, what might have seemed negatively lavatorial ('mess') is also, and more positively, the place where the character is metaphorically 'washed', or purified, corresponding to the original meaning of 'lavatory' as the place where one washes oneself. However, abjection, with its problematic and shifting identifications, makes this a profoundly *anxious* space, that functions to destabilise masculine identity, at the same time as it tries to affirm its inviolability on the higher, more allegorical level of ritual purification. We now turn to a closer analysis of the film, to show how it establishes an anxiously homoerotic rectal fantasy, rather than the paedophilic fantasy which offended US screen-testing audiences.

Léon and the rectal fantasy

The image we have of Léon at the start of the film is that of a self-sufficient loner, Thomas's idea of the self-made man. He depends on Tony, of course, but his samurai-like behaviour, so closely related to Jef Costello's in *Le Samouraï* (*The Godson*, Jean-Pierre Melville, 1967), suggests that he operates on a different plane of reality to the sordid mafia business centred on money and power. Léon is not interested in money, as his conversations with Tony make clear. He is, like Costello before him, a stylist; as his training programme suggests, he is dedicated to his profession. He is also unconnected to women at the start of the film. When Tony guesses that the changes in Léon's behaviour are down to meeting a woman, he reminds Léon of the 'dangers' of women, and we learn that Léon was 'rescued' from the clutches of a woman when he arrived in New York for the first time.

Léon comes across to us as even more 'self-made' by virtue of the way he is constructed. He is a curious compilation of images: on the one hand, as Bruzzi points out, he has all the right sartorial components of the gangster image, but they are unconventional, eccentric, individualist: 'Léon has a hat, but it is a woollen skull-cap, not a Fedora; he has braces (like Vito Corleone, for example), but they are over T-shirts and buttoned vests; he has pleated trousers, but they are threadbare and short; and he has a coat, but it is, tramp-like, several sizes too large' (Bruzzi 1997: 92).

In fact, the mix is even more complex, since certain items and events – the white T-shirt, the sewing-up of the wound in his chest – recall Jef

Costello in Melville's film; and the dark glasses combined with the weaponry evoke James Cameron's *Terminator* films (*The Terminator*, 1984; *Terminator 2: Judgment Day*, 1991). The sunglasses – one of the Terminator's trademarks – are very clearly intended to signal anonymity, and also function as a protective shield: Léon wears them when he goes on a hit, and, as if to underline this, he puts them on when he is trying to summon up the courage to kill Mathilda.

He is self-made, then, by virtue of lonely professionalism (let us not forget that the subtitle of the film for US audiences is 'the professional'), and by the eclecticism of his costume. He is also a version of the 'hard-bodied' action heroes of the 1980s and 1990s (the term comes from Susan Jeffords; see Jeffords, 1994), not so much by his muscular physique, as by his supposed indestructibility. Tony says to Léon, when Léon expresses the fear that he may die one day: 'You're indestructible, bullets slide over you, you play with them'. This reminds us, no less than the sunglasses might have done, of the Terminator, described by director James Cameron as 'an indestructible machine' (Cameron quoted in French 1996: 18), and, famously, turned father-protector in the second film in rather the same way that Léon protects Mathilda; indeed, Mathilda is the same age as John Conner in *Terminator 2*. As Sarah Conner says in this film:

> Watching John with the machine, it was suddenly so clear. The Terminator would never stop, it would never leave him and it would never hurt him, never shout at him or get drunk and hit him or say it was too busy to spend time with him. It would always be there and it would die to protect him. Of all the would be fathers who came and went over the years, this thing, this machine was the only one who measured up. In an insane world it was the sane choice.

A similar situation obtains in *Léon*. Unlike Mathilda's own father – whom she says to Léon she would have killed one day if no one else had – Léon does not 'get drunk and hit' her. Moreover, the second Terminator film and *Léon* have other features in common: their protagonists both learn from the children (morals in *Terminator 2*, reading in *Léon*); and their principal foes are the police who are either ineffectual or evil, as is the T1000 in *Terminator 2*, dressed as a cop throughout.

The protective image is in tune with the times. As Yvonne Tasker explains, when talking about the Terminator films, 'men have become, during the 1980s, more overtly targeted as consumers of lifestyle. The invitation extended to western men to define themselves through consumption brings with it a consequent stress on the fabrication of identity, a denaturalising of the supposed naturalness of male identity'

(Tasker 1993: 110). That denaturalising is of course a threat, and the principal cause of anxiety, expressed most forcefully, as we have argued above, by the constitution of confusing labyrinths full of 'mess', and private male spaces invaded by females.

One significant difference between the Terminator films and *Léon* is that whereas the Terminator films have been analysed as a commentary on the state of the family in the USA and men's position within it, *Léon*, we would suggest, is much more about the relationship between men, than it is about issues connected with the state of the family in France during the 1990s. It is a buddy-movie in the sense that the relationship between Léon and Stansfield is as important as that between Mathilda and Léon. While Mathilda enters Léon's life as an intruder, separated from him in age and temperament, Stansfield and Léon are locked into a binary relationship which is constantly underlined by stark contrast. Stansfield is a dandy, while Léon dresses like a tramp. Stansfield is cultured and articulate, waxing lyrical about classical composers, while Léon is unable to recognise even the most popular movie icons, including the one he resembles most, Chaplin, when he and Mathilda play charades; and, compared with Stansfield, he is relatively inarticulate. Their accents are in both cases slightly foreign, but Stansfield's is, like Stansfield himself, unstable, difficult to position in relation to place. Léon is referred to as 'Italian' by Stansfield when he is talking to Tony, but in fact his inflections are French, and consistently so, suggesting stability, in contrast with Stansfield's psychopathic, mercurial volatility. Stansfield's instability even extends to his name: he is called Stan (a Christian name) by his colleagues, but is referred to as Stansfield (a surname) by others. This instability is related to the moral dimension: Léon has a hitman's rule which is repeated several times in the film, including by Mathilda as she trains with him – no women or children – while Stansfield has no such qualms, as is demonstrated by his killing of the whole family, women and children included. He does not believe in rules, walking out on the investigators, and calling their enquiry, based on rules of engagement, 'mickey-mouse bullshit'.

The point of the film, it might be argued, is to bring Stansfield and Léon together climactically, in both the narrative and sexual sense. At the start of the film, Léon watches Stansfield and his men from the safety of his apartment, voyeuristically, with several close-ups of his eye applied to the judas in his door. Towards the end of the film, Stansfield also gazes on Léon voyeuristically as he sits in his SWAT costume being tended by the police doctor. The moment when they finally meet in the hotel corridor is constructed around a confusion of point of view, as the camera adopts the point of view of each man in turn: Léon first as he stumbles towards the light at the end of the tunnel formed by the corridor, followed by Stanfield whose face takes the place of Léon's as he follows Léon out, and then back to Léon before Stansfield shoots him, and the camera cants and falls as it readopts Léon's point of view. The death scene which follows is constructed as a scene between lovers, reminding us of the end of Godard's À bout de souffle (Breathless, 1960), as Michel Poiccard (Jean-Paul Belmondo) lies in the street after his long stumble along it, and murmurs his last words to his lover Patricia (Jean Seberg). It is worth rehearsing the details of this climactic scene before teasing out its implications (see Table 10.1 for a shot-by-shot breakdown).

Table 10.1 Shot-by-shot breakdown of the final explosion in *Léon*

Shot number	Angle	Event
1	medium	Stansfield rolls Léon over
2	medium/low	Stansfield stands over Léon
3	close up	Stansfield grasps Léon's right hand with his right hand
4	medium/high	Léon lying as if dead
5	close-up	Stansfield's face
6	close-up	Léon's face. Léon says: 'Stansfield'
7	medium/low	Stansfield holding Léon's hand looks down on him and says: 'At your service'
8	medium/high	Léon takes Stansfield's hand in both of his
9	close-up	Léon puts something in Stansfield's hand; blood on all three hands.
10	medium close-up	Léon's face; he says, haltingly, 'This is for Mathilda'
11	medium close-up	Stansfield's face
12	medium close-up	Léon removes his hands, and Stansfield's fisted hand hangs down between his legs
13	close up	Stansfield's hand comes into focus as Léon's face goes out of focus behind it. He opens it to see a grenade pin
14	close-up	Stansfield's worried face
15	medium/high	Stansfield opens Léon's coat and sees the grenades
16	close-up	Stansfield's face; he says 'shit'

It is perhaps worth remembering that the version of the film released in 1994 had been substantially modified after screentests with US audiences. One of the many changes relates to this sequence. In the first version of the film, Stansfield shoots Léon, and Mathilda returns to the scene; she hands Stansfield the grenade pin, and opens her coat which has the grenades.[3] The released version, therefore, concentrates on the man-to-man relationship rather than on the triangle formed in the original screenplay.

That relationship is homoerotic, as is suggested by the *mise-en-scène* and camerawork: the oscillation between high and low camera angles, corresponding to point of view, makes it clear that the relationship is one of domination and submission. The holding of hands covered in Léon's blood suggests more than 'blood-brotherhood', it suggests the exchange of bodily fluids, an engagement with the abject materiality of bodies (sweat, blood). This is something that Stansfield is not afraid of, particularly with men: we remember the way he 'sniffs' Mathilda's father, holding him close, ruffling his hair, and stroking his face.

This is to some extent emphasized by the explosion itself. Léon reasserts phallic mastery (the grenades which decorate his torso are not round but tubular) by metaphorically 'fucking' Stansfield when he blows him up; 'fucks' him so hard indeed that Stansfield is exploded through his own rectum. This may sound like a fantastical reading, but the explosion itself is fantastical: slowing the film down, we can see that shot 17 shows two cops standing close to the exit of the hotel, and cowering as the explosion occurs; this is immediately followed by a second shot which reprises the explosion, with the camera placed a few metres further back. The explosion therefore occurs twice, fantasmatically, confirming that we could read the scene as a rectal and homoerotic fantasy, an obsessive and excessive replay of a homoerotic scene.

The very excess of this explosion suggests a kind of hysterical displacement, whose origin is not difficult to find if we accept the reading proposed above: it is, as Thomas says, in his discussion of scatontological anxiety, the fear of homosexuality: 'a fear of the anus as phantasmatic origin ... and as destination of desire or locus of pleasure' (Thomas 1996: 88). The rectal fantasy could have been positively radical; as Shaviro points out, abjection can be productive:

> Film's radical potential to subvert social hierarchies and decompose relations of power lies in its extreme capacity for seduction and violence ... Film should neither be exalted as a medium of collective fantasy nor condemned as a mechanism of ideological mystification. It should rather be praised as a technology for intensifying and renewing experiences of passivity and abjection. (Shaviro 1993: 65)

For Shaviro, film (it is not altogether clear whether he means all films, or just the films he analyses, principally those of George Romero and

David Cronenberg) can put the spectators in touch with their body because of its seductiveness, and can therefore induce the abject, leading to cataclysmic excess:

> The more intensely my body is affected, and the more it is put in contact with appearances, the closer I approach abjection (which) is also an exaltation: there is deep, unresolvable ambivalence in the contact of the flesh, a continual affective oscillation. This indeterminacy is not empty, but overly, insufferably full: a hypertrophic surplus of irreconcilable sensations and passions, the bodily contours of my desire. (Shaviro 1993: 260)

Shaviro's analysis of Cronenberg's films points to monsters as embodiments of passion rather than repression (see Shaviro 1993: 130–3). Similarly we could see the monster who is Léon (he is after all a hitman) as an embodiment not so much of repression – his relative muteness characteristic of Steve Neale's definition of the 'hard' narcissistic male protecting his ego (Neale 1983)[4] – but of a surplus of archaic desires and passions, amongst them the paedophilic, although this is largely overshadowed by the homoerotics of the film's climax. In this analysis, then, Léon's compactness is fluidified by nascent sexual desire for the 'daughter' who is also his 'mother', Mathilda, bringer of milk, of speech, and even of play, as exemplified by the scene where he acts out John Wayne, and Mathilda mothers him as he walks away, disappointed that she had not recognised the charade.

It is clearly not a coincidence that his mimicry of this quintessentially masculine man is not recognised by Mathilda; this, and the playfulness which Mathilda brings into his life more generally, undermines his previously compacted masculine identity, predicated on muteness and on his almost magical capacity to make himself invisible. The explosion sequence, then, is as much an admission of failure, as it is of the reclaiming of phallic power over Stansfield. In Thomas's terms, it is *Durchfall*, which, we remember, means both failure, falling and the involuntary emptying of the bowels (Thomas 2004: 229). The phallic becomes the fecal, and the feminised; the compacted hard man, afraid of hard men's business and the homoerotics they imply, is expelled from the intestinal labyrinth, in a dizzyingly excessive display of splattered bodies; as Thomas colourfully says of the fragmentation of the phallic self through *Durchfall*, 'the hyperbolic self not only shatters but splatters' (Thomas 1996: 71).

'Léon' was, according to a piece in *Première*, the name Besson's mother gave to Besson 'when he did something naughty' (Besson and Reno 1994: 62). In this chapter we have seen how *Léon* works through a complex structure of abjection, establishing a cloacal labyrinth, where men's business and mess come together climactically in rectal homoerotics, 'shattering' and 'splattering' masculine identity. If the mawkish coda of the film is something profoundly unsatisfying and appears tacked on, as we pointed above, it is partly because it was not part of the original screenplay, in which Mathilda blew herself up with the two men. The coda's effect is that it offsets the explosive homoerotics of the previous sequence. Everything returns to 'normal'. Space is no longer the intestinal, rectal space of the previous sequence, filled with men's bodies and blood; it is an open space, filled exclusively with a woman (the headmistress) and young girls. Mathilda has returned to school, the headmistress treats her story as fiction, as too fantastical. Léon becomes a figment of a disturbed girl's imagination, figured by a houseplant which Mathilda plants in the lawn outside the school, where it will evidently not survive. The coda, in other words, full of mawkish sentimentality and improbable stories of the 'it was all just a dream' type, erases what has preceded, because what has preceded is too dangerous, too excessive, too 'naughty'. We could be forgiven for preferring naughtiness.

References

Battistini, A. (2002), 'Ariadne and the Minotaur: the cultural role of a philosophy of rhetoric', *Philosophy and Culture: Essays in Honor of Donald Phillip Verene*, ed. G. A. Magee (Charlottesville, VA: Philosophy Documentation Center), pp. 1–13.

Besson, L. and J. Reno (1994), 'Avant-avant-avant dernier film de Besson' (interview), *Première*, 211, pp. 62–71.

Bhabha, H. K. (1994), *The Location of Culture* (London: Routledge).

Bruzzi, S. (1997), *Undressing Cinema: Clothing and Identity in the Movies* (London and New York: Routledge).

French, S. (1996), *The Terminator* (London: BFI).

Hayward, S. (1998), *Luc Besson* (Manchester: Manchester University Press).

Jeffords, S. (1994), *Hard Bodies: Hollywood Masculinity in the Reagan Era* (New Brunswick, NJ: Rutgers).

Kennedy, B. M. (2001), 'Reconfiguring love. . .a Deleuzian travesty?: *Léon* and a molecular politics via the girl and the child', *Deleuze and Cinema: The Aesthetics of Sensation* (Edinburgh: Edinburgh University Press), pp. 193–214.

Kristeva, J. (1982) *Powers of Horror: An Essay on Abjection* (New York: Columbia University Press).

Longhurst, R. (2001) *Bodies: Exploring Fluid Boundaries* (London and New York: Routledge).

Moss, P. and Dyck, I. (1999) 'Body, corporeal space, and legitimating chronic illness: women diagnosed with M.E.', *Antipode* 31/4: 372–97.

Neale, S. (1983), 'Masculinity as spectacle: reflections on men and mainstream cinema', *Screen*, 24:6, pp. 2–16.
Purce, J. (1974), *The Mystic Spiral: Journey of the Soul* (New York: Avon).
Shaviro, S. (1993), *The Cinematic Body* (Minneapolis and London: University of Minnesota Press).
Tasker, Y. (1993), *Spectacular Bodies: Gender, Genre and the Action Cinema* (London and New York: Routledge).
Thomas, C. (1996), *Male Matters: Masculinity, Anxiety, and the Male Body on the Line* (Urbana and Chicago: University of Illinois Press).
Thomas, C. (1999), 'Last laughs: *Batman*, masculinity and the technology of abjection', *Men and Masculinities*, 2:1, pp. 26–46.
Thomas, C. (2004), '*Batman*, masculinity, and the technology of abjection', *The Trouble with Men: Masculinities in European and Hollywood Cinema*, eds P. Powrie, A. Davies and B. Babington (London: Wallflower Press), pp. 218–29.
Vincendeau, G. (1992), 'Family plots: the fathers and daughters of French cinema', *Sight & Sound*, 1:11, pp. 14–17.

Notes

1   Vincendeau's article focuses partly on *Nikita*. There is no substantial academic work on *Léon* apart from Hayward 1998, and a rather technically philosophical chapter in a volume on Deleuze (Kennedy 2001).
2   Although the two terms are often seen to be interchangeable, specialists tend to distinguish between the maze and the labyrinth. The labyrinth is normally unicursal, with only one path leading to the centre, whereas the maze is multicursal, with several possible paths and dead ends. The term used here is labyrinth, taken as a broad metaphor for labyrinthine or maze like spaces, without regard to distinctions between their design.
3   A translated version of the original screenplay was consulted on the Internet at www.geocities.com/ra_sully66/Léon.pdf, accessed on 2 March 2005.
4   Neale talks about Alain Delon's image in *Le Samouraï* as one 'marked not only by emotional reticence, but also by silence, a reticence with language. Theoretically, this silence, this absence of language can be further linked to narcissism and to the construction of an ideal ego. The acquisition of language is a process profoundly challenging to the narcissism of early childhood ... Language is a process (or set of processes) involving absence and lack, and these are what threaten any image of the self as totally enclosed, self-sufficient, omnipotent' (Neale 1983: 7).

11

Jeanne d'Arc:
high epic style and politicising camp

Susan Hayward

It was the imaginative, epic quality of the sci-fi saga *Le Cinquième élément*, with its substantial budget and cast of big international stars, that established Luc Besson as a visionary trade warrior for European cinema. The release of *Jeanne d'Arc* in France on 27 October 1999 was meant to cement the earlier film's huge success. However, by the time of its release, the controversies surrounding the film's inception and production, to say nothing of its actual release time had given the idea of Besson the Euro-warrior several new twists.

Besson's well-documented paranoia about the film led him to set up his own website (www.luc-besson.com) to counter what he termed disinformation. The most serious charge came from US filmmaker Kathryn Bigelow, who was down to direct a film about Joan of Arc with the help of Besson's backing, and including financing from a large Japanese electronic company (possibly JVC, a former funder of Besson's films). Bigelow had nurtured her project, *Company of Angels*, to be scripted by Jay Cocks, for more than a decade, and had conducted extensive research. In July 1996, contracts were exchanged: Besson was to receive a fee, a credit and the right to be consulted on casting. Morgan Creek also contributed monies. However, according to Bigelow (Honeycutt, 1998), when it became clear to Besson – some eight weeks before filming was due to start – that his then partner Milla Jovovich was not going to be cast as Joan (Bigelow preferred Claire Danes), Besson pulled the plug and with him went the Japanese money.[1] Bigelow threatened to sue, but eventually the matter was settled out of court (see Jermyn and Redmond 2003: 11).

The controversy around *Jeanne d'Arc* was compounded by the death of a stuntman during the first weeks of shooting on location in the Czech Republic. According to some press reports, Besson became seriously introverted after the accident, appearing on set only to shout orders (Holtz 1999: 34). He gave notice on his website that he would talk about the incident and all the 'stupid things that have been said about it', but nothing resembling an explanation emerged.[2]

Yet another controversy surrounded the question of the film's Frenchness, which was raised again and again (see for example Cotillon and Paumier 1999: 32). Dismissive, as always, of the idea that a French film can only be French if it is voiced in French, Besson argued that his project's Frenchness cannot be disputed. It was financed by Gaumont, to the tune of $60 million.[3] All the historical advisers were French. Many of the cast and technical crew were French. The sound-mixing was done at a new, purpose-built digital factory in France (SonyVision). The point, according to Besson, is to export French *culture* and to defend it – not language, which is another thing altogether. With 2,000 copies released in the USA, 400 in Japan and 595 in France (of which some 500 are French-language versions), Besson's claim that he is a cultural ambassador for his nation is not unreasonable (Cotillon and Paumier 1999: 32). His film received a standing ovation at its première on the opening night of the Tokyo Film Festival in November 1999.

Finally in this list of controversies, the film was dogged by problems when released. It was scheduled for release in France by mid-October 1999. But the French distributors of George Lucas's *Star Wars Episode 1: The Phantom Menace* (1999) declared war by obliging French exhibitors to agree to run their film through October, forcing Besson to await release of his film by two weeks. Besson wrote an open letter to Lucas, to no avail, and *Star Wars* had 800 screens in France at the time of *Jeanne d'Arc*'s release. Figures at the end of November 1999 gave the advantage to Lucas's film with 6.7 million entries over eight weeks to Besson's 2.5 million over three.[4]

In general terms, the film itself follows a tradition more readily associated with classical French cinema. It is in three parts, all focused on Jeanne: first, childhood, then the woman warrior, and finally, the trial. There are many mirrorings and repetitions with variations, reminiscent of Carné and Renoir's work of the 1930s. The film begins and ends with a confession (Jeanne's); her body is twice pierced by an arrow (connotations with the martyr Saint Sebastian should be allowed to stand); at the height of her power (after winning Orléans) she buys a prisoner with her ring (to spare his life), and later in the film is herself sold as a prisoner (and will lose her life). However, the film lacks the tight cohesion of classical film narrative, and has two major weaknesses. After the stunning second part (the battle scenes), with its brilliant pacing and fast editing, the pace of the third is far too slow. It does not have the slow-tempo aesthetics of a Bresson film. Indeed, this part, which is devoted to Jeanne's incarceration and trial, compares very unfavourably with Bresson's masterpiece, *Le Procès de Jeanne d'Arc/The Trial of Joan of Arc* (1962). The weaknesses are particularly apparent during Jeanne's moments in her cell which, whatever Besson himself might believe,[5] are reduced to silliness by Dustin Hoffman as her (free-floating) 'conscience'. He floats in and out of the cell like some embodied alter ego to challenge Jeanne's own version of the truth of her voices and God-given mission. The first encounter, where her mystical interpretation of the sword is reinterpreted within the discourse of logic and male reason by Hoffman, is frankly absurd and does not work. Jeanne's moments alone in the cell are none too convincing either. We do not sense her as caught in a struggle between mysticism and the sin of pride.

That said, there are strong moments when Jeanne emerges from her cell to confront her inquisitors, and exposes the church's hypocrisy with wit and irony. In these scenes Jovovich is remarkably reminiscent of the rebellious Nikita nine years earlier. Yet another major weakness, however, comes towards the end of the second part, when Jeanne lays an assault on Paris. Historically, Besson's facts are correct. Jeanne really did only have an army of hundreds (400 to be precise), not thousands. Furthermore, the Parisians did not want to be 'liberated' (to the Armagnacs and Charles VII), quite the opposite in fact. But the *mise-en-scène* is unusually weak for a filmmaker who has often been seen as a master of visual style: as Jeanne and her faithful follower Gilles de Rais discuss, in the foreground, the failing fortunes of her campaign (and he urges her to stop), background action is unconvincingly staged – indeed, it has vague resonances with a Monty Python farce (as in *Life of Brian*, Terry Jones, UK, 1979). And yet this is a crucial moment in the narrative, since it marks the beginning of Jeanne's fall from grace (with the king and his mother-in-law Yolande d'Aragon); even the voices have deserted her.

An epic film in the making and the nature of epics

When we consider the heritage of Besson's film, there is a monumental 'history/mythology' that has accrued around this historical personage. There are at least twenty-two filmic representations of her story. In this context (as in others), each interpretation is designed to suit the ideological cloth of either the filmmaker or the nation producing the film. This same phenomenon occurs with the political groupings within France itself. Both the left and the extreme right have claimed Jeanne as their icon. Besson undoubtedly thought that this quintessentially French yet internationally well-known story – told using English dialogue –

would be a breakthrough for the European historical epic. His film was liked by the French critics on the whole, but criticised for its historical inaccuracies by the Anglo-Americans.[6] In response to the criticisms, he pointed to the fact that, over the centuries, there has been an extraordinary conflation of Jeanne's true person and her myth, to the point where it is hard to distinguish the real Jeanne from the stories constructed around her. He claimed that he was striving with his film to understand the human being, not the myth: how could a young woman whom historical documents tell us cried and panicked over her victory at Orléans – reactions that signal doubt – still be at one with herself and her God? This is what he sought to investigate (see Cotillon and Paumier 1999: 30). Besson also insisted that the weaponry, battle scenes and trials were thoroughly researched. Yet history is falsified as early as the very beginning of the film when Jeanne witnesses the rape and murder of her sister by English soldiers, with the result that her drive to rid France of the English and install Charles VII as king seems motivated as much by revenge as by any pious belief in the voices she hears. In actual fact, it was the Burgundians who ransacked Jeanne's village. However, in this context of falsification, despite the fact that there is as much historical muddle here as in Victor Fleming's 1948 *Joan of Arc* (with Ingrid Bergman) or Otto Preminger's 1957 *Saint Joan* (with Jean Seberg), it has to be said that Besson does successfully show more clearly the extent of the collusion between the Burgundians and the English to gain control of France during what was in effect a civil war.

As the French weekly *Marianne* puts it so well, the true history of Jeanne can never be told, of course, because it is a taboo subject (Kahn 1999: 55). Though she has been extolled over the centuries as the ultimate icon of Frenchness by Republicans and Monarchists alike, she in fact sided with the ultra-conservative Armagnacs, anti-intellectuals hated by the university, the parliament, and the Parisian bourgeoisie. Since her canonisation by the Vatican in 1920 as a thanksgiving for France's victory over Germany, she has been appropriated by the extreme right, culminating in Jean-Marie Le Pen's choice of her and her national holiday as emblems of the xenophobic and racist *Front National*. And it was not the English, but the French who arrested Jeanne, sold her and condemned her to death. After the crowning of Charles, she went on to fight at Paris and Compiègne, disastrous campaigns, not supported by the king, which she led against the Parisians and Burgundians who shunned her 'liberating' zeal. Besson's version, then, goes part way towards correcting the abiding impression that it was perfidious Albion that burnt the French saint. Indeed, John Malkovich's greedy, narcissistic and cowardly Charles and Faye

Dunaway's ruthless Yolande d'Aragon make it clear that Jeanne is a pawn to be used by all within this very Franco-French civil war. In fact, one of the intriguing elements within the film is the unspoken struggle between Yolande and Jeanne. Both are given considerable agency. However, the former survives through her wit and hypocrisy; the latter perishes because of her candour and genuine confusion. Furthermore, Besson's version of Yolande takes on board certain historians' view that she was responsible for training Jeanne to become a warrior (see Kahn 1999). Having heard of her visions and voices, and desperately seeking a way to legitimise her son-in-law's claim to the French throne, she turned her prodigy, Jeanne, into a secret weapon: the virgin who could save France. In the end, as Besson's film makes clear, Jeanne was taken prisoner by the French and passed onto the Duke of Burgundy; subsequently, it was the University of Paris that demanded her transportation to the capital for trial and the Burgundian archbishop Cauchon who mercilessly conducted her prosecution.

Let us now consider the nature of epic films and Besson's own film. Epics are about grandeur and style, about casts of thousands, and they cost (naturally) millions. Often they are vehicles for monumental stars; or, rather, monumental stars are their vehicle. They pull history from a distant past – the further the better – so that ideological meanings and messages will pass unremittingly. It is in the nature of epics, however, to falsify – or at least simplify – the historical subject, or the momentous moment of history. The very thing epics are not about is historical truth, although they may well be grounded in historical realism. Thus, epics are rarely about coming to understand the historical persona they purport to represent; the motivation is always exterior to that persona, and often reveals more about the contemporary moment than it does about the past.

Besson is on record as saying that he was not interested in narrating history but in pulling out of that history a message that is relevant for us today (Cotillon and Philippe Paumier 1999: 28). In order to achieve this, Besson says he has pulled away from the 'factual' narrative of the *then* (the 1420s) and tried to get behind the 'exterior envelope' and into the emotional effect and affect of Jeanne (Cotillon and Philippe Paumier 1999: 30). In other words, he sought in his film to find the woman, to follow her emotionally, reveal her doubts and to show that you cannot come out of the experience of war intact. Thus, set against the epic background of her battles on the field and in the court (that is, set against *a* historical realism) is the investigation, or an attempt to understand the inner motivations (*a* reality) of this historical persona. Besson's portrayal of Jeanne represents a coming to understand. As such he is striving for something that epics do not normally set out to do.

However, the way in which Besson set about this investigation is not without some problems for historians because, according to Besson's version, Jeanne is as much motivated by a desire for vengeance – for the rape of her sister by the English – as she is by divine intervention (see Péron 1999: 33). And it is because she is doubly motivated (again according to Besson's version) that she swings between doubt and conviction, and can therefore be ambiguously represented. So this falsifying of 'history' allows Besson to give interior depth to Jeanne. In other words, he plays the epic card one way – falsifying history – in order to achieve something epics do not normally attempt, namely, the inner, psychological workings of the mind. This falsifying of 'history' also gives Besson the way in to shake down the myth of Jeanne d'Arc and bring the icon down to earth – again something that, traditionally, epics do not do. In so doing, Jeanne becomes accessible, human, full of contradictions. And as with Nikita before her, Besson's Jeanne is someone whose courage young women can identify with (as several interviews have made clear; see for example Eisenstein 2000: 61).

The question becomes: are we talking here of high epic style and dumbing down history? Not necessarily. Young French teenagers when interviewed, especially women, said that they knew nothing about Jeanne d'Arc until seeing this film (Eisenstein 2000: 61). Thus Besson's film as an epic has worked its ideological and pedagogical effect (for the nation) by bringing history to a new audience, to a new unknowing group of people. The spectacular functions here then as a defence of a nation's culture. But at the same time it offers a resistance to political appropriation, precisely because Jeanne is ambiguously represented and suffers terrible doubt. In essence, Besson's epic brings Jeanne back into an arena – the human one of moral ambiguity – where neither the left nor the right (in particular the racist and xenophobic *Front National*) can recuperate her. However, there is more to Jeanne's ambiguity than just the moral issue. As I shall now go on to discuss, sexual ambiguity comes into play and, with it, a visitation by Jeanne into the world of androgyny and camp – all of which make her even more ungraspable.

Jeanne's camp

I shall focus on two aspects of camp in relation to this film. First, Jeanne/Milla Jovovich's androgyny, about which Jovovich had the following to say: 'I could pass for a boy, from behind, actually I'm pretty buff' (Anon. 1999: 64; buff meaning expert at passing); given her flat-chest and slim body, she arguably 'passes' from in front just as well.[7] The second aspect is the visible presence in this film of camp amongst the

Jeanne d'Arc

male characters, as exemplified both by Charles the Dauphin and his noble warrior soldiers (Gilles de Rais, Dunois, Alençon).

Let us start with this second aspect first before weaving Jeanne's androgyny into this camp reading. Camp as a term has always had theatrical and performative connotations, deriving from the French expression 'camper son role', literally to install one's self in one's role, to take it on, however temporary or illusory that might be. And this in part is true of camp. But as a term it also has earlier military connotations, which are not divorced from theatricality or performance, as explained by Mark Booth (Booth, 1999). In France, at the time that it had monarchies (and Louis XIV is exemplary of this), courtiers, nobility, were kept from being a threat to the monarchy by having to be at court. Once at court, it was a politics of play, display, wit and amusement that prevailed, in other words, not true politics. Courtiers swanked. Authors put on plays, actors camped their roles. But so too did wits. In playing with language, they demonstrated linguistic swank.

In moments of battle, the whole court would 'move' camps and set up a temporary, artificial camp, made of tents. These tents, however temporary, were no small affair. As we know from looking at Besson's spectacular recreation of these camps, they were ornate, made of silks, satins and tapestries, and adorned with jewels. Flimsy though they were, they were expansive and expensive constructions of excess, which interestingly is a definition of camp ('se camper' meaning to present oneself in an expansive and flimsy manner). The (battle) camp became the pageant. In decamping to these artificial, temporary camps, the noble soldier warrior did not give up his posturing, but continued to display himself, to swank. Indeed, Booth tells us, 'camp behaviour was not thought incompatible with good soldiering . . . if anything, the reverse' (Booth 1999: 78).

So far, I have argued that camp is about spectacle, performance and excess. But it is also apolitical and male, apolitical because male courtiers turned to camp (that is, to display) as the mannered way of being when held as virtual prisoners in court. Thus, my next point begins with this idea that camp is apolitical, but it is also 'a self-mocking abdication of any pretension to power' (Booth 1999: 74), and because of this, traditionally, it has its original location in the feminine. So, to return to our courtiers, their camp is a self-mocking display of their impotence; it is, moreover, a recognised and recognisable admission (to the monarch) of their political impotence.[8] The repression of political potency takes on a certain pathological display, or camp, whereby the male courtier knowingly feminises his self, ironises his condition, makes it spectacular. However, if camp is a self-mocking abdication of any pretence to power, then this display raises interesting questions when transposed to the battlefield. In going to war, the courtiers disempowered status has been decamped from court to the battlefield (but let us not forget that they are still encamped, disempowered, at this temporary court). The difference is that here they are able to display masculine prowess, as well as perform and swank (now they joust, wield swords, etc.). Thus, their performance in battle is located both in the feminine and the masculine; in being camp they are now being *both/and*. Therefore camp, at least when on the battlefield, is itself located in the feminine and the masculine, suggesting that camp is more androgyne or bisexual than we might originally have believed; but, within the context of our courtiers, it is also a male strategy of performance when confronted with their own disempowerment.

Thus far in talking about camp, we have only been referring to it as a male performance. What happens, however, when the female androgyne comes upon the scene, as in the case of Jeanne? She unsettles a number of things, starting of course with the notion of gender. Androgyny is a parody of gender, it plays openly, in its bodily performance, on both the feminine and the masculine, and challenges assumptions around a normative relationship between biological sex and gender. Because it parodies and performs, androgyny is closely associated with camp sensibility. But it offers more than that. The androgyne, in this instance the female androgyne Jeanne, free-ranges between the masculine and the feminine. She shows that there is more space between feminine and masculine gendered identities than we might think; there is space for more, for a greater range of gendered identities. She signifies the fluidity of sexual characteristics because she holds them together in one performance. As such she disorientates. The female androgyne does not simply dress as a man. She performs androgyny – an in-between or even third or fourth way of sexual and gender identity. In so doing, she plays on the notion of gender's 'either/or-ness' suggesting it is rather a case of 'bothness'.[9]

We can see already how the female androgyne is doing something a little different from our previously mentioned male courtiers, who for their part, as I have argued, ironise their impotence in their courtly display of camp (located in the feminine) and who, once on the battlefield, occupy a position of bothness. It is not, then, a position they always already occupy – unlike the female androgyne – but one they find themselves occupying by dint of being at war. What the female androgyne refuses to do is to don the masquerade of womanliness (unlike the camp courtiers). But at the same time she expresses a sexual ambiguity. There is no pretence at being 'either/or', nor any pretence at being a man. Only a camping of bothness, an installing of one's self ('se camper') as sexually ambiguous, as feminine and masculine. Female androgyny as camp is not therefore about abdication, self-mockery or lack of power; it is the opposite.

So what of Besson's Jeanne in all of this? Jovovich may not be the best Joan of Arc we have seen – in the 90-minute battle section in particular, her voice lets her down – but she takes an admirable stab at the role, almost despite the circular self-reflexivity of her image: as model, as Leeloo (of *Le Cinquième élément*) and as a sexual (and especially lesbian) icon. The visual pleasure of Besson's film is derived as much from watching her androgynous body – flat-chested, short boyish haircut – as from the wonderfully shot landscapes and battle scenes. Besson's Jeanne is now the fourth in line of his strong female characterisations (Nikita, Mathilda, Leloo). Again she is marginal to society and, as Besson puts it, out of synch with society (Cotillon and Paumier 1999: 31). She also displays herself as androgyne, as to a degree do all his former women characters, which is part of their strength. When asked why there is this constant of the androgyne in his female characters, he answers that what interests him in the woman is her masculinity (and similarly, he adds, in man his femininity), and that what he wants to draw out in her is both her masculinity and her femininity (Cotillon and Paumier 1999: 31).[10] Jovovich's Jeanne is very much a woman of action. She may fall victim to the scurrility of the court and church, but the point of view is almost without exception hers: we are with her in the battles, viewing them through her initially elated and then horrified eyes. Finally, Jovovich cuts a new figure as the androgyne Jeanne from her earlier film counterparts, namely, Bergman and Seberg's Jeannes of the 1950s whose feminine shape was never 'allowed' to be fully disguised by their costumes, and whom we do not see camping at war (Bergman is merely perceived urging her troupes on; Seberg never makes it to the battle-fields). Bergman's Jeanne is costumed like the one illustrating Anatole France's book *La Vie de Jeanne d'Arc* (re-edited in 1999 by L'Atelier de l'Archer), with chain-mail skirts hanging at least to the knees, and strikes poses that are similar to these illustrations. Seberg's Jeanne has her hair shorn crew-cut gamine-style, unlike the basin-style cut of the soldiers and men at court (and more in tune with the new trendy late-1950s gamine look launched by Audrey Hepburn and Seberg herself); by way of contrast Jovovich's hair is identical in cut to those of her male warriors. Seberg continues to be distinct from her male warriors through her dress-code. Until the battle of Orleans, she wears a leather jerkin which highlights her breasts, and the length of which cuts off just above the buttocks so as to highlight her hips and the roundness of her bottom. After Orleans, she wears a longer chain-mail skirt like the men, although the jerkin still accentuates her breasts. Thus, Besson, in bringing out the inner person of Jeanne (which as we know was his intention), brings out more forcefully her androgyny, and, as we shall see more clearly in what follows, the ways in which she constituted a threat to the establishment of that time.

Milla Jovovich may not be a monumental star either (thinking about the definition of epics given above), but she certainly encodes and embodies as Jeanne the female androgyne, as she herself readily admits. Before considering how this affects the camping courtiers, it is worth bearing two points in mind.

First, once she is received into the Dauphin's confidence and provided with an army to attack Orleans, Jeanne rapidly enters into androgyny by making a public display of cutting her hair off. In the 1400s, exposed long hair would have been a sexual provocation when amongst armed soldiers, and furthermore in courtly society women were supposed to keep their hair hidden for decency's sake.[11] She cuts her long plaited hair off so that she may enter the male province of the warrior soldier (in an interesting reversal of roles, it is her male valet, Aulon, who tidies up her hair once she has cut it all off). Jeanne cuts her hair in order to be taken seriously, no longer to be thought of as a maid or as a girl, but as a soldier, a soldier who can fight and give orders, be taken as equal to a man. True, she is already cross-dressed as a soldier. But this is not enough. To be accepted, for the masquerade to be accepted, she must also make her hair correspond with masculine display. However, she makes no secret of this, any more than her cross-dressing; the masquerade is overt, there is no intention to deceive, merely to be equal. And this is the point. With androgyny, female androgyny in this case, there is no pretence at being a man, but a camping of bothness (masculine and feminine). Jeanne has to display this performance of androgyny in order to be taken seriously. Thus her public display of hair-cutting is an open display of bravura, of swank – as with male camp.

The second point concerns Jeanne's battle scenes. Here again she gets to swank. Thanks largely to Besson's camera work in these scenes (themselves a study in excess), we are right in the heart of the battle scenes. Besson said that in the battle scenes the idea was not to isolate Jeanne but to follow her; more significantly still, Besson stated that the battle scenes 'served to reveal her' (Cotillon and Paumier 1999: 31). It is her bravura against the English and Burgundians that inspires the men to fight. Her swank wins the day as she cuts a swathe through the enemy. It is her brilliance and wit when she turns the tower around, reversing/ inverting its intended battle function, and using it as a means of access into the (until then) impregnable fort. The point is that she is being 'revealed' to us (to take Besson's words) when she is performing her androgyny in the arena of the most intense form of camp, battle, when camp is located in both the feminine and the masculine. In these scenes that reveal her, then, her own female androgyny meets up with and mirrors the androgynic moment of camp.

Let us now return to Jeanne's androgyny in the world of camp. Jeanne's performance of androgyny challenges the 'ontological status' (Butler 1990: 136) of the gendered body, the notion that biological sex and gender are one and the same. And she is burnt as a witch for this. As the costume designer for Besson's film, Catherine Leterrier, puts it 'she was burnt for dressing like a man', she 'was the first fashion victim of history' (quoted in Besson 1999: 143). Viewed in this light, she was burnt for camping a role, for performing androgyny. But she is also burnt for more than this. She is burnt because she has a direct source line to God (through the voices of saints that she hears), whereas in accordance with canon law only the church possesses this line. Thus, in the church's eyes she is a transgressor and usurper of the Christian law of the Father. Further still, within this domain of the law of the Father, Jeanne, having transgressed into the world of camp, was the one who gave the orders at Orleans. It was she who possessed the legitimated voice of action. As such she was successful in being a woman encamping a male-warrior role (itself always already a camped role), and winning the battle – that is, possessing power, political power through camp (the legitimated, god-ordained, law of the Father's voice providing her with the power to win). She occupies, therefore, the very opposite position to that occupied by her noble male warriors of the time (which as explained above was an apolitical position). Thus she is burnt also for having possessed political power; for having, in a word, politicised camp. Camp, the very comportment that purports to display one's lack of power (a self-mocking abdication of any pretension to power) is turned around by her performance.

Jeanne's performing female androgyny, therefore, does more than disorientate, it disturbs fundamentally the social order of things of that time. Her masquerade is so transgressive because it is triple and so she must be erased completely. Her first transgression is the one outlined above: her challenge to the ontological status of the gendered body which leads her to politicise camp. Her second and third transgressions are also linked to this challenge to the ontological status of the gendered body through the notion of androgyny and masquerade. By performing androgyny, Jeanne inverts the double mimesis of womanliness. Instead of being the woman masquerading as the masquerade of womanliness (the double mimesis of womanliness), she masquerades as man, but specifically as man-as-camp, (man) as womanly. But she also puts the masquerade on show – she publicly exposes its fraudulence – because she plays doubly (in her performing androgyny) at what she is already publicly perceived to be (by those who surround her): a virgin (she has been probed in public and proved to be so) and a maid in drag as a male warrior. She is not attempting to pass as man. Indeed, when she cuts her hair, she does it so that her sex will not matter. Yet she cross-dresses, dresses up in clothes, male attire, that should matter, that should express desire, but which Jeanne refuses to express, precisely because she is not attempting to pass. She has to don these clothes so that she may fight. But we always know her sex. She always knows her sex. The diegetic audience always know her sex. However, the social order of things of that time could not accept that that knowledge (of her sex) was always already present – because to have this knowledge meant to acknowledge that Jeanne's blatant cross-dressing had no sexual purpose (she cuts her hair so her sex will not matter). Furthermore in being 'out' as female (albeit cross-dressed as male and, therefore, as phallic) this meant she could not be investigated – it is all out there already. That is, there is nothing to be curious about, she cannot be fetishised, or be an object of voyeurism. She is what she says she is: a woman performing androgyny.

Small wonder she has to be burnt for playing on the phallic economy and exposing it for what it is. Small wonder also that she must perish for her attempts at viewing the world as non-sexed, or rather as in sex not mattering. Small wonder, finally, that – because of all this performing and masquerading – Jeanne as a myth is adrift in the culture, and can be taken and remodelled to suit our own desire either as camp or as lesbian, just as much as she is constantly remodelled to suit political desire and purpose.

The powerful message of Besson's film remains, therefore, that in appropriating camp Besson's Jeanne problematises identity politics; she extends the limited possibilities of the subject and, by circumscribing the overtly simplistic gender divide, gives us a knowing link in which we can all delight.

References

Anon. (1999), '*Joan of Arc*', *Première*, 13:1, p. 64.
Besson, L (1999), *Aventure et découverte d'un film: l'histoire de Jeanne d'Arc* (Paris: Intervista).
Booth, M. (1999), '*Campe-toi!* On the origins and definitions of camp', *Camp: Queer Aesthetics and the Performing Subject* (ed. F. Cleto, Edinburgh: Edinburgh University Press), pp. 66–79.

Butler, J. (1990) *Gender Trouble: Feminism and the Subversion of Identity* (London and New York: Routledge).
Cotillon, L. and P. Paumier (1999), '*Jeanne d'Arc*, Luc Besson, son film, sa bataille', *CinéLive*, 29, pp. 28–34.
Eisenstein, Z. (2000), 'Jeanne d'Arc fait son cinéma' *Guardian*, 29 February 2000, p. 61.
Hayward, S. (1998), *Luc Besson* (Manchester: Manchester University Press).
Holtz, M. (1999), 'Les Grands bleus: la coterie de Besson et ses méthodes sont vertement dénoncés', *Libération*, 27 October 1999, p. 34.
Honeycutt, K. (1998), 'Directors in fight over *Joan of Arc*', *Hollywood Reporter*, 9–15 June, webpage www.kathrynbigelow.com/articles/hr.html, accessed 4 February 2005.
Jermyn, D. and S. Redmond (eds) (2003), *The Cinema of Kathryn Bigelow: Hollywood Transgressor* (London: Wallflower Press).
Kahn, J.-F. (1999), 'Ce qu'on n'a pas dit sur *Jeanne d'Arc*', *Marianne*, 131, pp. 55–61.
Maxwell, R. (1999), 'The messenger: "dumbed down dame"', webpage dated 12 November 1999: www.ronmaxwell.com/messenger.html, accessed 4 February 2005.
Péron. D. (1999), 'Jeanne dépucellée', *Libération,* 27 October, pp. 33–4.
Piggford, G. (1999), '"Who's that girl?": Annie Lennox, Woolf's *Orlando*, and female camp androgyny', *Camp: Queer Aesthetics and the Performing Subject* (ed. F. Cleto, Edinburgh: Edinburgh University Press), pp. 282–307.

Notes

1 Besson is no stranger to difficulties over film rights, having tussled with Warren Beatty over his marine-life epic, *Le Grand bleu* (see Hayward 1998: 43–4).
2 www.luc-besson.com, accessed 15 November 1999.
3 This is reasonably inexpensive for an epic of 160 minutes, and compares favourably with the $90million for *Le Cinquième élément*.
4 *Le Film français*, 19 November 1999, p. 23. The full figures for audiences in France were 2,984,144, a disappointing figure when compared with *Le Cinquième élément* which obtained over 7.5 million in France alone.
5 See Besson 1999: 52–4 where he sings the praises of Hoffman and the scenes with Jeanne.
6 For a comparison see Péron, 1999 and Maxwell, 1999.
7 Neither Bergman nor Seberg (despite the latter's tomboyish looks) could pass in the same androgynous way, if only because of their shapely feminine figures and curvaceous breasts.
8 Camp is now understood, partially, as a political act. In its earlier medieval to seventeenth-century forms it was an apolitical act; it was all that was allowed to courtly society.
9 Piggford, 1999 was helpful in shaping this part of the analysis.

10 When I asked Besson about the strong female characterisations that run through his films, he replied by saying that he found women more interesting to make films about. When asked why, he added that because they are not as strong as men, physically, what intrigues him are the strategies they adopt to have strength; it is that which makes them more interesting, he declared. (Informal interview after the *Guardian* interview at the National Film Theatre, 23 March 2000.)
11 Thus in Besson's film, Yolande/Faye Dunaway's striking hair style is historically appropriate.

12

An unpublished interview with Luc Besson

Gérard Dastugue

This interview was recorded in late 1999 when *Jeanne d'Arc* was released.[1]

Why did you decide to do a film about Joan of Arc?
I was interested by the duality between this young girl, this adolescent who shakes everything up, who dreams dreams like all adolescents about a perfect world, and reality. Between thought and action, there's often a gap, and Joan pays for her illusions. The reality is that once you start a war, it will always end the same way: there are only losers. That's the lesson that history gives us: Joan is a great historical figure, she is all those things, it's extraordinary, but the fact of the matter is that there were 800 dead at Orleans. It didn't free either France or England, it didn't solve any problems, it didn't prevent the two world wars afterwards... We've been knocking each other about for four thousand years, and we haven't changed anything. Perhaps the only solution is that you have to accept other people. Each of us sees the truth standing right in front of us, each of us sees our own immediate interests. If we want to live together, you have to see our own interests – that's perfectly normal – and at the same time sacrifice something to see other people's interests. What I have will end up being smaller, but it will allow everyone to live a little better together. It's the basis of religion. Religion is made up of quite beautiful texts which are there to teach us how to live together. 'Love each other', or 'Thou shalt not kill'. It's a fantastic philosophy! But it's true that some denature the texts by saying on the one hand 'Thou shalt not kill' and 'Love each other', and on the other hand 'If you disagree with me, I'll kill you!' It's the principle of wars of religion. People don't kill because someone likes the colour blue; they accept it.

Your film is a demystification of Joan of Arc...
She is human; she even understands where she has gone wrong. She has motivations which are fair and commendable: she doesn't want to kill, she doesn't want more land, more riches. She wants peace. But if you go to extremes to get that, you are wrong, because in the end you are at fault.

Nonetheless, you puncture a certain number of illusions...
Yes, but I think that I bolster others. There's hope, there's a message; it's up to us to organise ourselves. If everyone chips in, things should normally get better.

Your characters have wounds, cracks, and yet they also have a strength which keeps them going...
We all have cracks, and we would all like to have that strength. That's why heroes inspire us. We have something in common with heroes, and that's their weaknesses. Because we have the same weaknesses, we are a bit like them, and because we are a bit like them, we would like to have the same qualities they have. The more you see heroes like Bruce Willis or Schwarzenegger who manage to save widows and orphans, the more you need to ask yourself what effect this is having on us. Perhaps it might change us for the better, perhaps not, or perhaps not everybody...

Are Joan's strengths and weaknesses not one and the same thing? She isn't a child any more, but she isn't quite a woman either, she is at a pivotal moment of her life. You feel it in the battles: she manages to rally a whole army around her, and once it's all over, she loses everything. And then there are those visions...
Joan's visions are natural to start off with: wind, bells, doors, a stained-glass window which shatters... Except that it's there to show that the ordinary can be extraordinary, and that you can believe one thing rather than another. I built it up on purpose in the first part so that I could knock it down in the second, so that I could say: 'No, it was just bells, just wind. You saw what you wanted to see'. For example, when you see her lying down with the sword next to her, you think to yourself that it's a sign. Why? Because it's filmed in a particular way, with the music and the position, so it can't be just chance. There must be a meaning which escapes us, so a divine meaning. And her conscience comes to say to her: 'Why see the divine in this when there are a hundred reasons why the sword might have ended up there'. It's a question of probability. You fly a plane at 30,000 feet and you let a flowerpot go, it ends up killing

someone. Mathematically, it's a probablity. There's no particular sign which determines that it will fall on this person rather than that person.

The keystone of your film is the squence when the two armies face each other, would you say?
What's interesting in that sequence is that it's loaded by what's come before. We've lived through the horror with her. When you see them face to face in a field where there are flowers, you say to yourself that they can't possibly kill each other. A breath of humanity wafts through at that point for a few seconds.

It's something fragile in the middle of all that immensity, an immensity which often happens in your films...
I think it's always linked to a character. I was very interested in Jacques Mayol, and it's true that his story evolves in a vast décor. The most difficult thing is always to look into the character's soul. To come back to the sequence we were talking about, when Joan is waiting for the English to respond, the archers step forward, she thinks that they are going to attack, and we have to feel all that distress on her face, that's the most difficult thing to convey.

In *Léon* for example, the way you film New York is very interesting. There aren't that many shots of the city, and yet the city is very present throughout the film. From the credits onwards, you present New York as the remains of a lost civilisation...
New York is such a huge place that you can be invisible in it. It's a city lost in the jungle, huge and autonomous like a ship, and there are rats that live on the ship. But you never catch them. Léon is undetectable in this city. I couldn't film *Léon* in Paris, it would have been impossible. If you're in Paris, there's a concierge at the bottom of the building who knows everything, the walls are too thin, so the neighbour knows when he's in... There's a whole state of mind which means that he can't be invisible in Paris. In New York, I've seen a guy talk to himself completely naked in the middle of town in the afternoon! And no one stops!

After the gigantic scale of *Le Cinquième élément* and *Jeanne d'Arc*, what are you hoping to do now?
I think I am making films that are increasingly human, more and more intimate in the end, because I tend to focus on a single character. The gigantic scale doesn't alter that. What guides you through a film are the characters and the way they develop, the way I will convey such and such a feeling, a fear, a doubt. That's the heart of the film. The rest is just

logistics. There were supposed to be 1,500 of them in Orleans, so we took on 1,500 extras. That doesn't change what you have to say. I'm lucky enough to be able to make the films I want to. It's a privilege I'm very conscious of.

How does one measure the freedom of an auteur?
First there's a choice. You can choose to make a film or not. Some find this difficult. Because they can't do what they really want to do, they make concessions. From then on, each director tries to deal with a particular set of concessions. But you are always free to say no. I prefer not to do things than do things by half. It's a choice. Then freedom is something the spectator gives you. The spectator recognises the artist, respects the artists, and so follows the artist's work... Economically speaking, people say to themselves that the artist is profitable, so they're prepared to lend money so that the artist can make films.

You've said in the past that you wanted to stop your career after you'd made ten films. Why ten?
Because it's a round figure! The Ten Commandments, Snow White and the Ten Dwarves [laughter]... In the Ten Commandments, since we're speaking about them, I've always wondered why 'Thou shalt not kill' is in sixth position rather than first. Rather than saying 'You must believe in me' ['Thou shalt have no other gods before me'], we should have started with that...

Note

1   Translated by Phil Powrie

Filmography

The filmography includes British and American DVD and CD details where available (but not VHS). Each entry includes all available details, including the Amazon identity number (ASIN). Spectator figures are compiled from the Centre National de la Cinématographie.

La P'tite Sirène (*The Little Mermaid*), 1978, 10 min, colour
Voici (*Here You Are*), 1980, 4 min, colour (music clip)
Formule 2 (*Formula 2*), 1980, 50 min, colour (commissioned film)
L'Avant-Dernier (*Second Last*), 1981, 10 min, b/w, Cinemascope (Avoriaz Festival, 1982)
*Le Dernier Combat (*The Last Battle), 1983 (France) and 1984 (USA), 92 min, b/w, Cinemascope

Spectators week 1 (Paris):	13,238
Spectators in Paris to 2000:	91,297
Spectators in France to 2000:	236,189
Production company:	Les Films du Loup
Producers:	Luc Besson, Constantin Alexandrov
Production managers:	Eliane André, Alain Floris
Script:	Luc Besson, Pierre Jolivet
Camera:	Carlo Varini
Music:	Eric Serra
Editor:	Sophie Schmit
Set design:	Christian Grorichard, Thierry Flamand, Patrick Leberre
Frescos:	Claire Vaton
Costumes:	Martine Rapin, Marie Beau
Make-up:	Maud Baron
Sound editor:	Juliette Marchand
Sound recorder:	Jean-Paul Loublier, Richard Gallet
Sound effects:	André Naudin

Ambient sound:	Frédéric Ullman, François Waledisch
Music performed by:	Jean-Marie Courtois, Alain Guillard, Amaury Blanchard, Yvon Guillard
Script supervisor:	Véronique Cadet, Nadine Deichtman
Assistant directors:	Patrick Alessandrin, Didier Grousset, François Xavier Coutant
Assistant camera:	Vincent Jeannot, François Gentit, François Kotlarsky, Joëlle Malberg
Assistant editors/stagiaires montage:	Christine Dufour, Antoine Vaton
Principal actors:	Pierre Jolivet (Young Man), Jean Bouise (Old Doctor), Fritz Wepper (Gang Leader), Jean Reno (Swordsman), Maurice Lamy (Water Collector), Petra Moller (Woman in cell), Christiane Kruger (Gang Leader's Prisoner), Pierre Carrive, Jean-Michel Castanié, Michel Doset, Bernard Have, Marcel Berthomier, Garry Jode.
DVD details:	21 August 2001: Columbia Tri-star Studios; Region 1; 93 min; ASIN B00005M2C0
	1 March 2003: Columbia Tri-Star Home Video CDR17422; Region 2; 89min; ASIN B000087I29
	29 April 2003: Columbia Tri-Star Home Video (compilation with *Le Cinquième élément*); Region 1; ASIN B00008MTYG

Subway, 1985, 102 min, Eastmancolor, Cinemascope

Spectators week 1 (Paris):	189,286
Spectators in Paris to 2000:	615,045
Spectators in France to 2000:	2,920,588
Production company:	Les Films du Loup, TSF Productions, Gaumont, TF1 Films Production
Executive producer:	Louis Duchesne
Producers:	Luc Besson, François Ruggieri
Production supervisors:	Edith Volnel, Gisèle Thenaisie
Production manager:	Eliane André
Script:	Luc Besson, Pierre Jolivet, Alain Le Henry, Marc Perrier
Camera:	Carlo Varini
Music:	Eric Serra; 'Lucky Guy' Rickie Lee Jones
Telephone lyrics:	Corinne Marieneau
Editor:	Sophie Schmit
Set design:	Alexandre Trauner
Costumes supervisor:	Martine Rapin

Filmography

Costumes:	Magali Guidasci
Make-up supervisor:	Maud Baron
Make-up:	Geneviève Peyralade
Sound editor:	Gérard Hardy
Sound:	Harald Maury, Harrick Maury
Sound recorders:	Gérard Lamps, Bruno Bourgade
Sound effects:	André Naudin, Julien Naudin, Luc Perini
Assistant directors:	Dider Grousset, Patrick Alessandrin
Stunts:	Daniel Vérité, Lucien Fleurot
Roller-skater stunt double:	Didier Langlois
Principal actors:	Isabelle Adjani (Héléna), Christophe Lambert (Fred), Richard Bohringer (Florist), Michel Galabru (Commissioner Gesberg), Jean-Hughes Anglade (Roller-skater), Jean-Pierre Bacri (Batman), Jean-Claude Lecas (Robin), Jean Bouise (Station-master), Pierre-Ange Le Pogram (Jean), Jean Réno (Drummer), Arthur Simms (Singer), Constantin Alexandrov (Héléna's husband), Eric Serra (Bassist), Alain Guillard (Saxophonist), Christian Gomba (Big Bill), Jean-Michel Castanié (Minder).
DVD details:	6 November 2001: Columbia Tri-star Studios; Region 1; 98 min; ASIN B00005OSJO
	18 December 2001: Columbia Tri-star Studios (compilation with *Léon / Le Cinquième élément / Le Grand bleu / Jeanne d'Arc / Nikita*); Region 1; ASIN B00005Q65D
	31 March 2003: Columbia Tri-Star Home Video CDR28313; Region 2; 98 min; ASIN B000087I25
	29 April 2003: Columbia Tri-Star Home Video (compilation with *Léon*); Region 1; ASIN B00008MTYH

Le Grand Bleu (*The Big Blue*), 1988 (France and USA) and 1989 (UK), 136 min (long version: 162), b/w and Eastmancolor, Cinemascope

Spectators week 1 (Paris):	97,817
Spectators in Paris to 2000:	1,547,043
Spectators in France to 2000:	9,192,732
Production company:	Gaumont
Executive producer:	Les Films du Loup
Producer:	Patrice Ledoux
Production supervisors:	Bernard Grenet, Marc Maurette, Patrick Mille
Production managers:	Eric Vidart-Loeb, Valérie Simonin
Script:	Luc Besson, Robert Garland, Marilyn Goldin,

	Jacques Mayol, Marc Perrier (based on an original idea by Luc Besson)
Camera:	Carlo Varini
Underwater cameras:	Luc Besson, Christian Petron
Music:	Eric Serra (the song '*My Lady Blue*', was written by Luc Besson, sung by Eric Serra); film's soundtrack won the Golden Disc Award
Editor:	Olivier Mauffroy
Set design:	Dan Weil
Costumes:	Magali Guidasci, Mimi Lempika, Martine Rapin, Patricia Saalburg, Malika Khelfa, Brigitte Nierhaus, Blandine Boyer
Make-up:	Geneviève Peyralade
Make-up assistant:	Michèle Constantinides
Sound editors:	Patrice Grisolet, Stéphanie Granel, François Gedigier, Marion Monestier, Annick Marciniak
Sound recorders:	Gérard Lamps, François Groult
Sound effects:	Jérôme Lévy, Alain Lévy
Music performed by:	Eric Serra
Scripte 'girl'/Scripte:	Elisabeth Chochoy
Assistant directors:	Jérôme Chalou, Yann Michel, Patrick Halpine
Assistants camera:	Vincent Jeannot, Irène Champendal, François Gentit
Assistant editors:	Elisabeth Couque, Nicolette Barr, Bénédicte Mallet
Diving instructor:	Marc Biehler
Diving assistants:	Georges Latouche, Gilles Samanos, Jean Marc Bour
Principal actors:	Jacques Mayol (Jean-Marc Barr), Jean Reno (Enzo Molinari), Johana (Rosanna Arquette), Laurence (Paul Shenar), Novelli (Sergio Castellitto), Oncle Louis (Jean Bouise), Roberto (Marc Duret), Duffy (Griffin Dunne), Alfredo (Patrick Fontana), La Mamma (Alessandra Vazzoler), Jacques as a child (Bruce Guerre-Bertholet), Enzo as a child (Gregory Forstner), Jacques's father (Claude Besson), Dolphin trainer (Constantin Alexandrov).
DVD details:	15 August 2000: Columbia Tri-star Studios; Region 1; 168 min; ASIN B00004TWZF
	18 December 2001: Columbia Tri-star Studios (compilation with *Léon / Le Cinquième élément / Subway / Jeanne d'Arc / Nikita*); Region 1; ASIN B00005Q65D
	30 June 2003: 20th Century Fox Home Enter-

Filmography 183

	tainment 02298DVD; Region 2; 163 min; ASIN B00004TBSX
Audio CD details:	29 June 1992: Virgin Records 86078; ASIN B000000WGK
	6 March 6 1996: Emi International 787790; ASIN B0000070KB

Nikita (USA: *La Femme Nikita*; remade in USA as *Point of No Return (aka The Assassin)*, John Badham, 1992), 1990 (France) and 1991 (USA), 112 min, Kodak colour, Cinemascope

Spectators week 1 (Paris):	113,900
Spectators in Paris to 2000:	828,867
Spectators in France to 2000:	3,787,845
Production company:	A Franco-Italian production – Les Films du Loup, Gaumont/Gaumont Production/Cecchi Gori Group/Tiger Cinematografica
Producer:	Jérôme Chalou
Production manager:	Christine de Jekel
Script:	Luc Besson
Camera:	Thierry Arbogast
Music:	Eric Serra (the song 'The Dark Side of Time' written by Luc Besson, sung by Eric Serra)
Editor:	Olivier Mauffroy
Set design:	Dan Weil
Costumes:	Anne Angelini (assisted by: Valentine Breton des Loys, Mimi Lempicka)
Make-up:	Geneviève Peyralade
Sound editor:	Pierre Befve, Gérard Lamps
Sound recorder:	Michel Barliet
Sound effects:	Eric Mauer
Music performed by:	Eric Serra
Script supervisor:	Elisabeth Chochoy
Assistant directors:	Christophe Vassor, Guillaume de Bary, Coralie Roy
Assistant camera:	Jeanne Lapoirie, Germain Desmoulins
Assistant editor:	Fanchon Brulé, Catherine Constant, Nathalie Hureau, Annie Marciniak
Principal actors:	Anne Parillaud (Nikita) – César for best actress 1991, Tchéky Karyo (Bob), Jean-Hugues Anglade (Marco), Jeanne Moreau (Amande), Jean Reno (Victor). Jean Bouise, who makes a brief appearance in the film, died during the shooting.
DVD details:	16 September 1997: Pioneer Video; Region 1; 117 min; ASIN 6304615477

	3 October 2000: MGM/UA Studios; Region 1; 117 min; ASIN B00004XMSL
	18 December 2001: Columbia Tri-star Studios (compilation with *Léon / Le Cinquième élément / Le Grand bleu / Subway / Jeanne d'Arc*); Region 1; ASIN B00005Q65D
	31 March 2003: Columbia Tri-Star Home Video CDR13671; Region 2; 112'; ASIN B000087I27
	7 September 2004: Metro-Goldwyn-Mayer; Region 1; 117 min; ASIN B00008ZZ9E
Audio CD details:	19 March 1991: Varese Records 5314; ASIN B0000014S6

Atlantis, 1991, 75 min, Colour, Cinemascope

Spectators in Paris to 2000:	196,148
Spectators in France to 2000:	1,068,772
Production company:	Gaumont-Les Films du Dauphin, Cecchi Gori Group
Executive producer:	Claude Besson
Production manager:	Monique Pautas
Camera:	Christian Petron
Music:	Eric Serra (Music extracts from *La Somnambula*, performed by Maria Callas)
Editor:	Luc Besson
Sound recordist :	William Flageollet
Sound effects:	Eric Mauer, Marie Guesner
Chief diver:	Jean-Marc Bour
Assistant directors:	Vincent Ravalec, Marcia De Caviedes, Brent Spector, Pat Purcell, Catherine Thabourin
DVD details:	29 April 2003: Columbia Tri-star Home Video; Region 1; 78min; ASIN B0000844ML

Léon (USA: *The Professional*), 1994 (France and USA); 1995 (UK), 106 min (director's cut, 131 min, released in France, 1996), Technicolor, Cinemascope

Spectators week 1 (Paris):	243,285
Spectators in Paris to 2000:	595,114
Spectators in France to 2000:	3,546,077
Production company:	Gaumont-Les Films du Dauphin
Executive Producer:	Claude Besson
Producers:	Bernard Grenet, Luc Besson
Production managers:	(France) Thierry Guilmard, Sylvie Ménard
Script:	Luc Besson
Camera:	Thierry Arbogast
Music:	Eric Serra

Filmography

Editor:	Sylvie Landra
Set design:	Dan Weil
Costumes:	Laurence Glentzin
Make-up:	Geneviève Peyralade
Sound editor:	Patrice Grisolet
Sound recorders:	François Groult, Gérard Lamps, Bruno Tarrière
Sound effects:	John Morris
Special effects:	(France) Nicky Allder, (New York, USA) Al Griswold
Music mixer:	William Flageollet
Music performed by:	Eric Serra (soundtrack also includes songs by Sting ('Shape of my Heart' and Bjork's ('Venus as a Boy')
Script supervisor:	Sylvette Baudrot
Assistant directors:	(France) Pascal Chaumeil, Camille Lipmann, (New York, USA) Eric McGinty
Assistant camera:	Bernard Tissier, Laurent Delpech, Sarah Bouyain
Assistant editor:	Frédérique Recoque, Annie Marciniak, Santiago Thévenet
Principal actors:	Jean Reno (Léon), Nathalie Portman (Mathilde), Gary Oldman (Stansfield), Danny Aiello (Tony), Peter Appel (Malky).
DVD details:	15 May 2000: Touchstone Home Video D888223; Region 2; 109 min; ASIN B00004R84D 3 October 2000: Columbia Tri-Star; Director's Cut; Region 1; 132 min; ASIN B00004YYDI 18 December 2001: Columbia Tri-star Studios (compilation with *Le Cinquième élément / Le Grand bleu / Subway / Jeanne d'Arc / Nikita*); Region 1; ASIN B00005Q65D 29 April 2003: Columbia Tri-Star Home Video (compilation with *Subway*); Region 1; ASIN B00008MTYH 9 September 2003: Columbia Tri-Star Home Video; Uncut International Version (includes 24 minutes of footage not shown in the USA); Region 1; 132 min; ASIN B0000AGQ6Y 7 December 2004: Columbia Tri-star Studios; Region 1; 109'; ASIN 0767802519 11 January 2005: Columbia Tri-Star Home Video; Deluxe Edition; Region 1; 133 min; ASIN B0006GVJEE

Le Cinquième élément (*The Fifth Element*), 1997 (France, USA, UK) 126 min, colour, Cinemascope

Audio CD details:	25 October 1994: Tri-star 67201; ASIN B000005D8K
	30 January 1995: Sony; ASIN B00000813S
Spectators week 1 (Paris):	425,019
Spectators in Paris to 2000:	952,075
Spectators in France to 2000:	7,696,667
Production company:	Gaumont
Producer:	Patrice Ledoux
Associate producer:	Iain Smith
Production directors:	Sarah Bradshaw, Barrie Melrose
Production manager:	Monique Pautas
Script:	Luc Besson (adaptation and dialogues: Luc Besson and Robert Kamen)
Camera:	Thierry Arbogast
Music:	Eric Serra
Editor:	Sylvie Landra
Set design:	Dan Weil (cartoon designers: Jean-Claude Mézières and Jean 'Moebius' Giraud)
Costumes:	Jean-Paul Gaultier
Make-up:	Lois Burwell (Bruce Willis's make-up: Amanda Knight)
Sound editor:	Mark Magnini
Sound mixers:	Chris Jenkins, Mark Smith, Ron Bartlett
Sound engineer:	Daniel Brisseau
Script supervisor:	Jean Bourne
Music performed by:	Eric Serra
Supervisor of creatures' design:	Nick Dudman
Special effects and digital animation:	Digital Doman, Venice, California
Assistant directors:	Chris Carreras, Cliff Lanning, Fred Garson
Assistant camera:	David Bryant
Assistant editors:	Yann Hervé, Simon Cozens, Donald Likovich
Principal actors:	Milla Jovovich (Leeloo), Bruce Willis (Korben Dallas), Gary Oldman (Zorg), Ian Holm (Cornelius), Chris Tucker (Ruby Rhod), Billy (Luke Perry), Brion James (the General), Tiny Lister Jr. (the President), Maïwenn Le Besco (the Diva).
DVD details:	9 December 1997: Columbia Tri-star Studios; Region 1; 126 min; ASIN 0800195175
	9 December 1997: Columbia Tri-Star Home

Filmography 187

	Video; Region 1; 126 min; ASIN 0800195043
	25 October 1999: Pathe Distribution Ltd P8920DVD; Region 2; 121 min; ASIN B00004CZO2
	9 October 2001: Columbia Tri-star Studios (Superbit Collection); Region 1; 126 min; ASIN B00005NRNA
	9 October 2001: Columbia Tri-star Studios (compilation with *Crouching Tiger, Hidden Dragon / Desperado*); Region 1; ASIN B00005OCJR
	18 December 2001: Columbia Tri-star Studios (compilation with *Léon / Le Grand bleu / Subway / Jeanne d'Arc / Nikita*); Region 1; ASIN B00005Q65D
	17 December 2002: Columbia Tri-Star Home Video (compilation with *Starship Troopers*); Region 1; ASIN B00007149T
	29 April 2003: Columbia Tri-Star Home Video (compilation with *Le Dernier combat*); Region 1; ASIN B00008MTYG
	15 September 2003: 20th Century Fox Home Entertainment 25773DVD; compilation with *The Abyss* and *Aliens* Region 2; ASIN B0000CAPYK
	24 November 2003: Pathe Distribution Ltd P9056DVD (Special Edition); Region 2; 121 min; ASIN B0000CERTA
	28 September 2004: Columbia Tri-Star Home Video (compilation with *Gattaca*); Region 1; ASIN B0002IQNIS
	11 January 2005: Columbia Tri-Star Home Video (Ultimate Edition); Region 1; 126 min; ASIN B0006GVJE4
Audio CD details:	6 May 1997: Virgin Records 44203; ASIN B000000WE5

Jeanne d'Arc (UK: *Joan of Arc*, USA: *The Messenger: The Story of Joan of Arc*, 1999 (USA, France) and 2000 (UK), 160 min; USA: 148 min, colour

Spectators week 1 (Paris):	214,472
Spectators in Paris to 2000:	408,240
Spectators in France to 2000:	2,984,144
Production company:	Gaumont, Leeloo Productions
Executive producers:	Marc Jenny, Oldrich Mach
Producers:	Patrice Ledoux, Luc Besson

Production manager:	Bernard Grenet, Thierry Guilmard, Patrick Millet
Script:	Luc Besson, Andrew Birkin
Camera:	Thierry Arbogast
Music:	Eric Serra
Special effects:	Duboi, Pittof
Editors:	Sylvie Landra
Set design:	Hugues Tissandier
Costume supervisors:	Thierry Delettre, Patrick Lebreton
Costumes:	Catherine Leterrier
Make-up:	Kuno Schlegelmilch
Sound editors:	François Groult, Bruno Tarrière
Sound:	Vincent Tulli
Assistant director:	Gérard Krawczyk
Stunts:	Philippe Guégan
Principal actors:	Milla Jovovich (Joan of Arc), Dustin Hoffman (The Conscience), Faye Dunaway (Yolande D'Aragon), John Malkovich (Charles VII), Tchéky Karyo (Dunois), Vincent Cassel (Gilles de Rais), Pascal Greggory (The Duke of Alençon)
DVD details:	13 November 2000: Columbia Tri-Star Home Video CDR29081; Region 2; 155 min; ASIN B00004YA9W 30 October 2001: Columbia Tri-Star; Region 1; 158 min; ASIN 0767845722 18 December 2001: Columbia Tri-star Studios (compilation with *Léon / Le Cinquième élément / Le Grand bleu / Subway / Nikita*); Region 1; ASIN B00005Q65D 17 May 2004: Columbia Tri-Star Home Video CDRP1418 (compilation with *Glory / The Patriot*); Region 2; ASIN B0001HK0RU
Audio CD details:	2 November 1999: Sony 66537; ASIN B00002MZ52

Select bibliography

Books by Luc Besson
(1991) *Atlantis* (Paris: Arthaud).
(1992) *L'Histoire de Nikita* (Paris: Bordas).
(1993) *L'Histoire du dernier combat* (Paris: Bordas).
(1994) *L'Histoire du Grand Bleu* (Paris: Intervista).
(1995) *L'Histoire de Léon* (Paris: Intervista).
(1997) *L'Histoire du Cinquième Élément* (Paris: Intervista); *The Story of The Fifth Element* (London: Titan, 1997).
(1999) *En attendant Jeanne* (Paris: Intervista).
(1999) *L'Histoire de Jeanne d'Arc* (Paris: Intervista).
(2000) *L'Histoire de Subway* (Paris: Intervista).
(2001) *Wasabi, la petite moutarde qui monte au nez: un film* (Paris: Intervista).
(2001) *Yamakasi, samouraï des temps modernes* (Paris: Intervista).
(2002) *Arthur et les minimoys* (Paris: Intervista). Trans. by E. Sowchek as *Arthur and the Minimoys* (London: Faber & Faber, 2005).
(2003) *Arthur et la cité interdite* (Paris: Intervista). Trans as *Arthur and the Forbidden City* (London: HarperCollins, 2005).
(2004) *Arthur et la vengeance de Maltazard* (Paris: Intervista).
(2004) *Pour David* (Bruxelles: Graton, 'Michel Vaillant' 67).

Film tie-in
Gillot, A. (1988), *Le Grand Bleu* (Paris: Ramsay).

Novelisations
Bisson, T. (1997), *The Fifth Element* (London: HarperCollins). Trans. by D. Hass as *Le Cinquième élément* (Paris: France loisirs, 1997).
Maréchal, D. (1990), *Nikita* (Paris: G. de Villiers).
Parillaud, P. and B. Clope (1998), *Le Grand bleu* (Paris: Intervista).

Academic work on the films of Luc Besson

Books

Giraldi, M. (2004), *Luc Besson* (Roma: Gremese, 'Collana I Grandi registi del cinema').

Hayward, S. (1998), *Luc Besson* (Manchester: Manchester University Press, French Film Directors series).

Martani, M. (1997), *Luc Besson: l'iniziazione, i sentimenti e la forma* (Roma: S. Sorbini, 'Sentieri selvaggi', 9)

Obayashi, C. (1997), *Luc Besson* (Tokyo: Kinema Junposha, 'Kinema junpo', 1237; 'Filmmakers', 1).

Sojcher, F. (2005), *Luc Besson: un Don Quichotte face à Hollywood* (Paris: Séguier, Carré noir').

Articles in journals

Dallos, N. (1997), 'Nikita: the coolest, hippest, most stylish French thriller in ages ... und was daraus wurde!', *Maske und Kothurn: Internationale Beiträge zur Theaterwissenschaft*, 43:4, pp. 75–81.

Grindstaff, L. (2001), 'A Pygmalion tale retold: remaking *La Femme Nikita*', *Camera Obscura*, 16:2, pp. 133–75.

Hayward, S. (1998), 'Sex violence surveillance: questions of containment and displacement in Besson's film *Nikita*', *Journal of the Institute of Romance Studies*, 5, pp. 245–60.

Knabel, K. (2002), 'Geschichte auf der Leinwand: Der Fall Jeanne d'Arc', *Romanistische Zeitschrift für Literaturgeschichte/Cahiers d'Histoire des Littératures Romanes*, 26:3–4, pp. 377–93.

MacRory, P. (1999), 'Excusing the violence of Hollywood women: music in *Nikita* and *Point of No Return*', *Screen*, 40:1, pp. 51–65.

Maddox, P. (2003), 'Retiring the maid: the last Joan of Arc movie', *Journal of Religion and Popular Culture*, 3, www.usask.ca/relst/jrpc/art-joanofarc.html.

Méjean, J.-M. (2000), '*Le Grand bleu* ou le ciel renversé', *CinémAction*, 94 ('Philosophie et cinéma'), pp. 139–43.

Mongin, O. (1990), '*Le Grand bleu* ou le trou noir de nos passions', *Esprit*, 158, pp. 84–99.

Ott, B., and Aoki, E. (2004), 'Counter-imagination as interpretive practice: futuristic fantasy and *The Fifth Element*', *Women's Studies in Communication*, 27:2, pp. 149–76.

Reader, K. A. (1992), 'How to avoid becoming a middle-aged fogey, with reference to three recent popular French films', *Paragraph: A Journal of Modern Critical Theory*, 15:1, pp. 97–104.

Scalia, B. (2004), 'Contrasting visions of a saint: Carl Dreyer's *The Passion of Joan of Arc* and Luc Besson's *The Messenger*', *Literature/Film Quarterly*, 32:3, pp. 181–5.

Sojcher, F. (2002), 'Luc Besson ou les contradictions du cinéma français face à Hollywood', *CinémAction*, hors-série 'Quelle diversité face à Hollywood', pp. 142–56.

Vincendeau, G. (1992), 'Family plot: the fathers and daughters of French cinema', *Screen*, 1:11, pp. 14–17.
Wiles, M. M. (1997), 'Mapping the contours of cyborg space in the conspiracy film: the feminine ecology of Luc Besson's *La Femme Nikita*', *Post Identity*, 1:1, pp. 39–65.

Chapters in books

Buckland, W. (2001), 'S/Z, the "readerly" film and video game logic (*The Fifth Element*)', in T. Elsaesser and W. Buckland (eds), *Studying Contemporary American Film: A Guide to Movie Analysis* (London: Arnold), pp. 146–67.
Grindstaff, L. (2002), 'Pretty woman with a gun: *La Femme Nikita* and the textual politics of "the remake"', in J. Forrest and L. Koos (eds), *Dead Ringers: The Remake in Theory and Practice* (New York: State University of New York, 'Cultural Studies in Cinema/Video' series), pp. 273–308.
Hawk, B. (2003), 'Hyperrhetoric and the inventive spectator: remotivating *The Fifth Element*', in D. Blakesley (ed.), *The Terministic Screen: Rhetorical Perspectives on Film* (Carbondale, IL: Southern Illinois UP), pp. 70–91.
Hayward, S. (1997), 'Luc Besson's *Cinquième élément* (1997) and the spectacular: the city-body and the sci-fi movie', in W. Everett (ed.), *The Seeing Century: Film, Vision, and Identity* (Amsterdam: Rodopi, 'Critical Studies' series), pp. 136–46.
Hayward, S. (1998), '*Luc Besson*', in J. Hill and P. Church Gibson (eds), *The Oxford Guide to Film Studies* (Oxford/New York: Oxford Universty Press), pp. 594–6.
Hayward. S. (1999), 'Besson's "mission elastoplast": *Le Cinquième élément* (1997)', in P. Powrie (ed.), *French Cinema in the 1990s: Continuity and Difference* (Oxford: Oxford University Press), pp. 246–57.
Hayward, S. (2000), 'Recycled woman and the postmodern aesthetic: Luc Besson's *Nikita*', in S. Hayward and G. Vincendeau (eds), *French Film Texts and Contexts* (London and New York: Routledge), pp. 297–309.
Hayward. S. (2002), 'Luc Besson: bard and filmmaker', in Y. Tasker (ed.), *Fifty Contemporary Film-Makers* (London: Routledge), pp. 51–8.
Powrie, P. (1997), '*Subway*: identity and inarticulacy', *French Cinema in the 1980s: Nostalgia and the Crisis of Masculinity* (Oxford: Clarendon Press), pp. 121–9.
Powrie, P. (2006), '*Nikita*', in P. Powrie (ed.), *The Cinema of France* (London: Wallflower Press), pp. 197–205
Reader, K. A. (2000), 'Subtext: Paris of Alexandre Trauner', in M. Konstantarakos (ed.), *Spaces in European Cinema* (Exeter: Intellect), pp. 35–41.
Smith, A. (2001), 'Nikita as social fantasy', in L. Mazdon (ed.), *France on Film* (London: Wallflower), pp. 27–40.
Vincendeau, G. (1993), 'Fathers and daughters in French cinema: from the 20s to *La Belle Noiseuse*', in P. Cook and P. Dodd (eds), *Women and Film: A Sight and Sound Reader* (London: Scarlet Press/Philadelphia, PA: Temple University Press), pp. 156–63.

Sections in books

Austin, G. (1996), *Contemporary French Cinema: An Introduction* (Manchester: Manchester University Press); 'Luc Besson', pp. 126–32.

Bruzzi, S. (1997), *Undressing Cinema* (London and New York: Routledge), pp. 91–3 (*Léon*).

Durham, C. A. (1998), *Double Takes: Culture and Gender in French Films and their American Remakes* (Hanover and London: University Press of New England), pp. 175–80 (*Nikita*).

Frodon, J.-M. (1995), *L'Âge moderne du cinéma français: de la Nouvelle Vague à nos jours* (Paris: Flammarion), pp. 689–91.

Hayward. S. (1998), 'Luc Besson', J. Hill and P. Gibson (eds), *The Oxford Guide to Film Studies* (Oxford: Oxford University Press), pp. 494–6.

Journot, M.-T. (2005), *L'Esthétique publicitaire dans le cinéma français des années 80: la modernité en crise, Beineix, Besson, Carax* (Paris: L'Harmattan).

Lanzoni, R. F. (2002), *French Cinema: From its Beginnings to the Present* (New York and London: Continuum), pp. 341–46.

Mazdon, L. (2000), *Encore Hollywood: Remaking French Cinema* (London: BFI), pp. 108–23 (*Nikita*).

Prédal, R. (1991), *Le Cinéma des Français depuis 1945* (Paris: Nathan); 'Luc Besson', pp. 469–70.

Revie, I. (1994), 'Paris remythologized in *Diva* and *Subway*: *nanas néopolarisées* and *Orphées aux enfers*', in *Mythologies of Paris* (Stirling French Publications, 2, 1994), pp. 28–43; 'Paris as topos: *Subway*', pp. 33–8.

Wilson, E. (1999), *French Cinema since 1950: Personal Histories* (London: Duckworth); 'A girl and a gun' (*Nikita*), pp. 74–82.

Index

Note: 'n' after a page number indicates the number of a note on that page

15 Août 35
37°2, le matin 15, 17, 19
400 coups, Les 116, 120
2001: A Space Odyssey 100

À bout de souffle 16, 155
Adjani, Isabelle 15–17, 55, 76
Abyss, The 114, 116
Alessendrin, Patrick 35
Alexander, Geoffrey 69
Alien 103
Alien 3 103
Aliens 96, 100
Allen, Woody 57
Almodóvar, Pedro 57, 73
Altman, Rick 4
Andersson, Harriett 116
Anglade, Jean-Hugues 79
Antonioni, Michelangelo 18
Arcady, Alexandre 40
Arquette, Rosanna 16, 78
Artificial Intelligence: A.I. 114
Assayas, Olivier 33
Atlantis 43–4, 47
À ton image 36

Bacri, Jean-Pierre 79
Baiser du dragon 3
Bar, Jean-Michel 40
Bardot, Brigitte 136, 141–2, 145

Barocco 11
Barr, Jean-Marc 78
Barthes, Roland 89
Bartkowiak, Andrzej 37
Bartok, Bela 71
Beatty, Warren 173n1
Beethoven, Ludwig van 49
Beineix, Jean-Jacques 2–3, 11, 14–15, 18–20, 40, 75–6
Belmondo, Jean-Paul 76, 155
Berceau de cristal, Le 11
Bergman, Ingmar 116
Bergman, Ingrid 169, 173
Berry, Richard 35–6
Bertolucci, Bernardo 73
Bidasses aux grandes manœuvres, Les 40
Bigelow, Kathryn 40, 100, 107, 161
Björk 53, 67
Blade Runner 1, 98–9
Blanche 36
Blier, Bertrand 35
Bloch-Laîné, Nathalie 34
Bohringer, Richard 76
Bont, Jan de 28
Bonvoisin, Bernard 35–6
Bouise, Jean 93
Boy meets girl 12, 15, 17, 20
Braque, Georges 18
Bresson, Robert 163

Briand, Manon 35–6
Broca, Philippe de 76
Buena Vista 30
Burton, Tim 43
Burwell, Carter 71

Calopresti, Mimmo 3, 35–6
Cameron, James 96, 103, 107, 114, 139, 153
Campbell, Martin 43
Canal+ 31, 33, 40
Carax, Leos 2–3, 11–13, 15, 18–20, 40, 75–6
Carné, Marcel 1, 162
Cartouche 76
Cavalier, Alain 112
Cézanne, Paul 19
Chan, Jackie 89
Chanel, Coco 84, 104
Chaplin, Charlie 154
Cheeky 35
Chion, Michel 4, 53–4
Cinquième élément, Le 1, 4–5, 24, 39, 43–5, 47–8, 53, 57, 68–70, 77–8, 80–8, 91–2, 96–105, 113, 149, 169, 173, 177
Clockwork Orange, A 49
Cocks, Jay 107, 161
Cocteau, Jean 20
Coen Brothers 71
Coppola, Francis Ford 48
Corbiau, Gérard 34
Côtelettes, Les 35
Cousteau, Jacques 111, 113
Cronenberg, David 43, 157
Cruise, Tom 26
Cruz, Penélope 36

Dahan, Olivier 35
Dall'Anese, Gilbert 62
Danes, Clare 161
Daney, Serge 13–15, 111, 143
Danny the Dog 35
Debussy, Claude 55
Décalage horaire 43
Delacorta 19
Delahaye, Valérie 97

Delon, Alain 79, 160
Demy, Jacques 116
Dernier combat, Le 4–5, 16–17, 19, 44–5, 47, 55, 57–62, 78, 81, 87, 91–6, 98–9, 105, 148–9
Deux 2
Die Hard 87–8
Digital Domain 96–7, 106
Digital Factory 3, 33–4
Disney 32, 34, 106
Diva 11–14, 16, 18–21, 75–6
Djian, Philippe 19
Donner, Richard 37
Dorléac, Françoise 135–6, 138
Doval, Isabelle 36
Dreyer, Carl 20
Duelle 11
Dunaway, Faye 165, 174
Dutartre, Alain 41

Elfman, Danny 43
Enfant de l'hiver, L' 33
Enfants du paradis, Les 133
Epstein, Jean 18
Et Dieu créa la femme 141
Europa 3, 24, 27, 32–8, 41

Fabuleux destin d'Amélie Poulain, Le 28
Fanfan la Tulipe 36
Faraldo, Claude 40
Farmer, Mylène 55
Felicitá non costa niente, La 35–6
Feller, Michel 33
Fellini, Federico 43
Filles uniques 55
Fincher, David 103
Fleming, Victor 164
Fonda, Bridget 40
Force majeure 55
Fox 3, 23, 30, 34
France, Anatole 169
Fred 55
Freeman, Morgan 35
Frère du guerrier, Le 55
Freud, Sigmund 84, 101, 115–16, 150–1

Index

Gabriel, Peter 53, 63
Gainsbourg, Serge 55
Galabru, Michel 79
Garcia, José 36
Garrel, Philippe 11, 20
Gaultier, Jean-Paul 85, 96, 104
Gaumont 25, 30, 32-3, 162
G.I. Jane 139
Godard, Jean-Luc 2, 16, 18, 20, 113, 155
Godfather, The 48
Gohatto 73
Goldeneye 43
Goodfellas 48
Goodis, David 19
Graduate, The 113
Grand bleu, Le 3, 16-17, 20, 43, 45, 47-8, 55, 57, 62-4, 70, 76, 78, 82-4, 87, 109-18, 124, 149, 173
Grand carnaval, Le 40
Gray, F. Gary 89
Grousset, Didier 55

Haine, La 75
Hamilton, Linda 139-40
Hepburn, Audrey 169
Herrmann, Bernard 71
Hirosue, Ryoko 35, 37
Hitchcock, Alfred 71
Hoffman, Dustin 163, 173
Holst, Gustav 70
Hoskins, Bob 35
House Party 89
Hudlin, Reginald 89

Immortal Beloved 49, 55
IP5 40

Jackson, Michael 85
Jackson, Samuel L. 89
Jeanne d'Arc 4, 7, 24, 33, 35-6, 39, 40, 43, 47, 53-4, 57, 69-70, 83-4, 113, 149, 161-72, 175-8
Jeunet, Jean-Pierre 28
Jian gui 36
Joan of Arc 164
Jolivet, Pierre 43, 45, 55, 57, 78, 93

Jones, Terry 163
Jones, Rickie Lee 61
Jovovich, Milla 83, 161, 163, 166, 169-70
Jurassic Park 96, 106

Kamikaze 55
Karyo, Tchéky 40, 78
Kelly, Gene 66
Khaled, Cheb 53
Kiss of the Dragon 32-3, 35, 37
Krawczyck, Gérard 3, 34, 36, 55
Kubrick, Stanley 49, 100

Lambert, Christophe 16, 45
Lang, Fritz 1
Lang, Jack 30
Last Emperor, The 73
Legally Blonde 138
Lelouch, Claude 18
Léon 23, 28, 37, 39, 43, 47-55, 57, 65-7, 70, 77-8, 80, 82-3, 89, 146-58, 169, 177
Leone, Sergio 43
Le Pen, Jean-Marie 164
Le Pogam, Pierre-Ange 32
Lescure, Pierre 34
Leterrier, Louis 35
Lethal Weapon 4 37
Li, Jet 35, 37
Life of Brian 163
Lions au soleil 40
Little Buddha 73
Little Richard 105
Lost World: Jurassic Park, The 106
Lucas, George 57, 71, 97, 106, 162
Lune dans le caniveau, La 15, 17, 19
Lynch, David 57
Lyon, Philippe 40

McTiernan, John 43
Mafart, Henri 144
Malkovich, John 164
Malle, Louis 116
Malraux, André 19
Ma petite enterprise 55
Marais, Jean 84

Marshall, Garry 146
Mauvais sang 12–13, 15, 17–18, 20–1, 76
Mechanic, Bill 34
Melville, Jean-Pierre 79, 152–3
Merry Christmas Mr Lawrence 73
Messier, Jean-Marie 31, 33–4, 40
Metropolis 1
Michel Vaillant 35
Moi César, 10 ans ½, 1 m 39 35–6
Montand, Yves 40
Moore, Demi 139–40
Moreau, Jeanne 137
Morricone, Ennio 43
Mortel transfert 40

Nahon, Chris 3, 32
Nash, Johnny 46, 61
Negotiator, The 89
Nichols, Mike 116
Nikita 6, 28, 37, 40, 43, 47–8, 64–5, 67, 76, 78, 80, 89, 121, 126–32, 134–44, 149–50, 159, 166, 169

Oldman, Gary 48, 80
Orff, Carl 70
Oshima, Nagisa 73
Otaku 40
Othello 133

Pang Brothers 36
Parapluies de Cherbourg, Les 116
Parillaud, Anne 64, 136–7, 140, 146
Peau d'ange 35
Peau douce, La 135–6, 138, 142
Perez, Vincent 35–6
Picasso, Pablo 18–19
Pirès, Gérard 28
Pola X 40
Preminger, Otto 164
Pretty Woman 137, 146
Prieur, Dominique 144
Prince 53, 85, 105
Procès de Jeanne d'Arc, Le 163

Ratner, Brett 89
Ravel, Maurice 153–4

Ray, Nicholas 117
Rebel Without a Cause 117
Reno, Jean 35, 37, 43, 45, 78, 80–2, 93, 141, 146
Renoir, Jean 162
Richie, Lionel 53
Rigaut, Jacques 116–17
Rire et châtiment 36
Rivette, Jacques 11
Rivières pourpres, Les 35
Rivières pourpres 2: Les anges de l'Apocalypse, Les 35
Roi danse, Le 34
Rollerball 43
Romeo Must Die 37
Romero, George 157
Rose, Bernard 49
Rota, Nino 43, 48
Rush Hour 89
Rush Hour 2 89

Sagan, Françoise 136
Saint Joan 164
Saint Theresa 112
Sakamoto, Ryuichi 68, 73
Samouraï, Le 79–80, 152–3, 160
Sarafian, Richard C. 116
Schwarzenegger, Arnold 176
Scorsese, Martin 48, 57
Scott, Ridley 1, 98, 103, 139
Seberg, Jean 155, 169, 173
Séri, Julien 40
Serra, Eric 4, 43–4, 47–8, 57–71, 112
Shore, Howard 43
Silla, Virginie 33
Simms, Arthur 46
Simon & Garfunkel 116
Sinatra, Frank 60
Singh, Talvin 67
Sommaren med Monika 116
Sony 3, 23, 26
Speed 28
Spielberg, Steven 23, 26, 57, 71, 96, 106, 114
Star Wars 93
Star Wars Episode 1: The Phantom Menace 162

Stetson, Mark 97
Sting 53
Strange Days 100, 197
Strictement personnel 55
Subway 1, 6, 12, 15–16, 18, 20, 43–5, 47, 49, 55, 57, 60–2, 76–80, 83, 121–8, 132–4, 149

Tarantino, Quentin 2
Taxi 28
Taxi 2 41
Téchiné, André 11
Terminator 2: Judgment Day 96, 139–40, 153–4
Thérèse 112
Thewlis, David 35
Thompson, Danielle 43
Toscan du Plantier, Daniel 30
Transporter, The 35
Trauner, Alexandre 1, 133
Truffaut, François 116, 135
Tucker, Chris 76, 84–5
Turbulence des fluids, La 35

UGC 30

Vadim, Roger 141
Valenti, Jack 30
Vanishing Point 116
Versois, Odile 76
Villiers, Aruna 36
Vivendi-Universel 33–4, 38, 40

Warner 3, 23, 26
Wasabi 3, 35, 37, 55
Wayne, John 157
Welles, Orson 133
Wepper, Fritz 78, 93
Williams, John 71
Willis, Bruce 78, 84–5, 87, 103, 176
Witherspoon, Reese 138
World of Silence 113

Yamakasi 35, 40
Yuen, Corey 35–6

Zeitoun, Ariel 35
Zidi, Claude 20
Zorn, Fritz 117